Peoples of the River Valleys

EARLY AMERICAN STUDIES

Daniel K. Richter and Kathleen M. Brown, Series Editors

Exploring neglected aspects of our colonial, revolutionary, and early
national history and culture, Early American Studies reinterprets familiar
themes and events in fresh ways. Interdisciplinary in character, and with a
special emphasis on the period from about 1600 to 1850, the series is
published in partnership with the McNeil Center for Early American
Studies.

A complete list of books in the series is available from the publisher.

Peoples of the River Valleys

The Odyssey of the Delaware Indians

Amy C. Schutt

PENN

University of Pennsylvania Press

Philadelphia

10   9   8   7   6   5   4   3   2   1

Published by
University of Pennsylvania Press
Philadelphia, Pennsylvania 19104–4112

Library of Congress Cataloging-in-Publication Data

Schutt, Amy C.
  Peoples of the river valleys : the odyssey of the Delaware Indians / Amy C. Schutt.
    p. cm. — (Early American studies)
  Includes bibliographical references and index.

  ISBN: 978-0-8122-2024-7

    1. Delaware Indians—History.   2. Delaware Indians—Social life and customs.   3. Middle-Atlantic States—History.   4. Middle-Atlantic States—Social life and customs.   I. Title.   II. Series.

E99.D2S34   2007
974.004'97345—dc22

                                                          2006050917

To Rob

Contents

Prologue
"Sachems from nine different places"

One day in early January 1633 a Dutch crew of seven men on a whaling vessel called the *Squirrel* traveled up the Delaware River. Along the way the crew traded with the Indian inhabitants of the area. The *Squirrel* anchored at the mouth of Newton Creek in the area of present-day Gloucester City, New Jersey, where it was boarded by more than forty Indians, with "a portion of them" commencing "to play tunes with reeds." A sachem attempted to give "an armful of beaver-skins" to the Dutch, an offer that would have signaled the construction of a relationship between allies and trading partners. Suspecting the Indians of recently attacking an English crew, the Dutch refused the gift, which their visitors may have interpreted as a call to war. Indeed, the Dutch accompanied their refusal with a warlike pronouncement, commanding the Indians "to go ashore immediately" or else the sailors "would shoot them all."[1]

The Indians, who came from nearby Mantua Creek, possibly did not take this threat seriously since they significantly outnumbered the Dutch. They also may have known that the Dutch were in a weak position without Native assistance. The *Squirrel*'s crew had used up all their "stock-fish," and their supply of porridge was dwindling. Their survival depended on obtaining food from Indians. Probably used to trading with ships coming down from Manhattan, the Indians did not give up on building a friendly relationship with the Dutch, who might provide access to a variety of European goods. After the Mantua Creek sachem was rebuffed, a leader named Zee Pentor from "the Armewanninge, another but neighboring nation," tried to reopen channels with the *Squirrel*'s sailors. Through his intervention, a second meeting was set near the Dutch Fort Nassau in the country of the Armewanninge (or Arrowamex) just below Newton Creek.[2]

The following day Indians poured into Fort Nassau, with "more and more constantly coming." After the crowd had gathered, "nine chiefs, sachems from nine different places" set out from the fort in a dugout canoe, "a boat hollowed out of a tree," to meet the Dutch aboard the *Squirrel*. The crew remained suspicious, but the sachems calmed their fears. David de Vries, a Dutch witness of the event, wrote, "The nine seated themselves in a circle and called us to them, saying they saw that we were afraid of them, but that they came to make a lasting peace with us." This time the Indians successfully presented their gift of peltry. Through a designated speaker, "they made us a present of ten beaver-skins," De Vries reported. They seemed to follow a prescribed ritual, with the speaker carrying out "a ceremony with each skin, saying in whose name he presented it." The goal, the speaker explained, "was for a perpetual peace," to ensure that the Dutch would "banish all evil thoughts" and would know that the Indians "had now thrown away all evil."[3]

These few days in the winter of 1633 offer a glimpse at alliance building between Indians and Europeans in the Delaware Valley. The Indians probably saw the act of sitting down with the Dutch as deeply significant. To "sit down" meant to choose peace. The expression symbolized a truce, perhaps leading to an alliance. The meeting with the nine sachems appears to have been a preliminary event preparing the way for a trading partnership. Soon the Indians around Fort Nassau began to trade with the Dutch. They exchanged "Indian corn of different colors" for European cloth ("duffels"), "kettles, and axes." The Dutch also received some additional beaver pelts.[4]

But this event suggests something more than an Indian-European encounter. Embedded in the event is a story of Indians' contacts with other Indians, some of which would have likely predated the arrival of the Dutch. When relations with the crew of the *Squirrel* were in jeopardy, Indians from "nine different places" coordinated their actions in order to establish a peace agreement with the Dutch. The Armewanninge leader Zee Pentor stepped forward to help after his neighbors from Mantua Creek, known as "Mantes" Indians, had initially failed to secure the alliance. The collection and presentation of gifts to the Dutch also required a certain amount of cooperation among Indians. The fact that there were ten skins seems significant. Probably nine of them came from each of the sachems and the groups they represented. The tenth possibly represented the joint donation of the assembled Indians, with a single presenter acting and speaking for all. What is only hinted at here, but should not be overlooked, are the ways in which alliances among Indian groups preceded and accompanied alliances between Europeans and Indians. When they met with the Dutch, Indians apparently had already established some sort of agreement among communities and sachems, symbolized by their leaders' sitting down together in a circle aboard the *Squirrel*.[5]

Because terminology was fluid, I do not employ one neat label to discuss the Native peoples central to this book—peoples who came from the Delaware and portions of the Hudson Valley. Indians in these areas shared linguistic and other cultural patterns. Many of them have been called "Lenape" or "Delaware." Given the importance of these terms down to the present day, I have incorporated both. "Lenape," a Native term of self-identification, can be translated as "original person" or "real person." "Delaware" originally referred to Indians associated with the river named for the Virginia governor, Sir Thomas West, Lord de la Warr; however, it also came to include some peoples with Hudson Valley origins. No term should be used to imply political or tribal unity across an extensive homeland region in the seventeenth century. There were many different communities and political groupings among peoples typically called "Lenapes" or "Delawares," and I stress this diversity by using a variety of group labels (such as "Armewanninge" and "Mantes"), which especially appeared in seventeenth-century records. "Lenapes" or "Delawares" have been placed within the very broad linguistic classification "Algonquian," marking a distinction from neighboring Iroquoian speakers. Because my concern, especially in opening chapters, is not just with Lenapes but also with closely connected Mahicans, I sometimes use the more inclusive term "Algonquian" to refer to Indians from the Delaware and mid to lower Hudson valleys generally. As the story moves forward in time, I rely increasingly on "Delaware," as it gained in importance as an ethnic/political designation in the course of the eighteenth century.[6]

Through years of researching, writing, and revising, I have grappled with the problems presented by the social complexity of the peoples under investigation and the fluid nature of the groups involved. Early on, I viewed my project as one that concerned identity and ethnogenesis, specifically how Indians came together to forge a Delaware identity from the seventeenth into the eighteenth centuries. Nevertheless, the more I pondered the project and talked with others about it, the more I became aware of the distance between myself and the people whose identity I had so confidently expected to reveal. A major difficulty was the shortage of accounts written by colonial-era Lenapes themselves, making it highly difficult to understand their mindsets and personal identities. Also, the hand of European writers lay heavily on the available documents, further obscuring the internal world of Delawares and their identity formation. Often the best-documented Delawares were those who had a relationship with Euro-Americans, requiring speculation about other Delawares who appeared only briefly in records.

Yet, in some ways, the available records were surprisingly useful. True, they were filtered through Europeans' biases, which required me to read skeptically. True, also, they did not answer a number of my questions, so that I often have had to write with the qualifiers "probably," "possibly," and "perhaps" when I would have preferred more definite statements. Nevertheless, a range of commentators usefully reported on actions and words of Lenape/Delaware peoples. Recorders of treaty minutes documented the alliances they formed. Missionaries, especially German-speaking Moravians, detailed the relationships that they constructed. Travelers described how Delawares settled the land and organized themselves into communities. By close readings of numerous documents, I was able to discern patterns of behavior and approaches to relating to others that told a significant story about Lenapes/Delawares over a substantial period of time. From less tangible questions about identity, then, I shifted my focus to Delawares' recorded actions toward other Indians and toward Euro-Americans. Through examining many incidents such as the one involving the *Squirrel* in 1633, I was struck by the profound significance of alliance formation in the shaping of the Delawares as a people. This story of alliance building appears throughout the following chapters and in two short narrative interludes designed to highlight this process.

Alliances were fundamentally about relationship construction. For the Delawares and their Indian neighbors, success in life required careful tending of a variety of relationships, not just with humans but also with the natural world. Relationships could provide access to power—that is, "successful interaction" or "the ability of an individual to influence other people and other beings." In the Delawares' world, respectful relationships promised a connection with spirit forces that could come to people's aid. Those who built alliances drew especially upon mediation skills. For Indian peoples, mediation was not just a helpful tool; it could also be "a source of influence." Thus, in the eighteenth century, when Delawares thought of ways they could be effective leaders, they sought the roles of mediator and alliance builder.[7]

Delawares organized themselves around kin and community, typically living in relatively small settlements. Nevertheless, their small residential groups were not isolated between 1609 and 1783, the main period I examine. Building networks of communication across a substantial region, moving between and among communities, and constructing alliances and sometimes merging with neighboring Indian groups were approaches that Delawares utilized in the seventeenth century and beyond. Certain of these patterns likely predated the arrival of Europeans, but they played a special role in helping Delawares survive postcontact wars, epidemics, and land dispossession. In response to Euro-American encroachment, Delawares formed alliances to oppose land loss.[8]

Particularly in the mid-eighteenth century, leading up to the American Revolution, Delawares developed explanations about who they were as a people, even though they remained a group with permeable boundaries and even though they were not monolithic in viewpoint and organization. As increasing numbers of Delawares moved west and gathered in the Ohio Valley, their leaders used oral traditions to define their people as alliance builders who had claims to Ohio lands. These alliances involved relations with other Indians and sometimes with Euro-Americans. Delawares turned to the story of their historical connection with the Quakers and the colony of Pennsylvania in defining themselves as alliance makers. Their growing association with Moravian missionaries also became interwoven with this process. Especially in certain periods, however, some Delawares opposed alliance formation with Euro-American neighbors. Too much damage had accompanied Euro-American expansion for these Delawares to embrace such friendships. Delawares' experiences, even before the outbreak of the Seven Years' War in the 1750s, reveal that Pennsylvania was "less peaceful than legend would have it," as tensions over land and trade strained Indians' relations with Euro-Americans.[9]

Over the years Delawares attempted repeatedly to find ways to "sit down" with others in different places and under different circumstances. A Delaware leader might demonstrate a desire for peace by agreeing to "sit down and smoak my Pipe." A negotiator might symbolically prepare a treaty site by telling would-be allies, "I clear the Ground, and the Leaves that you may sit down with Quietness." Chiefs who desired that warriors cease fighting might urge them "to sit down and not to revenge themselves." And even if warriors were intent on fighting, they might promise to "sit down and Listen to their Chiefs" once short-term military goals had been achieved. When Delawares sought a leading role in peacemaking and alliance building, they did so having long invested hope in the possibilities of people sitting down together.[10]

Chapter 1
Communities and Kin

During the seventeenth century Algonquians of the Hudson and Delaware valleys oriented their lives around small communities and kin groups, which gained reinforcement from two other sources: leaders known as "sachems" whose authority was tied to their role within a group of kin traced through the female line, and rituals aimed at promoting the health and welfare of a people. The intersection of these two cultural elements—leaders and rituals—strengthened relationships within communities and kin groups as sachems maintained integrative ceremonies for the people they represented. Although deeply rooted among Indian peoples of the Hudson and Delaware valleys, kin and community groups were not unchanging entities. Their makeup fluctuated as Algonquians adapted to various conditions. Algonquians re-created their lives out of a merging of the old and the new as communities broke apart and reconnected and kin groups combined, separated, and overlapped.

Peoples of River Valleys

One fall day in 1679 Tantaqué, an elderly man of the Hackensack region on the lower Hudson, related his beliefs about the origin of the world in a conversation with Dutch traveler Jasper Danckaerts. After Tantaqué had settled by the fire, Danckaerts asked the old Indian "where he believed he came from." Pulling a chunk of coal out of the hearth, Tantaqué "began to write upon the floor." He drew "a little oval, to which he made four paws or feet, a head and a tail." " 'This,' said he, 'is a tortoise, lying in the water around it,' and he moved his hand round the figure, continuing, 'This was or is all water, and so at first was the world or the earth, when the tortoise gradually raised its round back up high, and the water ran off of it, and thus the earth became dry.' " Placing a straw in the center of the oval, he said, " 'The earth was now dry, and there grew a tree in the middle of the earth, and the root of this tree sent forth a sprout beside it and there grew upon it a man, who was the first male. This man was left alone, and would have remained alone; but the tree bent over until its top touched the earth, and there shot therein another root, from which came forth another sprout, and there grew upon it the woman, and from these two are all men produced.' "[1]

This and other origin stories told by peoples from the Hudson as well as the Delaware Valley included water as a central motif. In another account reported in the eighteenth century, Algonquians depicted their ancestors as living "under a lake." "One of their men made of a hole, through which he ascended to the surface." There "he found a deer," which he took to his friends below the lake. "He and his companions found the meat so good," the story went, "that they unanimously determined to leave their dark abode, and remove to a place where they could enjoy the light of heaven and have such excellent game in abundance." Seemingly a variation on Tantaqué's account, an origin story repeated in the early twentieth century depicted a great flood and the actions of Gicelamu'kaong, or the Great Spirit, to carry dirt from the bottom of the submerged earth to create a new world on the back of a turtle.[2]

The peoples who told these stories oriented their lives around water, specifically around the Hudson and Delaware rivers and the many small streams and creeks nearby. In some cases, they lived along the rivers' banks and at other times they built communities on islands. Their islands, both large and small, rose out of the river like the turtle's back from the depths of the water. Given their settlement patterns, it is not surprising that water emerged as a vital part of each origin story that these Indians handed down. By virtue of the explorations of Henry Hudson in 1609, the Dutch staked a claim in Algonquian homelands and established New Netherland. Early colonizers reported on the riverine settlements of Indian peoples in the Hudson and Delaware valleys. "Some of our navigators are well acquainted with these rivers, which they discovered and have visited for several years," one Dutch report stated. These navigators concluded, "several nations" of Indians "inhabit the banks of these rivers." Europeans who first encountered these peoples recognized their riverine orientation when they referred to them as "River Indians." This general term sometimes appeared in early seventeenth-century documents as shorthand for Hudson or Delaware Valley peoples, though by late in the century, Europeans increasingly applied it to New England Indians migrating into New York. Although Algonquians from the

Hudson and Delaware valleys did not spend all their days along rivers and tributaries, sometimes moving inland to hunting territories, the areas around rivers were central to their lives. Rivers created floodplains where the soil was rich for planting. They provided fish of many varieties. They led to ocean bays and sounds where people could gather the sea's bounty. And they provided a pathway for travel and trade that helped people build relationships throughout the region.[3]

Hudson and Delaware Valley Algonquians included a wide diversity of groups and communities. According to an early historian of New Sweden, a Delaware Valley colony in competition with New Netherland between 1638 and 1655, "there were ten or eleven separate tribes, each having its own *Sackheman* [sachem], or king" in the region. In the present Philadelphia area, between Pennypack Creek and the Falls of the Schuylkill, a Swedish observer in the 1650s found "six different places . . . settled, under six sachems or chiefs, each one commanding his tribe or people under him." New Netherlanders also catalogued a multiplicity of communities and groups along both the Delaware—or "South River" as they called it—and the Hudson—the "North River" or "Great River."[4]

At the time of early contacts with Europeans, most of these river-based peoples do not seem to have oriented their lives around large-scale warfare. A likely factor affecting the need for war and defense was the nature of Algonquians' relationships with the Iroquois or the People of the Longhouse (Haudenosaunee, meaning "the whole house"). Iroquois peoples consisted of the Mohawks, Cayugas, Oneidas, Onondagas, and Senecas, and their homelands included the Mohawk Valley, the area south of Oneida Lake, the Finger Lakes region, and the area east of the Genesee River—all within the bounds of present upstate New York. These peoples appear in seventeenth- and early eighteenth-century records as the "Five Nations"; later they became the "Six Nations" with the addition of the Tuscaroras to the Iroquois Confederacy. About the time of their first encounters with Europeans, many Hudson Valley Algonquians, whose lands bordered on Iroquoia, may have had relatively peaceful relations with their Iroquois neighbors. While the Iroquois engaged in sixteenth-century wars with the Wendats to the northwest, Susquehannocks to the south, and Indian groups along the St. Lawrence, they seemingly had fewer conflicts with Hudson Valley Indians. Competition related to the rise of the fur trade sparked conflict between Delaware Valley Algonquians and Susquehannocks in the seventeenth century; however, this hostility does not appear to have been of long duration.[5]

When it occurred, warfare involving Hudson and Delaware Valley Algonquians appears to have been decentralized and small scale. With some exceptions, they were less likely than neighboring Iroquoian peoples—the Five Nations and the Susquehannocks—to utilize military stockades. The seventeenth-century Swedish commentator Peter Lindeström, a student of mathematics and of "the art of fortification," noted this difference between Lenapes of the Delaware Valley and Iroquoians, whom he considered "somewhat cleverer in building" compared to "river Indians who live closer to us," because the former used "palisades around their dwellings." By implication, Lindeström let his readers know that Lenape settlements lacked what he considered to be superior defensive construction. When Hudson and Delaware Valley groups engaged in war, it may often have been limited to raids by small numbers of warriors who were responding in kind to the killing of relatives in an earlier attack. "The next of kin is the avenger," a New Netherland chronicler reported. Lindeström hinted that warfare for Lenapes meant limited retaliation. As he explained, when an Indian "of one nation kills one of another, immediately he sends one of his subjects to the same nation and stealthily has one of them killed." When Indian peoples along Delaware Bay in the early 1630s destroyed a small Dutch colony, Swanendael, they acted as an aggrieved group of "friends," perhaps kin, who blamed the Dutch for the death of one of their sachems. Discovering the ruins of the Dutch settlement soon before his visit to Fort Nassau, David de Vries was told, "the friends of the murdered chief [had] incited their friends . . . to set about the work of vengeance."[6]

Trade was a powerful factor influencing relations among Algonquians and their neighbors, both Indian and European. In addition to furs, which Europeans found especially desirable, wampum (or *sewan*), a type of shell bead, was a major trading item. After obtaining iron tools from Europeans, coastal Indians used them to drill holes in certain types of shells to produce wampum. Hudson-area Indians manufactured these beads in winter, using white and even more valuable black (or dark purple) shells. The Dutch lawyer and commentator Adriaen van der Donck explained bead production: "They strike off the thin parts of those shells and preserve the pillars or standards, which they grind smooth and even and reduce the same according to their thickness, and drill a hole through every piece and string the same on strings." Wampum became a form of currency in colonial America at a time when coins were scarce.[7]

Native North Americans, however, attached additional meaning to wampum. Believing that sacred power resided in wampum, they often kept this power close at hand by adorning themselves with it. Van der Donck described Indian women's dress as beautifully made with wampum: "The women . . . wear a cloth around their bodies, fastened by a girdle which extends down below their knees, and is as much an under-coat; but next to the body, under this coat, they wear a dressed deer-skin coat, girt around the waist. The lower border of this skirt they ornament with great art, and nestle the same with strips, which are tastefully decorated with wampum." A European correspondent from the 1620s explained that the Indians considered wampum "as valuable as we do money . . . they string it, and wear it around the neck and hands; they also make bands of it, which the women wear on the forehead under the hair, and the men around the body; and they are as particular about the stringing and the sorting as we can be here about pearls." Lindeström noted that Delaware Valley Indians of the 1650s greased their hair with bear fat so that "it shines so that one can see one's reflection in it." Then "the locks they bind up with braids and ribbons and their threaded money [wampum]. On the ends of their hair they string money and tie a knot to [it]." Wampum surrounded the wearer with spiritual power. No wonder that, according to a description from New Netherland, "They twine both white and black wampum around their heads . . . they wear Wampum in the ears, around the neck and around the waist."[8]

Wampum represented the spoken word, a sacred force for Indian peoples steeped in oral traditions. It added power to messages and speeches that constructed relationships. To give words legitimacy in negotiations, statements required the backing of wampum strings or belts. A 1645 treaty between the French, the Iroquois, and other Indian groups indicated the importance of wampum in representing the words that forged ties among these people. At the courtyard of the Three Rivers Fort on the St. Lawrence, "large sails" were "spread to keep off the heat of the Sun." A Jesuit priest described this event: "In the center was a large space, somewhat longer than wide, in which the Iroquois caused two poles to be planted, and a cord to be stretched from one to the other on which to hang and tie the words that they were to bring us." The "words" were wampum collars or belts, "a portion of which were on their bodies." Wampum was a signifier and authorizer of language, as a multitude of treaties demonstrated.[9]

Delaware Valley Algonquians had less access to wampum than did those in the Hudson Valley. New Sweden's governor, Johan Printz, complained in 1644 that the lower-Delaware groups "are poor, so that one can secure from them only little or hardly any *sevant*, hence we must buy *sevant* from

Manathans and of the North English [New Englanders], where *sevant* is made, and it can be bought cheaply there." Unlike the Hudson, the Delaware River did not provide a direct route to Long Island Sound, a major source of wampum. The difficulty in obtaining wampum may have minimized Delaware Valley Indians' trade in this sought-after commodity.[10]

It is possible that Hudson Valley peoples engaged in trade networks involved with the distribution of copper, which, like wampum, had ceremonial value. An officer on Henry Hudson's 1609 voyage saw copper items among Hudson Valley Indians. The people he encountered had "red Copper Tobacco pipes, and other things of Copper they did weare about their neckes." This officer also mentioned that the Indians "have yellow Copper." Hudson himself noted similarly that on the lower Hudson River "the people had copper tobacco pipes." The sources for this copper are uncertain, and it is also possible that the Dutch were misinformed, confusing red shale and clay items for copper. If the Hudson Valley Indians had copper, it may have been from the Great Lakes, reaching them via the Iroquois, who in turn obtained it from the Wenros and Neutrals living along the western end of Lake Ontario and the eastern end of Lake Erie. However, there were also copper deposits much closer to home—in areas of present-day Connecticut, Massachusetts, Pennsylvania, and New Jersey. Later Euro-American discoveries of copper indicate that Indians could have had sources in the region. In the eighteenth century a significant amount of copper was unearthed in the New Brunswick area, and copper was also mined in the Watchung Mountains of northern New Jersey.[11]

Communities and Kin Groups

When it came to obtaining the basic necessities of life, Hudson and Delaware Valley Algonquians of the seventeenth century depended greatly on their own considerable skills in planting and harvesting crops, hunting, fishing, and gathering wild foods. In the process of providing for their needs, Indians of the river valleys established numerous localized community-based associations. We should avoid narrow definitions of community for these Indians. Within a delimited territory, they constituted and reconstituted different types of communities, serving different functions and different sizes of population. Thus Hudson and Delaware Valley Indians took an adaptive and flexible approach to community building.

At least two major variables influenced the diversity in community formation. The first variable was seasonal change, to which Algonquians adjusted by occupying and reoccupying different places according to subsistence cycles. Arriving in 1682 to establish the colony of Pennsylvania, William Penn observed the round of seasons in the Delaware Valley. Fall was like a "mild Spring" in England; winter was "sharp" and "Frosty" with a "Skie as clear as in Summer, and the Air dry, cold, piercing and hungry"; spring was "sweet" with "no Gusts, but gentle Showers, and a fine Skie"; and summer "had extraordinary Heats, yet mitigated sometimes by Cool Breezese. . . . And whatever Mists, Fogs or Vapours foul the Heavens by Easterly or Southerly Winds, in two Hours time are blown away." Algonquians adapted to this seasonal round. They formed hamlets around cultivation of the soil, making good use of the growing season approximately between May and October, and they established hunting communities and fishing stations that corresponded with the seasonal migrations of animals. The second variable was the absence or presence of war. Algonquians appear to have frequently continued their dispersed settlement patterns during wartime; however, Hudson Valley Indians occasionally constructed stockades. Thus at least four types of community—planting settlements, hunting communities, fishing stations, and occasionally stockaded towns—emerged from these variables. It is important to note, however, that a location could serve more than one function, allowing for overlaps among these types.[12]

There was probably variation in the degree to which seventeenth-century Hudson and Delaware Valley Algonquians relied on crops. Coastal peoples may have devoted less attention to growing crops in comparison to groups farther inland because of less fertile soils. Nevertheless, the documentary record provides important examples of Algonquians' field production by the seventeenth century. The Jesuit father Isaac Jogues commented that when the first Dutch colonists arrived, they "found lands fit for use," left by the Indians "who formerly had fields here."[13]

Indians in the Hudson and Delaware valleys cultivated three principal crops—corn (or maize), beans, and squash. Van der Donck found squash (or *quaasiens*) a fascinating new type of food. "It is a delightful fruit," he rhapsodized, "as well to the eye on account of its fine variety of colours, as to the mouth for its agreeable taste. The ease with which it is cooked renders it a favourite too with the young women. . . . [I]t is incredible, when one watches the vines, how many will grow on them in the course of a single season." Other crops included gourds, pumpkins, tobacco, and sunflowers. In 1609,

Hudson River Indians boarded Hudson's ship, the *Half Moon*, and traded "eares of Indian Corne, and Pompions, and Tabacco" with the sailors. An English traveler in 1634 described the Delaware Valley as "covered over with woods and stately timber, except only in those places, where the Indians had planted their corne." There were accounts suggesting sizable production in certain areas. Hudson claimed that a Native community with about fifty-seven adults had produced a crop substantial "enough to load three ships." And the Siconese (or "Sironesack") Indians living on Delaware Bay near Cape Henlopen were reportedly "rich in maize plantations." Other evidence suggests, however, that cultivated fields were often small scale. Rocky terrain sometimes prevented large-scale planting, according to the mid-seventeenth-century notes of David de Vries. On the lower Hudson he encountered an area "little capable of sustaining a population, as there are only cliffs and stones along the river. . . . There is here and there some maize-land" where Indians were working to "remove the stones and cultivate it."[14]

On fertile riverine flats, women were responsible for raising crops throughout the growing season. Proximity linked homes with cultivated lands. "They plant Indian corn and beans round about their huts," wrote German immigrant Daniel Francis Pastorius about Delaware Valley Indians. Proximity was useful because corn needed frequent and careful attention to prevent damage from wildlife. Particularly troublesome was "a species of black bird which makes its appearance at harvest, when the corn named maize is ripe." De Vries noted that "these birds are called maize-thieves, because they fall upon the corn by thousands, and do great damage." Revealing the interconnections between residences and cultivated areas, Indians on the Schuylkill had "their dwellings side by side one another, wherefore also this land is thereby being cleared and cultivated with great power." These communities probably continued in a particular location until planting and re-planting limited the productivity of the fields, after perhaps a dozen years, at which time Algonquians would resettle in a new place.[15]

Various commentators discussed the production of corn or maize. Lindeström noted its colorful appearance in "white, red, blue, flesh-colored, brown, yellow and spotted ears" with "6 or 7 ears" per stalk. Delaware Valley Indians, he observed, planted this corn "in square hills" between which "one can conveniently walk." Isaak de Rasieres, a commercial agent in New Netherland, wrote about corn in the Hudson Valley: "It is a grain to which much labor must be given, with weeding and earthing-up, or it does not thrive; and to this the women must attend very closely." Women planted corn in "heaps like molehills, each about two and a half feet from the others." "In each heap," they placed "five or six grains." Later, "when the maize is the height of a finger or more, they plant in each heap three or four Turkish beans, which then grow up with and against the maize, which serves for props, for the maize grows on stalks similar to sugarcane." David de Vries also described "beans of different colors, which they plant among their maize." In contrast to De Rasieres, he judged that the distance between corn plants was greater, as much as "three or four feet apart, in order to make room to weed it thoroughly."[16]

Corn was the source of meal that Hudson and Delaware Valley women used in making bread and porridge. De Rasieres explained that the bread makers first boiled the grain and "then beat it flat upon a stone; then they put it into a wooden mortar, which they know how to hollow out by fire, and then they have a stone pestle . . . with which they pound it small." Baskets made of hemp or rushes formed sieves for sifting cornmeal. "The finest meal they mix with lukewarm water, and knead it into dough," De Rasieres wrote, "then they make round flat little cakes of it, of the thickness of an inch or a little more, which they bury in hot ashes, and so bake into bread." After the loaves were baked, they needed to be cleaned: "They have some clean fresh water by them in which they wash them while hot, one after another, and it is good bread, but heavy." According to De Vries, Indians baked the bread "in the ashes, first wrapping a vine-leaf or maize-leaf around them."[17]

By boiling the "coarsest meal," Indians made a type of porridge, called *sapaen* or *homine*. "We seldom visit an Indian lodge at any time of the day, without seeing their *sapaen* preparing, or seeing them eating the same," Van der Donck noted. "It is the common food of all; young and old eat it; and they are so well accustomed to it, and fond of it, that when they visit our people, or each other, they consider themselves neglected unless they are treated with *sapaen*." To create a specialty dish, women "mix this, also, thoroughly with little beans, of different colors, raised by themselves; this is esteemed by them rather as a dainty, than as a daily dish."[18]

Besides using corn for porridge and bread, Native peoples also "Roasted [it] in the Ashes," according to Penn. Stored corn could support families during lean winter months. De Vries explained, "They gather their maize and French beans the last of September and October, and when they have gathered and shelled the corn, they bury it in holes, which they have previously lined with mats, and so keep as much as they want for the winter and while hunting." And dried corn kept hunters and travelers alive on long journeys away from home. Van der Donck noted its essential role on these trips. "When they intend to go a great distance on a hunting excursion, or to war, where they expect to find no food," he wrote, "then they provide themselves severally with a small bag of parched corn meal, which is so nutritious that they can subsist on the same many days." A minimal amount of this corn made a huge difference for travelers: "A quarter of a pound of the meal is sufficient for a day's subsistence; for as it shrinks much in drying, it also swells out again with moisture. When they are hungry, they eat a small handful of the meal, after which they take a drink of water, and then they are so well fed, that they can travel a day."[19]

Variations in housing throughout the Delaware and Hudson valleys suggest that differences in community type and function resulted in different forms of dwellings. In communities oriented around planting and harvesting, bark longhouses may have been one of the principal forms. Archaeologists have excavated sites of round-ended longhouses in the upper Delaware Valley in New Jersey. Their findings indicate that these longhouses had "a single opening on one of the long sides," and "room partitions extended from one of the long walls to within about three feet of the opposite wall, providing a passageway along one side of the house and access to family compartments and storage areas." One of the more sizable house patterns discovered through excavation in the Delaware Valley is of a dwelling sixty feet by twenty feet. Generally smaller than Iroquois longhouses, which averaged one hundred feet long, these dwellings would have been convenient to cultivated fields and would have accommodated Indians as they gathered in their villages at the end of the growing season to celebrate the harvest. Given reports of diversity in construction, there probably was variation in housing within planting communities. For example, archaeological work in New Jersey uncovered patterns for eighteen longhouses less than sixty feet in length and for even smaller oval buildings.[20]

Planting settlements with longhouses or some other form of semipermanent dwellings seem the most obvious community type because they may have included the largest gatherings of people, which probably peaked at harvest time; however, other forms of community were just as important to the life of the people. Of major significance were hunting groups. Although the period after the harvest and through the winter was the primary hunting season, Indians also hunted in the spring and summer.[21]

The size of hunting parties varied greatly. Some communal hunts involved large numbers of hunters who set up fire rings to flush out and contain game. Lindeström described a communal hunt in late winter or early spring:

Now at that time of the year the grass which grows there . . . is as dry as hay. When now the sachem wants to arrange his hunt, then he commands his people [to take a position] close together in a circle, . . . In the first place each one roots up the grass in the position, [assigned to him] in the circumference . . . so that the fire will not be able to run back, each one then beginning to set fire to the grass, which is mightily ignited, so that the fire travels away, in towards the center of the circle, which the Indians follow with great noise, and all the animals which are found within the circle, flee from the fire and the cries of the Indians, traveling away, whereby the circle through its decreasing is more and more contracted towards the center. When now the Indians have surrounded the center with a small circle, so that they mutually cannot do each other any harm, then they break loose with guns and bows on the animals.

When from aboard his ship, De Vries saw "great fires on the land" in the Delaware Valley, he may have been observing this type of activity.[22]

In the Hudson Valley, Adriaen van der Donck also observed hunting parties burning brush. "The Indians have a yearly custom," he wrote, "of burning the woods, plains and meadows in the fall of the year, when the leaves have fallen, and when the grass and vegetable substances are dry." Another burning took place again in the spring. This schedule perhaps varied— along the Delaware the fires observed by De Vries occurred between January and early February. Besides allowing hunters "to circumscribe and enclose the game within the lines of the fire," burning also made "the game . . . more easily tracked." "Notwithstanding the apparent danger of the entire destruction of the woodlands by the burning, still the green trees do not suffer," Van der Donck explained. "The outside bark is scorched three or four feet high, which does them no injury, for the trees are not killed." The fires created quite a spectacle for travelers in boats along the Hudson. These conflagrations "appear grand at night . . . when the woods are burning on both sides of the same," he marveled. "Then we can see a great distance by the light of the blazing trees, the flames being driven by the wind, and fed by the tops of the trees. But the dead and dying trees remain burning in their standing positions, which appear sublime and beautiful when seen at a distance."[23]

One last example of large-scale hunting comes from De Vries, who described "a hundred more or less joining in the hunt." At these big gatherings, the hunters "stand a hundred paces more or less from each other, and holding flat thigh-bones in the hand, beat them with a stick, and so drive the creatures before them to the river." As the hunters "approach the river, they close nearer to each other, and whatever is between any two of them, is at the mercy of their bows and arrows, or must take to the river." If the animal jumped into the river, other Indians waiting in canoes threw ropes "around their necks, and tighten, whereupon the deer lie down and float with the rump upwards, as they cannot draw breath."[24]

Smaller hunting groups were probably more frequent than these large-scale enterprises, which may have involved multiple kin groups. At times a few individuals may have hunted together, and at other times a single family, perhaps just a wife, husband, and children, constituted a hunting party. Following the harvest, families left the planting settlement to visit hunting territories. Having stored grain in "baskets woven of rushes or wild hemp," the women "went with their husbands and children in October to hunt deer, leaving at home with their maize the old people who cannot follow." From late fall into winter, hunting families worked together, with men and women fulfilling their respective functions. Indian men hunted the animals; women cleaned and prepared skins and meat, cooked for the camp, and cared for the children. Small groups of hunting families created communities in territories where their kin had probably found game for generations, given the repetition in animals' migration patterns. Nuclear families may have set up dome-shaped lodges in interior regions along the bases of mountains. Some of these were perhaps constructed quickly, as Penn implied: "In Travel they lodge in the Woods about a great Fire, with a Mantle of Duffills they wear by day wrapt about them," and "a few Boughs" arranged into a temporary dwelling. A Dutch report from 1624 described "dwellings . . . commonly circular, with a vent hole above to let out the smoke, closed with four doors, and made mostly of the bark of trees." "Their dwellings are constructed of hickory poles set in the ground and bent bow fashion, like arches," explained another Dutch account, "and then covered with bark which they peel in quantities for that purpose." Variations on such dome-shaped houses could have not only served planting communities as an alternative to the longhouse but also housed wintering families in interior regions.[25]

Hunting provided both food and clothing for peoples all along the Hudson and Delaware valleys, making the hunt a major focus of their lives. Among the animals hunted were deer, bear, wild turkeys, partridges, pigeons, and geese. For the Indians of Long Island, Daniel Denton noted in 1670 that they also killed and ate "Skunks, Racoon, Possum, Turtles, and the like." Indians obtained pelts for clothing from some of these animals, as well as from beavers, fox, otters, lynxes, and minks. Meat was normally boiled without salt or oil. River valley peoples sometimes dried meat to a hard consistency, pounded it, and boiled it with *sapaen*. "Dry beans, which they consider dainties," were also "boil[ed] soft with fresh meat."[26]

Early Hudson and Delaware Valley peoples traditionally made their clothes out of furs, feathers, and skins. On a voyage with Hudson, Robert Juet described the people who came aboard the *Half Moon*, "some in Mantles of Feathers, and some in Skinnes of divers sorts of good Furres." According to De Rasieres, "In the winter time they usually wear a dressed deer skin; some have a bear's skin about the body." Of the Indians on the lower Hudson, De Vries observed that "their clothing is a coat of beaver-skins over the body, with the fur inside in winter, and outside in summer; they have, also, sometimes a bear's hide, or a coat of the skins of wild cats, or *hesspanen* [raccoon], which is an animal almost as hairy as a wild cat, and is also very good to eat." In the Delaware Valley, Pastorius reported that "instead of shoes," the Indians "use thin deer skin." Lindeström provided a more detailed description of their footwear: "On their feet they use *sippackor* or laced shoes of deer skin, bordered and decorated with their money [wampum]."[27]

In addition to constructing communities around hunting, Hudson and Delaware Valley peoples formed communities and attachments around fishing stations, which provided another key dietary staple. Archaeological evidence demonstrates the importance of fish and shellfish to the nutrition of riverine peoples from at least the Early Woodland period (ca. 1000 to 500 B.C.E.). Excavations of refuse pits on the upper Delaware from the Late Woodland period (beginning about 900 C.E.) reveal some scales and fish bones as well as the remains of freshwater mussels by the thousand. In this same area, archaeologists have recovered a variety of netsinkers dating back to Early Woodlanders who utilized these weights to catch fish. River-based Indians in the seventeenth century continued this ancient practice of netting fish. According to De Rasieres, "In April, May, and June, they follow the course of these [the fish], which they catch with a drag-net they themselves knit very neatly, of the wild hemp, from which the women and old men spin the thread." Netted fish were "principally . . . shad" and "the largest fish is a sort of white salmon, which is of very good flavor." By another account, fishermen used "seines from seventy to eighty fathoms in length, which they braid themselves, and on which, in place of lead, they hang stones, and instead of the corks . . . they fasten small sticks of an ell in length, round and sharp at the end." An alternative method was creek damming. At fishing stations in the Delaware drainage Native peoples worked together to construct fish traps, or dams, on creeks that emptied into the river. Lindeström reported, "when the river rises and the water is highest they close up the opening, but when the water is run out and the ebb is lowest then the fish remains behind in the low water, where they either catch them with their hands or shoot it [*sic*]."[28]

Fish and shellfish were abundant and came in many varieties. On the Delaware, De Vries found "a great plenty of fish," including "perch, roach, pike, sturgeon," and "along the sea-coast . . . codfish." An English contemporary made similar observations along the Delaware. "Of fish heere is plenty," he stated, "but especially sturgeon all the sommer time." Expounding on ocean-side collection, Van der Donck reported, "Sometimes towards the spring of the year, they [the Indians] come in multitudes to the sea shores and bays, to take oysters, clams, and every kind of shell-fish." Juet said matter-of-factly about the Hudson, "The River is full of fish," and he included salmon, mullets, and bass among the available types.[29]

Although fishing appeared to European observers to be mainly a male occupation, communities of women and men sometimes gathered at fishing stations, especially when they overlapped with planting settlements. One commentator referred to "villages near the water sides, at fishing places, where they plant some vegetables." In such settings men fished and constructed nets, and women cooked and tended crops. Children were present to learn from adults about the craft of fishing. Pastorius noted that very young Delaware Valley children "are made to catch fish with hooks." Danckaerts probably encountered one of these fishing families in the lower Hudson Valley in March 1680. On a small creek, he visited "a hut of the Indians, of whom there is only one family on this whole tract." These Indians seemed to consist of more than one nuclear family because they included at least two men and some women and children. They lived within a few hours of a rich fishing area—"a basin" below the falls at Passaic "so full of all kinds of [fish] . . . that you can catch them with your hands, because they are stopped there, and collect together, refreshing themselves, and sporting in and under the falling fresh water, which brings with it, from above, bushes, green leaves, earth, and mire, in which they find food." Danckaerts and his companion Peter Sluyter presented to "each man four fish-hooks, and the women and children each two," perhaps recognizing the timeliness of their gift after viewing the fish sporting below Passaic falls. Groups of related individuals probably returned year after year to fishing stations at the same falls or the same shoreline that had yielded successful catches in the past. In this way, fishing stations became places that represented the sustenance and welfare of communities whose boundaries shifted seasonally, as groups overlapped and separated.[30]

Algonquians probably spent only limited, if any, time in the fourth type of community—the fortified town. The small, dispersed settlement in planting, hunting, and fishing areas appears to have been their overwhelming choice. Nevertheless, there were some stockaded sites in the Hudson Valley, where war broke out between Euro-Americans and Algonquians and sometimes among Indians. Hudson Valley Algonquian fortifications may have borne some resemblance to the palisaded hilltop towns of neighboring Iroquois. A 1632 map of Hudson Valley lands purchased by the Dutch patroon Kiliaen van Rensselaer located two fortified Indian towns—Monemin's Castle and Unuwat's Castle. Lower on the Hudson at Wecquaesgeek (or Wetquescheck) in 1644, there were three forts with stockades "of plank five inches thick, nine feet high, and braced around with thick balk full of port-holes." Van der Donck described a Native method of fortification in New Netherland, which may have applied to some Hudson Valley Algonquians:

For the erection of these castles or strong holds, they usually select a situation on the side of a steep high hill near a stream or river, which is difficult of access, except from the water, and inaccessible on every other side, with a level plain on the crown of the hill, which they enclose with a strong stockade work in a singular manner. First, they lay along the ground large logs of wood, and frequently smaller logs upon the lower logs, which serve for the foundation of the work. Then they place strong oak palisades in the ground on both sides of the foundation, the upper ends of which cross each other, and are joined together. In the upper cross of the palisades they then place the bodies of trees, which makes the work strong.

He added that one of these stockaded communities might include twenty or thirty houses.[31]

Connections to specific places of community formation overlapped with connections to kin groups. The basic unit of kinship was the matrilineage, an exogamous descent group traced through the female line. It is possible that each lineage or combinations of lineages as clans had a name that referred to an attribute of the group's common ancestress or to a place relevant to her. Indirect evidence comes from kin group names among nineteenth-century descendants of Delaware Valley peoples. Names such as *O-ka-ho'ki* ("Ruler"), *Ta-ko-ong'o-to* ("High Bank Shore"), *Kwin-eek'cha* ("Long Body"), *Tong-o-nä'-o-to* ("Drift Log"), *Toosh-war-ka'-ma* ("Across the River"), and *Koo-wä-ho'ke* ("Pine Region") marked matriclans or matrilineages of the

Delawares of Kansas. In this system, ties between mothers and their children were especially strong.[32]

One of the oldest female members of the matrilineage may have been a lineage matron who selected the sachem as a leader for the matrilineage. Seventeenth-century evidence for this is lacking, and the argument for the role of lineage matron rests on later sources. In the eighteenth century the Moravian missionary David Zeisberger reported on the involvement of various women in a ceremony installing a new sachem, although he was not explicit about the functions of these women in this event. Delawares living on the Six Nations Reserve in Ontario in the early twentieth century told of the female " 'chief-maker,' in whose family lineage rested the power of selecting the ruling chief when the office was vacant." This woman, according to their hereditary chief, Joseph Montour, "had higher power than the chief himself." These bits of evidence suggest that, as was true among the Iroquois, female elders among the Delaware and Hudson Valley peoples may have selected sachems.[33]

Crosscutting these matrilineal relations were associations formed within nuclear families, including relations between children and parents of both sexes and between husbands and wives. Husbands and wives belonged to different matrilineages; thus the household was "a mixture of affinal and consanguine relatives." Spouses had a fundamental bond with their own mother's family, which cut across the ties they created with marriage partners. Divorce did occur, and links between husbands and wives may not have been as deeply rooted as relationships formed within matrilineages. When divorce took place, Van der Donck wrote, "children follow their mother," a practice that underscored the matrilineal relation.[34]

Relatives in matrilineages probably influenced the choice of a spouse and a couple's life after marriage. The following account of a marriage agreement shows that two people did not decide to marry each other as two isolated and independent individuals; instead, "friends" of the bride, perhaps members of her matrilineage, played significant roles in advising and approving of the marriage. De Rasieres explained, "They have a marriage custom amongst them, namely: when there is one who resolves to take a particular person for his wife, he collects a fathom or two of sewan." Then this man went not to the woman alone but "to the nearest friends of the person whom he desires, to whom he declares his object in her presence." The "friends" had to give their consent: "If they are satisfied with him, he agrees with them how much sewan he shall give her for a bridal present; that being done, he then gives her all the Dutch beads he has, which they call *Machampe*, and also all sorts of trinkets." "If she be a young virgin," they did not marry immediately. "He must wait six weeks more before he can sleep with her," De Rasieres wrote, and "all this time she sits with a blanket over her head, without wishing to look at any one, or any one being permitted to look at her." When the marriage finally occurred, her "friends" again entered into the arrangement: "they then eat together with the friends, and sing and dance together." Van der Donck noted the role of "the counsel and advice of their relatives" when a couple married.[35]

This union involved important reciprocal relations between the woman and the man. The prospective husband brought the fruits of his hunting to the woman when it came time for their marriage, underscoring his obligation to provide meat and skins throughout their years together. "That being done," De Rasieres wrote, "the wife must provide food for herself and her husband, as far as breadstuffs are concerned, and [should they fall short] she must buy what is wanting with her sewan." Thus the woman contributed her share as well to the new family unit being formed—planting, hoeing, harvesting, cooking, and baking, among many other duties. After marriage, the husband and wife may have lived with the wife's family, given the obvious importance of her "friends" or relatives in the marital agreement; but matrilocal residence, that is, the husband moving to the wife's family, lacks documentation. Penn mentioned that "Girls stay with their Mothers, and help to hoe the Ground, plant Corn and carry Burthens" and sometimes married at very young ages, such as thirteen or fourteen, but he and other European commentators never explicitly stated that matrilocal residence was the norm. As with the Iroquois, who also followed a matrilineal kinship system, matrilocal residence may have been "the ideal," though not always followed in practice.[36]

The visit of Danckaerts and Sluyter to Indians in the vicinity of the Millstone River near the Falls of the Delaware one December day in 1679 seems to offer a window on a world in which membership in a nuclear family overlapped with membership in matrilineal groups. Traveling through the area, the two Dutch travelers sought help from local Indians to assist them in traversing the Millstone, which was running high with a swift current. It had been raining, and both men were completely soaked as they came upon some Indian houses. Entering one of the residences, they saw that the dwelling consisted of two "households," possibly two related nuclear family units. One "household," a wife and husband with one or more children, sat together around one fire. All of a sudden "a little naked child fell from its mother's lap, and received a cut in its head." What happened next appeared to startle Danckaerts, who wrote, "All who sat around that fire, and belonged to that household, began to cry, husband and wife, young and old, and scream more than the child, and as if they themselves had broken their arms or legs." Around another fire "in another corner of this house" sat members of the other "household." This group was grieving over the loss of a loved one. Their "faces were entirely blackened," and they "observed a gloomy silence and looked very singular." As Danckaerts explained, "They were in mourning for a deceased friend."[37]

This account portrays two family groups, distinct but also linked, as they shared the same house. Although he tended toward full descriptions, Danckaerts mentioned no other houses in the community, except some "houses of the Indians on the right." From this lack of detail, we might assume that the Indians lived in a fairly small settlement. A larger place would likely have elicited more comment from Danckaerts. As two families in a small place, each group probably depended on the other for subsistence and survival. Yet there also seemed to be an emotional separation between the two families. With blackened faces one group mourned, while the other group did not. When the child fell and cut its head, one family reacted in pain, while the other continued its own separate bereavement ritual, apparently fixed on the spirit of a dead friend or relative whom they mourned. Thus each nuclear family appeared to be in its own distinct emotional world.[38]

Despite the obvious importance of the nuclear family here, Danckaerts's account also hints at the significance of crosscutting matrilineal ties. Apparently some, or all, of the members of the house were part of a matrilineal kin group that linked their settlement to another one in the area. At least several of the residents of the house considered a sachem a few miles away to be their leader. Sachems were kin-based leaders who followed matrilineal lines of succession. As Penn wrote, "Their Government is by Kings, which they call *Sachema*, and those by Succession, but always of the Mothers side; for Instance, the Children of him that is now King, will not succeed, but his Brother by the Mother, or the Children of his Sister, whose Sons (and after them the Children of her Daughters) will reign." A Native man in the house near Millstone River conducted Danckaerts and Sluyter to "their king or *sackemaker* [sachem] who lived two or three miles from there." In addition to this sachem at the second settlement, a "queen" resided with the sachem, possibly the lineage matron for the group, or alternatively, the wife of the sachem whom the Europeans viewed as the queen. After they arrived, the "queen" immediately greeted Danckaerts and Sluyter, offering the men "a piece of their bread, that is, pounded maize kneaded into a cake and baked under the ashes." After paying the sachem with some wampum and offering "fishhooks to several of them, but especially to the queen who had entertained us," Danckaerts and Sluyter then went with the sachem across the river.[39]

This example of the families along the Millstone suggests that these Algonquians formed kinship relations in varied ways. Nuclear family units were an essential source of emotional strength, economic survival, and residential focus. Matrilineal kin groups, headed by particular sachems, were also fundamental to community organization. When a Dutch commentator wrote that "the Indians . . . dwell together, mostly from friendship, in tribes commanded by a chief . . . usually called Sachemay," he was probably referring to communities in which members of a particular matrilineage with their sachem predominated among the residents. This tendency to organize around kin groups suggests that a matrilineal connection may have existed among at least some of the individuals in the first house that Danckaerts described. Yet matrilineages could link people not just within but also across different communities, as the two settlements visited by Danckaerts and Sluyter seem to indicate.[40]

Throughout the Hudson and Delaware valleys, Algonquians' approach of both subdividing and uniting enabled them to adapt to geographical and seasonal diversity and respond to outside threats. Small family groups—nuclear households or other small kin-based groups—worked as hunting units during the long winter months. At times larger gatherings formed, such as at ceremonies marking the annual harvest. At least occasionally in wartime, stockaded towns could provide protective space for multiple kin groups. In places with sizable longhouses, there seems to have been a careful arrangement of space recognizing different nuclear families. As Van der Donck observed of one of these places, "From sixteen to eighteen families frequently dwell in one house, according to its size. The fire being kept in the middle, the people lay on either side thereof, and *each family has its own place*."[41]

Leaders and Rituals

Leaders reinforced relationships formed within kin and community groups. Among Hudson and Delaware Valley Algonquians, leaders were typically heads of matrilineally related kin. Struck by this kin-based leadership though ignorant of its political significance, one Dutch writer stated, "They have no form of political leadership, except that they have their chiefs, whom they call *sackmos* and *sagamos*, who are not much more than heads of families, for they rarely exceed the limits of one family connexion." Along with the lineage matrons who may have appointed them, these sachems, who were usually male, were the leading representatives of their particular kin group. As part of a matrilineal tradition, which Penn had noted, sachems often succeeded their own brother or their mother's brother; succession thereby remained in the maternal line. "Rank descends in families," Van der Donck believed, "and continues as long as any one in the family is fit to rule."[42]

Sachems aided their people by representing them to outsiders. For this, they needed wealth great enough to offer the gifts and hospitality that created relationships with those beyond their lineage. "All travellers who stop over night come to the Sackima, if they have no acquaintances there, and are entertained by the expenditure of as much sewan as is allowed for that purpose," De Rasieres explained. Tobacco was often involved in the gift giving that strengthened ties between peoples. Before any words were spoken to a visiting stranger, the visitor and the sachem smoked a pipe of tobacco. "That being done, the Sackima asks: 'Whence do you come?' The stranger then states that, and further what he has to say, before all who are present or choose to come." Some seventeenth-century sachems had more than one wife, who assisted them in fulfilling their obligations of hospitality. According to one Dutch report, "Ordinarily" the Indians "have but one wife, sometimes two or three, but this is generally among the chiefs." "The Sackimas generally have three or four wives," De Rasieres wrote, "each of whom has to furnish her own seed-corn," obviously increasing the resources available for distribution. Lindeström noted the importance of the sachem's wife in providing for the needs of large numbers: "She is the housekeeper for the whole crowd," assigning cooking duties to various women "each in her turn."[43]

Leaders were also expected to work for the health and welfare of their own group. A proven ability to distribute and redistribute goods throughout the community was another sign of legitimate leadership. Access to wealth, particularly wampum, enabled sachems to promote their people's welfare by keeping goods flowing to those who could benefit from them. "Wealth circulateth like the Blood, all parts partake," Penn wrote. He also observed that upon receiving a portion of wealth, a sachem or "King sub-divideth it in like manner among his Dependents, they hardly leaving themselves an Equal share with one of their Subjects: and be it on such occasions, at Festivals, or at their common Meals, the Kings distribute, and to themselves last."[44]

A mark of sound leadership was the successful performance of rituals that preserved the health and safety of the group. As lineage heads, sachems took particular responsibility for conducting rituals aimed at the well-being of their people. Hudson and Delaware Valley Indians believed in a world of *manitou*, that is, one containing powerful spirit beings. "Every thing that is wonderful and strange or that surpasses human understanding, that they . . . call Menutto," stated one Dutch account. In order to aid those in relationship with them, sachems handled ceremonies honoring or appeasing spirits. Evidence of carvings, presumably of these spirits, within sachems' houses suggests the leader's importance in maintaining the group's ritual connection with deities. "Principally the chief's houses, have, inside, portraits and pictures somewhat rudely carved," a New Netherland chronicle revealed. Sometimes sachems were also shamans with special healing powers. Hans, an Indian guide for Danckaerts and Sluyter, called himself a "*Sakemaker* among the Indians, and also a medicine-man." "I . . . have performed many good cures," Hans declared. In order to maintain their position, leaders needed to persuade their people that they served the group's welfare; success in healing would have helped demonstrate the leader's legitimacy.[45]

Algonquians developed a long-standing tradition of family rituals to honor spirit beings, and older well-respected kin-group leaders were essential to maintaining this tradition. For the seventeenth century, evidence is limited, although the carved figures in sachems' houses provide indirect evidence of the role of kin-group leaders in the maintenance of rituals. The main sources for kin-based rituals, however, come from later centuries. In the eighteenth century Zeisberger described rituals that depended on family or lineage heads for their performance. Emphasizing the role of familial bonds, he used the word "Freundschaft" repeatedly, which might be translated as "kin," "kin group," or "relatives"—probably typically meaning "lineage." "The *Freundschaft* is very extensive among them," he wrote. "Such a sacrifice is held by a *Freundschaft* every other year. . . . They are usually held in the autumn or even perhaps in winter. . . . The headman of each *Freundschaft* knows the time and he must provide for it." Well over one hundred years later, the anthropologist M. R. Harrington reported on a variety of family rites still practiced among the Delawares. One of these, an Otter Ceremony, also occurred every other year, though in the spring, not the fall or winter as in Zeisberger's account. A particular family, probably a matrilineage, maintained this ceremony with otter-skin regalia that was passed down from generation to generation. "The oldest survivor of the family," akin to the lineage headman in earlier times, treasured this regalia, which was "kept in the belief that it would benefit the health of all of them."[46]

A range of rituals reinforced kin as well as community associations. The few extant references to seventeenth-century death rituals mention the role of family members in these events. When people died, Penn wrote, Indians "bury them with their Apparel, be they Men or Women, and the nearest Kin fling in something precious with them, as a token of their Love." It is unclear from this reference what was meant by "nearest Kin," but the reference may be either to members of the nuclear family, particularly a spouse and her relatives, or to the dead person's own matrilineal relations. De Vries suggested the spouse was involved. "They make a large grave, and line it inside with boughs of trees, in which they lay the corpse, so that no earth can touch it," he wrote. "They then cover this with clay," De Vries continued, "and form the grave, seven or eight feet high, in the shape of a sugar loaf, and place palisades around it. I have frequently seen the wife of the deceased come daily to the grave, weeping and crying, creeping around it with extended body, and grieving for the death of her husband." Indians sometimes integrated graves within communities, at least in parts of the Delaware Valley. In the northern Delaware Valley, Indians placed graves close to houses, apparently scattered throughout villages. Ongoing grave tending could also root ritual concerns about the dead in the daily life of the community. Penn noted, "They are choice of the Graves of their Dead; for least they should be lost by time, and fall to common use, they pick off the Grass that grows upon them, and heap up the fallen Earth with great care and exactness." In the Hudson Valley this care might include planting "a certain Tree by their Graves which keeps green all the year."[47]

Rituals could imbue specific communities and localities with spiritual significance. Sacred spaces would have been well known to community members. Around ritual fires Native peoples celebrated the first fruits of the hunt. "Their Sacrifice is their first Fruits," Penn wrote, "the first and fattest Buck they kill, goeth to the fire, where he is all burnt with a Mournful Ditty of him that performeth the Ceremony." Repetitive singing and dancing wove invisible bonds from person to person. "*Hägginj, hä, hä, hä; Hägginj, hä; Hägginj, hä; Hägginj, hä, hä, hä, hä*," chanted celebrants of a seventeenth-century first fruits ritual. "They sing and dance and when they become jolly and happy then they cry and sing," Lindeström reported, "thus repeating and continuing so long a time, so that it reaches well over the forest." Strenuous physicality heightened the significance and emotion of these events. Penn observed "such marvelous Fervency and Labour of Body" that the celebrant "will even sweat to a foam."[48]

Fall harvest festivals brought people together, perhaps offering opportunities for multiple lineages to host ceremonies for each other. According to Penn, "In the Fall, when the Corn cometh in, they begin to feast one another." In the Delaware Valley he himself had seen "two great Festivals . . . to which all come that will." One of these events involved feeding a sizable crowd with "twenty Bucks" and "hot Cakes of new Corn." "Round-Dances" with "Singing and Drumming on a Board" constructed a sacred space at this large gathering. "A green Seat by a Spring, under some shady Trees" was the ritual site for the harvest festival. Such examples parallel many aspects of ritual life among other northeastern river and coastal peoples. The New England Narragansetts apparently held ceremonies in similar arboreal settings.[49]

Other sacred places might have been sweathouses, which combined physical and spiritual purification. This purification may have corresponded with the completion of the harvest and the beginning of the fall hunt for, as De Vries noted, "when they wish to cleanse themselves of their foulness, they go in the autumn, when it begins to grow cold, and make, away off, near a running brook, a small oven, large enough for three or four men to lie in it." To construct this sweathouse, "they first take twigs of trees, and then cover them tight with clay, so that smoke cannot escape. This being done, they take a parcel of stones, which they heat in a fire, and then put in the oven, and when they think that it is sufficiently hot, they take the stones out again, and go and lie in it." Such events apparently affected the entire community since "men and women, boys and girls" all used the sweathouse "and come out so perspiring, that every hair has a drop of sweat on it. In this state they plunge into the cold water; saying that it is healthy." In Lindeström's account, when they started "to pour water upon the stones," each person cried out in a voice imitating a personal guardian spirit.[50]

Rituals combined individual and group dimensions, as in the sweathouse purification. The individual's quest for a spirit to guard and help the person through life was a noteworthy private ritual; however, even this quest had a public dimension, as individuals told the story of their quest or spoke in the voice of their guardian spirit, calling out "like a bear . . . a wild boar, wolf, dog, [or] goose." Rituals could be integrative, recognizing the diverse spiritual experiences of individuals while creating a sacred unity out of the diversity. Sacred places provided a means to accomplish this integration. Groves of trees with their circles of worship and dance, sweathouses, ritual fires, burial places, and sachems' houses with their carved images of deities created the sacred territory in which communities were embedded. These places were sites of repetition, continuity, and communication—all elements that bound kin and community members together. Rituals shaped and reinforced community in many ways. Communities were linked to the land, specifically to places that had provided sustenance to a group. For land to sustain a people, manitous had to be honored and feted. Rituals brought people together in the act of creating the proper relationship with the spirits of the land. Thus rituals tied to subsistence and the satisfaction of manitous strengthened the bonds linking people to deities, people to places, and people to people. These linkages structured communities and bolstered localized relationships.[51]

Community and kin provided fundamental sources of connection among Hudson and Delaware Valley Algonquians. Localized orientations offered stability and flexibility, key tools for responding to the dislocations after European colonization. Indians from the Hudson and Delaware valleys would use their long experience with diverse forms of community and their tradition of adjusting to varying environments for years to come. These Algonquians utilized kin networks to adjust to life away from their homelands. They built on flexible arrangements of kin, which structured interactions among peoples from different backgrounds. Responding to dispossession and depopulation, Algonquians drew upon their experience of cooperating and allying with outsiders while maintaining nuclear family and lineage distinctions that set them apart from others.

The Hudson and Delaware Valley Indians' story throughout the colonial era shows the continuation of a tradition of creating multiple group associations. This tradition had deep roots. In the seventeenth century, kin and community groups were distinct but not isolated. Despite the dominance of small corporate entities, there were larger gatherings when people apparently from different places and from a range of kin groups gathered. This tradition of cooperating across boundaries while maintaining localized distinctions continued, as Algonquians survived by constructing broader alliances that overlapped with fundamental orientations to kin and community.

Chapter 2
Reorganizations and Relationships in the Hudson and Delaware Valleys, 1609–82

Although seventeenth-century European commentators referred to numerous "nations" or "tribes" of Hudson and Delaware Valley peoples, the precise makeup and extent of these groups are unknown; thus the most appropriate language to describe these groups lies beyond our reach.[1] Whatever label is used for them, they might be loosely described as corporate entities associated with particular territories, such as a stream valley or small district near the Hudson or Delaware rivers. At times they may not have been much larger than a town or a group of relatives, and at other times they may have encompassed a somewhat wider sphere. These groups were dynamic in nature. Algonquians responded to the warfare, epidemic disease, and other tumultuous events of the seventeenth century by developing and using networks of trade and other forms of exchange, creating new alliances, sharing territories, and in some cases merging with other groups. A traditionally flexible approach to social organization promoted intergroup cooperation and a layering of multiple associations. What seemed to strengthen this approach was a tendency to consider land in dynamic terms and to perceive its possession in terms of a complex system of overlapping ownership rights. Out of this flexible approach, new associations formed—especially with other Indian peoples and to a lesser extent with Euro-Americans.

Defining and Possessing the Land

Algonquians approached land as "an element, a medium of existence, like the air and the sunlight and the rivers." Land was thought of in active terms, in relation to its use and to the people utilizing it, more than as a passive object to be possessed and conceptualized apart from its function. When seventeenth-century Hudson and Delaware Valley Algonquians sold land, what they may have been offering was shared land use rather than an inalienable, "irrevocable," and "exclusive" ownership of a territory. In this context it seems that particularly crucial elements of land sales for Algonquians were the building and renewal of relationships through processes of exchange.[2]

Early negotiations with Euro-Americans suggested that Indians viewed land ownership in terms of usage rights, some of which were retained by the seller at the time of deeding. Col. George Talbot, Maryland's surveyor general, explained in 1684 that rather than relinquishing use of a tract, Indian sellers typically reserved their right to obtain sustenance from parcels they were conveying. Regarding lands west of the Delaware, he stated, "Some of these Territories are Seated by the English by Consent and Composition with the Natives who in all treaties reserved to themselves the rights of hunting, fishing, and fowling in all the lands they sould or gave away." When four sachems—Amattehooren, Peminackan, Ackehoorn, and Sinquees—conveyed a tract on the Delaware between the Christina River and Bombay Hook, their agreement indicated that "hunting and fishing" rights were "excepted" from the sale. The sachem Mechowot retained even more extensive usage rights in 1639 when he sold territory on Long Island to the Dutch West India Company "under the express condition, that he, Mechowot, may be allowed, with his people and friends, to remain upon the aforesaid land, plant corn, fish, hunt and make a living there as well as they can."[3]

Wesakesons cutte, Pesakeson, Colehickamin, and Ojerickqua, four Indians who sold "the great Island Lying before" the Lenape village Shackamaxon to Elizabeth Kinsey, clearly expected to continue to benefit from the island's resources after the sale. In the deed, dated 1678, the Indian sellers reserved their "Liberty of Hunting Fishing and getting takaht [the root tuckahoe]," in exchange promising to try to be good neighbors toward Kinsey. Wesakesons cutte and the others agreed that they would attempt "as far as we Can to Save hir Hoggs from Killing and hir Hay from Burning." This comment hints that the Indians expected to continue planting on the island, although the deed did not stipulate agricultural rights. Hog killing and hay burning both had a possible connection to Native agriculture, as Indians sometimes threatened livestock that trampled their cornfields and may have used slash-and-burn techniques to prepare fields for their crops. That the Indians said they would *try* to prevent, but did not *guarantee* against, damage to Kinsey's property suggests that the Indians left open the possibility of using the island for planting as well as hunting, fishing, and gathering the edible tuckahoe.[4]

Additional evidence indicates Algonquians' perception of lands in terms of usage rights. At Hempstead on Long Island, Indians declared "that they had not sold the land, but only the grass upon it." When the sachem Tapusagh complained in 1660 that Hempstead residents were impinging on his lands and "doeth . . . make fenses uppon his plantinge lands & had threatened him & his people to burne theyre houses," he seemed to believe that his people had sold only "the grass," apparently restricting the Hempstead purchasers to grazing rights. Algonquians on the Brandywine Creek in the lower Delaware Valley claimed certain usage rights for themselves on lands sold to William Penn. As more and more Euro-Americans settled in the area, Brandywine-area Algonquians insisted that "tho' they sold the Lands on the Creek below their Settlements yet they never sold the Water or Creek itself, for they had ever reserved the use of it for fishing."[5]

This view of an area in terms of its usage apparently contributed to a complex ownership system. A specific territory might have been claimed in various ways by multiple owners so that "different groups of people could have different claims on the same tract of land depending on how they used it." Overlapping rights to a particular piece of land were apparently quite common in the Delaware Valley, as William Penn discovered when he made the purchases for his colony and agreed to buy some areas more than once from different owners. His acquisition of a portion of the region north of Philadelphia offers a useful example of this process. In 1683 the sachem Tamanen agreed to sell his "Lands betwixt Pemmapecka [Pennypack] and Nessaminehs [Neshaminy] Creeks, and all along Nesheminehs" to Penn. On the same day, Essepenaike, Swanpees, Okettarickon, and Wessapoat sold a roughly similar area, lands between the Pennypack and the Neshaminy and "all along" the Neshaminy. Their deed contained some additional information—the land they sold ran "backward" of the Neshaminy "two days Journey with an Horse up into the Country as the s[ai]d River doeth goe." Tamanen stated that his parcel was "much smaller than" that of Essepenaike and Swanpees. It appears, then, that Tamanen owned a tract within, or overlapping with, a larger area owned by Essepenaike and Swanpees, whose territory extended farther up the Neshaminy.[6]

In some cases a leader may have owned a specific territory while sharing in the ownership of, responsibility for, and rights to a larger tract within which the individual's smaller holding lay. It was possible that "communal territories were subdivided into smaller . . . 'individual' territories, whose 'owners' were limited in their right to the land by community sanction." Cottamack, Nawanemit, Abantsene, Sagiskwa, and Kanamoack were "owners and proprietors of their respective parcels of land" on the west side of the Hudson around Fort Orange (later Albany). Their sale of lands to the patroon Kiliaen van Rensselaer for his colony Rensselaerswyck seemed to indicate that these Indians had a sense of responsibility, not just for their individual holdings but for the entire tract along the river being sold. They appeared to work communally in selling this larger territory. The deed reinforced this sense of collective ownership by omitting a description of the boundaries of each of their "respective parcels" within the westside tract. It appears that this omission was not the result of sloppiness in recording, because at another point the document's scribe carefully specified the limits of an individual Algonquian's parcel across the river.[7]

Indians seemed to define land not only in terms of usage rights but also in terms of the people and the relationships created on the land. They apparently viewed early land sales as elements in the creation of relationships. Exchanging European goods for land or for rights to its use was not unlike exchanging presents to establish or renew treaty relationships between peoples. An account from Henry Hudson's voyage of 1609 suggests how Algonquians may have included access to land and its resources as part of the gift giving that they hoped would create an alliance as they met in the Catskill area with the crew of the Dutch vessel. Not only did the Indians in the Catskills present Hudson with tobacco and beads, but they also "shewed him all the Countrey round about." There are hints that this exhibition was far more than a bit of sightseeing because it was preceded by "an Oration"— probably a lengthy and formal speech that was a significant part of Indian treaties. After the Algonquians had pointed out their countryside, "they sent one of their companie on land, who presently returned, and brought a great Platter full of Venison dressed by themselves." Possibly Indians employed this ceremony to offer a share in the use of the land that they had just displayed to Hudson. The platter of venison suggested the fruitfulness of their territory, thus highlighting the quality of their gift. In return, the Catskill Indians would have expected a sound trading partnership that gave them ready access to European goods, such as the knives and hatchets that Hudson had brought with him.[8]

There are other examples that suggest that Algonquians approached land conveyances as forms of gift giving between peoples. Native oral traditions recorded in later centuries described how, upon first meeting Europeans, Indians granted or presented the newcomers with a small piece of land. Referring to the tract between the Christina River and Bombay Hook, Peminackan in the 1650s told the West India Company's director general Peter Stuyvesant, "We will rather present than sell . . . the land." Shortly thereafter the sachem Wappanghzewan, owner of a neighboring area above the Christina on both sides of the Delaware, informed Stuyvesant that he too was "willing to present him the land and, the property thereof." Sassoonan, a leader who as a child had witnessed one of Penn's treaties, recalled years later, "When Wm. Penn first came in he called the Indians together he proposed to purchase their Lands but they Said they would give it to him." Penn himself indicated that some Lenapes described their conveyances in terms of gift giving. Although he believed that some sachems "Sold" him land at early treaties, "others," he stated, "presented me with several parcels of Land."[9]

For Algonquians, concluding land agreements did not just mean developing relationships with Europeans but also meant recognizing and strengthening relationships among Native residents, some of whom were actual owners of the land and some of whom were witnesses to the sale. In places where a number of Indians shared ownership of a particular tract being sold, there must have been meetings among the owners and their kin in preparation for the sale. These meetings would have required a careful tending of various relationships in order to arrive at a joint decision. Broad involvement was essential to validating deeds, as a commentator on New Sweden explained: "If the kings or chiefs of the Indians signed such an agreement in the presence of a number of their people, then it was legitimate on their side." Indians who were technically not sellers of the land also played a role in the proceedings. Typically these were Native witnesses, who were on hand to place their marks on the deed and to observe the disposition of lands that may have overlapped with or bordered their own tracts.[10]

The distribution of the goods that constituted payment for land hinted at the web of Native relationships involved in sales. Payment goods might include a variety of items such as wampum, different types of cloth, kettles, shirts, coats, stockings, hoes, axes, hatchets, guns, lead and powder, knives, shoes, pipes, awls, fish hooks, and various alcoholic beverages. Penn noted that one of the main questions Indians asked themselves when they contemplated the payment goods was "what and to whom they should give them." They distributed items in such a way as to recognize the various social components among their own people and to strengthen their bonds with their

Native neighbors. "The Pay or Presents I made them," Penn said, "were not hoarded by the particular Owners, but the neighbouring Kings and their Clans being present when the Goods were brought out, the Parties chiefly concerned [were] consulted" about who should receive various items. Nutimus, an eighteenth-century leader from the Delaware Valley, explained a similar process of sachems using land sales to maintain social relationships among their own people and with their Indian neighbors. When a sachem agreed to a sale, Nutimus said, "he called together the heads of the families who had any Right in the Land sold & divided among them [the?] Goods he got for the Land . . . then the Heads of the families again divide their portion among the Young people of this Family & inform them of the Sale & thus every individual, who have any right [must?] be fully acquainted with the Matter." Furthermore, witnesses who were from "neighbouring Tribes," but who did not own the land, received a "share of the Goods."[11]

Relationships had to be tended over time and alliances renewed. Thus Indians likely did not see land agreements as one-time events but rather as part of an ongoing process that entailed obligations of further gift giving. The Dutch noted that Peminackan had added a requirement in his land agreement that "whenever anything is the matter with his gun, it shall be repaired for nothing, and when he come[s] empty among our people, they shall remember [to give] him some maize, and again a token of friendship." The land conveyance thus formalized an ongoing friendship between Peminackan and the Dutch, one that required periodic renewals through gifts of maize and gun repair. Elizabeth Kinsey's purchase of the island across from Shackamaxon also included arrangements that reinforced the notion that land was not a mere commodity to be transferred in a single instance but rather was a component in a continuing relationship. Kinsey agreed to pay Wesakesons cutte, Pesakeson, Colehickamin, and Ojerickqua powder and rum on a yearly basis in addition to an overall payment of six hundred guilders, although it seems that her husband Thomas Fairman later substituted an annual payment of an article of clothing known as a matchcoat for the stipulated powder and rum. Whatever the actual items presented, the land agreement was originally structured to ensure a periodical refreshing of the relationship between Kinsey and the Shackamaxon-area Indians.[12]

Penn's deeds, like certain others of the time, included statements that the Indians named in the documents granted and disposed of their parcels "for Ever," apparently as a way of preventing future claims against the property; nevertheless, the proprietor's practice of offering earnest with a promise of added payments later may also have encouraged a notion of sales not as terminal agreements but as part of ongoing relationships. Pursuing the acquisition of land "a days Journy" above Conshohocken on the east side of the Schuylkill, Penn provided the sachem Sickotickon a preliminary payment with the promise that "I am comeing shartly with ten great ships," presumably to pay more of what was owed. Meanwhile he sent Sickotickon and his people "some caps," leaving instructions to tell the Indians "as they use me, we shall use them." Two months later Penn indicated he was sending Sickotickon a cap that apparently displayed the proprietor's coat of arms, and he gave more caps, some adorned with tassels, to other Indians engaged in land negotiations.[13]

Financially strapped, Penn delayed full payments. In November 1686 Penn's surveyor general described land negotiations with Indians in Bucks County as "long & chargeable" and did not expect they would receive payment until the following spring. By May 1688 Penn was struggling with debts. His agent, William Markham, informed him, "The Indians . . . sent downe to us . . . to have what wee owed them," but Markham added pessimistically, "I am sure all the Cargo you sent was not able to Discharge [the debt]." Although Markham wrote with an expectation of Penn eventually being "out of the Indians Debts," the proprietor's financial problems led him to stretch out his dealings in ways that situated land sales within a lengthy process of building, monitoring, and tending relationships with Indians.[14]

Some disgruntled Philadelphians who had bought lots on Front Street along the Delaware seemed to see Penn's actions as gift giving that might strengthen relationships with Indians but would not necessarily lead to their own firm and unquestioned possession of the land. Complaining of the proprietor's approach, these colonists remonstrated, "As we bought our Land in England to be free from Indian Title & Incumbrances . . . We cannot but be concerned that of s[u]ch title the Land be clear'd by plain & Reguler purchases." They perceived Penn as engaged in "Reciprocall kindenesse . . . in his daily gifts & presents to the Indians," but, they argued, "These present Acts of Civillitie & Courtesie between the Proprietary and the Indians" were "no Reguler purchase nor clearing of Indian Title." Hence the goal of clearing land of Indian titles came up against practices that reinforced the notion that land agreements did not seem to have a clear endpoint because of the procedure of repeatedly presenting gifts.[15]

It is reasonable to speculate that because of the stress on land as process, Algonquians may have had a sense of a relationship commencing rather than of a deal closing when they placed their signature marks on some of the earliest deeds. One of the first agreements had a particularly personal and fluid quality. Hudson Valley Indians approached their early sale of the land at Fort Orange as a limited arrangement, not with the West India Company or the Dutch nation, but rather with a specific individual—the company's commissary, Bastian Jansz Crol—"for as long a time as he, Crol, should continue to live at the Fort." Although the legal language of many other agreements included assertions of permanence, as mentioned earlier, there were ways in which the fluctuations present during the seventeenth century fit well with a sense of land as process. Certain tracts were purchased and then repurchased from Algonquians as power shifted from the Dutch to the English in the Hudson Valley and among the Dutch, Swedes, and English (including governance under the Duke of York and under William Penn) in the Delaware Valley. Furthermore, the threat that colonial governments might require purchasers to forfeit their lands if they failed to seat sufficient numbers of European settlers on them probably added to a sense of impermanence in landholding.[16]

The history of Matinneconck Island (later Burlington Island) on the Delaware demonstrates the process of purchasing and repurchasing lands. A desirable piece of property, Matinneconck lay just below the falls in a portion of the Delaware that was "safely navigable with large vessels," making it accessible to European craft. Within its approximately four hundred acres, a significant portion was level arable land. At the same time, the island was suited for defense because its lower end rose up twenty feet, making possible a lookout and raised fortification to fend off attacks from downriver enemies. It was *Schoon Eylandt*, or the "Beautiful Island," to the Dutch, who it is believed attempted to establish a colony of Walloons there in the mid-1620s. Later in the century, the Labadist traveler Danckaerts enthused, "It is the best and largest island in the South River."[17]

Not surprisingly, given the island's attributes, many tried to use and possess Matinneconck. In 1649 Symon Root and other New Netherlanders obtained a deed for it along with land above the Rancocas Creek from an Indian named Kickeeu-sickenom. According to Danckaerts, Matinneconck attracted a Dutch governor, who "made it a pleasure ground or garden, built good houses upon it, and sowed and planted it. He also dyked and cultivated a large piece of meadow or marsh, from which he gathered more grain than from any land which had been made from woodland into tillable land." By 1671, the island was claimed by Peter Alrichs, a Dutch landholder who had

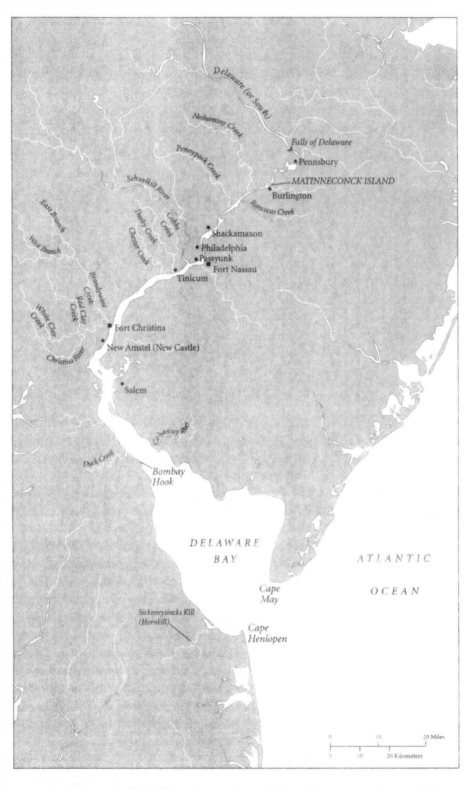

Map 1. Delaware (or South) River. Derived from *NYHM* 1981, opposite title page; *PP*, 2: 307, 334; *NYHM* 1977, fold-out map.

become influential in the recently established English colony. Eight years later Governor Edmund Andros "held it for himself, and had hired it out to some Quakers, who were living upon it." Finally, as part of his acquisition of lands along the falls and southward to the Neshaminy in 1682, William Penn bought Matinneconck Island from Idquahon, Janottowe, Idquoqueywon, Sahoppe, Swanpees (or "Swanpisse"), and several others.[18]

Expectations that land agreements needed renewal, that different usage rights overlapped, and that territories might be owned by a large group but also subdivided into smaller parcels belonging to individual leaders and their groups—all of these notions suggest a complex system of land possession. Relationships among many different peoples were embedded in such a system, and indeed, a concern for relationship construction and maintenance would have been one of its significant features. This system of overlapping possession created a mechanism for adjusting to outsiders, bringing them into an alliance while retaining older group affiliations. In the rapidly shifting world of the seventeenth century, the notion of land as process rather than commodity would have shaped how Algonquians adapted and responded to change.

The Effects of Disease and War

Undoubtedly some of the examples of overlapping land possession were the result of the major reorganizations, movements of peoples, and societal reconstructions that occurred in response to the traumas and turmoil of the seventeenth century. Algonquians coped with significant alterations and sometimes catastrophic events such as depopulating epidemics. Particularly in the Hudson Valley, wars with Euro-Americans had a devastating impact. Seeking support in troubled times, Native groups sought new and safer locations, split apart, merged, shared territories, and worked out new arrangements with their neighbors. Algonquians responded to crises by forming new groups and alliances to promote survival and, if possible, turn loss to advantage.

Hudson and Delaware Valley Algonquians were profoundly affected by epidemics following European contact. We can only guess at the numbers of people infected and the numbers of lives destroyed; however, the few records available indicate a severe demographic impact. In the Delaware Valley, Lindeström stated that by 1654 "whole tribes had died out" because "sickness had formerly often been among them." During the late 1650s, the lower Delaware Valley was probably a hotbed of infection that could have easily spread to Indians when "fully more than 100" colonists "perished" from the "continual sickness, fevers and langours" in the Dutch province. Some lower-Delaware Valley Algonquians may have become infected not just locally but also on trips to Manhattan or elsewhere in the north. Not long before the Delaware Valley changed to English control in 1664, a Dutch official reported that "the small-pox is drifting down the river with the Indians." Certainly Native Americans of the Hudson Valley saw their share of disease, as a report from the 1650s stated: "Indians . . . affirm, that before the arrival of the Christians, and before the small pox broke out amongst them, they were ten times as numerous as they now are, and that their population had been melted down by this disease, whereof nine-tenths of them have died." Indians brought reports to Fort Orange in 1661 of a "mortality at and around the *Manhatans*," which may have been striking Algonquians as well as Euro-Americans. In his publication of 1670, Daniel Denton claimed that the population of Long Island Indians had been drastically reduced: "where there were six towns, they are reduced to two small Villages, and it hath been observed, that where the *English* come to settle, a Divine Hand makes way for them, by removing or cutting off the *Indians*, either by Wars one with the other, or by some raging mortal Disease."[19]

Like Denton, Algonquians described the devastation and attributed it to a supernatural source, seemingly believing that Christians brought evil spiritual forces to attack their people. Lenapes appeared to suspect the Swedes had unleashed a manitou that was the source of the illness among the Indians. After the English conquest over the Dutch, a sachem summarized the waves of devastation that had struck his people on the Delaware and, by pointing to the heavens, seemed to indicate that a manitou, possibly the Christians' god, was the culprit. He stated, "In my grandfather's time the small-pox came: In my father's time the small-pox came; and now in my time the small-pox is come." With outstretched arms and "hands towards the skies," the sachem added, "it came from thence." Grieving over the death of his sister, perhaps from disease, a Delaware Valley Indian, Tashiowycam, declared, "The Manetto hath kill'd my Sister & I will go and kill the Christians." With the help of an individual named Wywaannattamo, Tashiowycam then killed two colonists on Matinneconck Island in 1671.[20]

A new burst of Native infections and deaths occurred after Quaker migrations to the English colony of West New Jersey. Between approximately

1677 and 1682 about 1,760 Quakers arrived in the area, with devastating effects on the health of the local Indian population. After English settlers arrived at Burlington in 1678 aboard a ship called the *Shield*, illness ravaged Indians east of the Delaware. Apparently referring to this epidemic, the Yorkshire Quaker Mahlon Stacy wrote from the Falls area, "'Tis hardly credible to believe, how the Indians are wasted in Two Years Time; and especiall the last Summer." Burlington resident Mary Murfin Smith, who like Stacy had been one of the *Shield*'s passengers, later remembered a "distemper" that had been "so mortal that" the Indians "could not bury all the dead." As had been true under the Swedes, Indians now looked to Euro-Americans for the source of these troubles. Thomas Budd, a West Jersey colonist, explained that the local Algonquians blamed the English for passing on smallpox with trade goods: "Shortly after we came into the country," Budd stated, the Indians heard rumors "that we sold them the small pox, with the matchcoat they had bought of us."[21]

Epidemics that in some cases may have left only remnants of communities and groups would have triggered reorganizations, such as the merging of neighboring villages and reconstitution of communities in new locations. Also causing major upheavals were warfare and the threat of war. War affected Native peoples in numerous ways. As in the case of epidemics, it led to population decline, sometimes on a large scale. It led to new alliances with neighbors. It forced Algonquians to relocate, and in the process exposed them to other groups, with whom connections could be formed and populations consolidated. In so doing, Algonquians demonstrated their flexible attitudes toward land and their tendency to form overlapping associations.[22]

Naming the groups that constructed alliances and reorganized is problematic because we cannot be sure how members of these groups referred to themselves or defined the extent of their territory at any given time. Place names and Native group names were often used interchangeably by Europeans, but all the Indians living in a particular place may or may not have thought of themselves as a distinct unit. Group names appeared and disappeared, sometimes in a fairly short period of time, calling into question the significance of some of these labels. Struggling with nomenclature, Europeans offered various labels for the different peoples they met in the Hudson and Delaware valleys. Johan de Laet, a West India Company director, gathered information about Indian groups, mentioning Sanhicans, Naratekons, Armeomecks, Matanackouses, and many others living along the Delaware and its tributaries. At the mouth of the Hudson, he reported, was the group called the Manhatthans and "within the first reach, on the western bank of the river, where the land is low" lived the Tappans. Farther up the Hudson were yet more groups, De Laet noted, including the Pachami, Waoranecks, Waranawankougs, and finally the Mahicans ("Mohicans") near present Albany.[23]

More than most of the group names that De Laet mentioned, the Mahican label had staying power. In one version or another, such as "Mahican," "Mohican," "Mahikan," and "Mahikander," the name was attached to a corporate entity throughout the seventeenth and subsequent centuries. With homelands near the Dutch post in the future vicinity of Albany, the Mahicans had early access to trade with New Netherland. Mahicans had close relations with other Algonquian speakers living in the Connecticut River Valley. Apparently alliances with these neighbors to the east involved Mahicans in war against the Mohawks in the 1620s. Later, during much of the 1660s and into the 1670s, the Mahicans fought frequently with the Mohawks and simultaneously held on to ties with New England Algonquians. Sharing lands for hunting and other purposes was probably an element of these alliances. In 1678 the Mahican Wattawyt, who had recently sold Hudson Valley lands, was reported hunting with his sons near Windsor in the Connecticut River Valley. Long-standing ties between Hudson Valley Mahicans and Connecticut Valley groups likely made such instances frequent.[24]

The Mahicans' ties to neighboring eastern Algonquians became a factor during Metacom's (or King Philip's) War. In 1675–76 New England Indians led by the Wampanoag Metacom stirred an intertribal assault against English colonists. Edmund Andros, recently named governor of the new English colony of New York, constructed a counteralliance with the Mohawks. Drawn into war again out of their long-standing friendship with New England Indians and their enmity toward the Mohawks, some Mahicans joined Metacom's forces. By the end of this war—a defeat for Metacom and his supporters—the Mahicans were in a weakened state; however, many continued to live in or near their old homelands in the Hudson Valley. A number of Mahicans who said they had never taken part in Metacom's War welcomed New England Indians to settle near them at Schaghticoke northeast of Albany, which Andros had designated as a place of protection for Indian war refugees. At Schaghticoke, Mahicans continued to forge alliances with other Algonquian peoples, with whom they shared the title "River Indians." Mahicans survived by sharing lands with these and other neighbors.[25]

Of growing importance were the alliances that Mahicans created with other Algonquian peoples on the lower Hudson and in the Housatonic Valley to the east. In the 1670s, Mahican sachems explained their close relationship with neighboring groups. First noting the rapid change between Dutch and English governance in New Netherland/New York, they said, "the English and Dutch are now one and the Dutch are now English." What they may have feared was the power of a possible Dutch-English alliance, and they tried to respond from a position of strength themselves. Asserting their own alliances, they stated, "we Mahikanders, the highland Indians, and the 'western corner' Indians are now one also." The Highland Indians included lower-Hudson Wappingers and Wecquaesgeeks. The Western Corner Indians came from Wnahktukook or Westenhoek on the Housatonic in the vicinity of later Stockbridge, Massachusetts. We know little about the dynamics and functioning of this alliance, but the Mahicans' statement in the 1670s hints at how the creation of broader relationships and connections became especially crucial for the Mahicans as they struggled through difficult times.[26]

Relations between Mahicans and lower–Hudson Valley Algonquians had not been friendly in every instance. In the 1640s, a sequence of conflicts had been set in motion, including a brief outbreak of violence between the Mahicans and two downriver groups—the Wecquaesgeeks from present-day Greenburgh Township, Westchester County, and the Tappans from present-day Orangetown Township, Rockland County. This combat, however, was far less consequential for lower–Hudson Valley Algonquians than was their subsequent warfare with the Dutch. Over several decades, conflict built upon conflict, resulting in new alignments and reorganizations by which Indian peoples reshaped their societies.[27]

In early 1643, about "eighty to ninety" Mahicans attacked downriver Algonquians. The full rationale behind the assault is unknown; however, De Vries stated that the Mahicans "wanted to levy a contribution" on the Wecquaesgeeks and Tappans. Why the Mahicans chose to force this contribution at this time probably relates to several developments. Just the year before, Dutch-Mohawk relations had been strengthened when Arent van Curler, as representative of Rensselaerswyck, undertook a diplomatic mission among the Mohawks. It seems likely that the Mahicans watched these activities carefully and considered ways to make themselves valuable to the Dutch at a time when the Mohawks were gaining an advantage. Even as the Mohawks consolidated their trading position upriver, the Mahicans sought to strengthen their own role downriver near the Dutch Fort Amsterdam on Manhattan Island. Lower-Hudson Algonquians probably had wampum and corn to trade.

When the Mahicans sought "to levy a contribution" on the lower-Hudson Algonquians, they may have been trying to control the Algonquian-Dutch trade in items such as these.[28]

The Mahicans probably thought the time was ripe for an attack because of Dutch anger at the downriver Algonquians. There was reason to think that the Dutch might approve of a Mahican attack and might even encourage it. Relations between lower-Hudson Indians and the Dutch were at a low point. These Algonquians resented a corn tax placed on them by West India Company director general William Kieft. Tappans complained that Kieft "must be a very mean fellow to come to live in this country without being invited by them, and now [he] wish[es] to compel them to give him their corn for nothing." Algonquians saw their corn yield threatened in another way as well. The colonists' "cattle usually roamed thrugh the woods without a herdsman" and "frequently came into the corn of the Indians, which was unfenced on all sides, committing great damage there." In response, some Indians took "revenge on the cattle without sparing even the horses," according to one Dutch account. Relations worsened when one Indian, who had been drinking, shot a colonist thatching his barn in the Hackensack Valley and when another, possibly a Wecquaesgeek, killed a wheelwright named Claes Smits on Turtle Bay in the East River. In the period before the Mahican attack, Kieft tried unsuccessfully to retaliate militarily against the lower-Hudson Indians. Thus, when the Mahican assault occurred, some Dutch would have welcomed it, viewing it, in the terms of one report, as God's "vengeance" fulfilled.[29]

There were likely other reasons for the timing of the Mahicans' attack. The Mahicans and Mohawks were not at war during the 1640s; hence the Mahicans would have been reasonably secure on their western flank as they launched their campaign downriver. At the same time, the Mahicans were possibly reacting to economic pressures, because it seems the Mohawks were requiring "a yearly contribution" from them. Mahican attempts to leverage their own contribution from downriver Algonquians may have been a counterbalance to this requirement. Finally, like the Mohawks, the Mahicans had acquired firearms and may have seen them as an advantage over other New Netherland Indians who complained about their lack of guns. This armament disparity meant that a relatively small Mahican force of eighty or ninety warriors "each with a gun on his shoulder" could hope for quick results against larger numbers of downriver Algonquians, who might then be swiftly persuaded to provide the Mahicans with a regular "contribution."[30]

The brief Mahican campaign reportedly led to the flight and relocation of some of the downriver Algonquians. Nevertheless, the subsequent war with the Dutch had a farther reaching and longer term impact than that with the Mahicans. Indeed, warfare between Mahicans and lower-Hudson Natives seems to have quickly subsided. Following the Mahican foray, Kieft and his soldiers took advantage of the vulnerable position of the lower-Hudson Indians and viciously struck Algonquians at Pavonia on the Bayonne peninsula near Staten Island and Corlaer's Hook on Manhattan. Outraged Indians burned Dutch farms at Pavonia and attacked European settlements in Westchester and on western Long Island. With the help of English colonists, the Dutch lashed back at the Indians in these areas. At Mespath and another nearby Indian village on Long Island, soldiers slew "about one hundred and twenty men." A staggering total of five to seven hundred Hudson Valley Natives died in an attack in present-day Westchester County. There "in a low recess protected by the hills," Indians had laid out a town with three rows of houses, "each row eighty paces long." The combined Dutch and English forces surrounded this town so "that it was impossible for one to escape." Before long there were "one hundred and eighty dead outside," and the rest remained "within the houses, discharging arrows through the holes." Perhaps the majority of those slaughtered were burned alive.[31]

By the time a treaty was signed in 1645, Euro-Americans had devastated Native communities west, north, and east of Manhattan, and Kieft and his supporters had embittered Hudson Valley Indians for years to come. Although angry Algonquians did not unite in a single force against the Dutch, there is evidence that Indians responded to war by forging alliances among themselves and seeking safety in each other's company. Hudson Valley Algonquians organized sizable gatherings that would have brought together Indians from various communities and districts. When the Dutch and English soldiers attacked Algonquians in the Westchester area, they found that hundreds had "collected together . . . to celebrate one of their festivals." During turbulent times, Indians probably assembled in large numbers to hold ceremonies aimed at driving off evil spirits plaguing their people. Like those suffering from epidemic diseases, Algonquians may have blamed a dangerous manitou among Europeans for the wartime destruction of their communities. The "feasts and great assemblages" held "to hunt or drive the devil," mentioned in Van der Donck's writings, likely included rituals meant to turn the tide of violence away from Indian communities.[32]

Hudson Valley Indians also gathered sizable numbers when they used diplomacy to stop wartime destruction. Large assemblages might have been

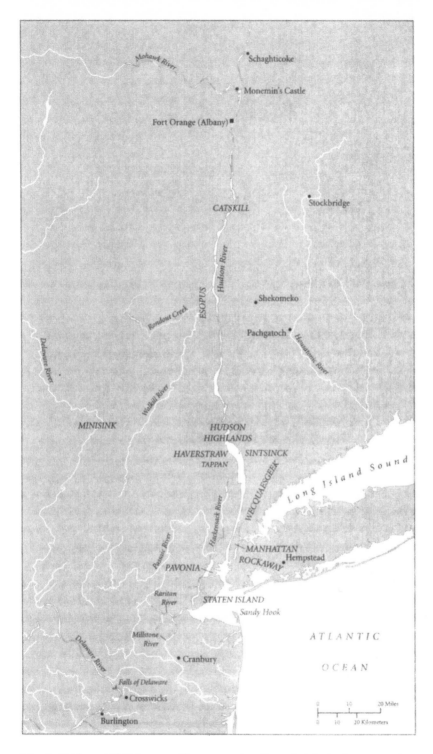

Map 2. Hudson and Delaware valleys—seventeenth- and eighteenth-century sites. Derived from Trelease, *Indian Affairs*, 6; Patrick Frazier, *The Mohicans of Stockbridge* (Lincoln: University of Nebraska Press, 1992), opposite title page; Dunn, *Mohicans and Their Land*, 103-5; NYHM 1977, fold-out map.

seen as a way to attract the aid of spiritual forces to promote peacemaking, and these would have gained serious attention from the Dutch. Before any Europeans arrived on the scene, peace treaties may have included rituals aimed at gaining spiritual power to strengthen and bind together the many Indians attending a treaty. In the aftermath of the Dutch attacks at Pavonia and on Manhattan, "two or three hundred Indians" with sixteen sachems sat down at Rockaway on Long Island to negotiate with the Dutch. Like the encounter at Fort Nassau in 1633, this meeting reflected alliances among different Native groups as well as the potential for an alliance between Algonquians and Euro-Americans. David de Vries, who was again on hand, reported that sixteen sachems "seated themselves around us, so that we sat within a ring."[33]

Algonquians in the Hudson Valley also cooperated across groups by sharing territories as they faced depopulation and the need to relocate for survival during and after wars. At such times Algonquians probably employed notions of land that allowed different groups to use a territory in various ways. There is evidence that in 1643 Indians from north of Fort Amsterdam were sharing hunting territories on Long Island with Rockaway-area Natives. When De Vries inquired "how they came so far from their dwelling," they responded that "they were out a hunting with these [Long Island] Indians, and had friends among them." Raritan Indians, described in 1640 as a "nation" residing "where a little stream runs up about five leagues behind Staten Island," mingled with Algonquians in the present-day Westchester (or Wecquaesgeek) area.[34]

Some important examples of responses to war came from the Esopus area (present-day Kingston, New York) in the 1650s and 1660s. The Esopus Algonquians dealt with the circumstances of wartime by sharing territories with their Indian neighbors and by moving flexibly among larger and smaller units of organization. Although the Dutch at midcentury typically referred to the Esopus Indians as a single unit, there is evidence that they actually consisted of a complex and shifting set of groups. According to one account, there had been "two or three tribes" near "Esopes" in the 1620s. By the late 1650s some of the Indians living at Esopus were probably former residents of areas nearer Manhattan, from which they had fled at the time of Kieft's attacks. Esopus Indians remembered well the war with Kieft and expressed resentment about "how many of their people had then been killed." At least one Indian at Esopus in 1658 reportedly came from Nevesink, an area southeast of the Raritan in the Atlantic Highlands. Other Esopus residents had apparently migrated from the Minisink in the upper Delaware Valley. As the Esopus became a dangerous place, a Minisink sachem said that "some of his friends have planted among the *Esopus* a long time ago" and were now ready to return home.[35]

Indians of the Esopus bore the brunt of Dutch expansion into interior regions. The Dutch viewed the Esopus lands in terms of agricultural production. Thomas Chambers, an early Euro-American purchaser at Esopus, extolled its virtues to the West India Company's director general, Peter Stuyvesant. Looking for support from the Company at a time when relations with the local Indians were deteriorating, Chambers wrote, "this *Aesopus* is a place, which if well peopled could feed the whole of *New-Netherland* and it would be, so to say, a sin, which could be avoided, if we should have to leave such splendid country."[36]

Besides their resentment over Kieft's actions, the Esopus Indians had other grievances and frustrations. They chided the Dutch for the damage they incurred by selling the Indians brandy, saying that it made the Indians "*cacheus*, that is crazy, mad or drunk and then [they] committed outrages." Although the Indians agreed to give a portion of "a certain piece of land" to compensate for Dutch livestock they had killed and other property they had ruined while intoxicated, Stuyvesant failed to send the expected presents to seal the agreement, causing the disgruntled Indians "to murmur on that account." The Esopus Algonquians also complained "that their corn-pits were robbed by the Dutch last winter and some beaverskins were taken" and that a man named Boertsen "had badly beaten an Indian and pointing a knife to his breast had threatened to kill him." Two wars broke out between the Esopus Indians and the Dutch in the period 1658–64.[37]

Both wars ended badly for the Indians. To try to survive, Esopus leaders utilized ties with neighboring Indians. Some Minisink Indians from the upper Delaware gave their lives to help the Esopus. A trader reported in 1660 that "eleven Menissing Indians had been killed with the Esopus Indians." The Esopus sachem Seweckenamo was probably one of the leaders who "tried to involve the *Menissinghs*" or Minisinks in helping his people fight the Dutch. Council minutes from Fort Amsterdam listed him as among the five sachems governing when the Esopus Indians approached the Minisinks. Toward the end of the war, Seweckenamo traveled to the Delaware, possibly to strengthen or renew connections with Minisinks, some of whom may have had family members living at Esopus. Seweckenamo and other sachems would have been able to build on these connections in seeking Minisink allies. Although the Minisinks did not unite behind the Esopus Indians in the war, there were reports of Minisink warriors among the Esopus. In summer 1663 Capt. Martin Cregier reported that "40 *Manissing* Indians" had joined the Esopus warriors and "40 more" would soon arrive. In addition, it was later said that "Christians" taken as prisoners were being kept "near the Menissingh."[38]

Esopus Indians also had ties with the Indians at Haverstraw, a territory downriver from Esopus on the west side of the Hudson. Kinship linked the two groups: the Esopus sachem Semackese (probably Seweckenamo) was a relative of a Haverstraw sachem. Indians from Haverstraw intervened in negotiations on behalf of their Esopus neighbors. When Seweckenamo made peace overtures at the end of the first Esopus-Dutch war, a Haverstraw sachem, Corruspin, served as one of the intermediaries who passed along the Esopus leader's words to the Dutch.[39]

During wartime the Esopus depended on the willingness of their Indian neighbors to share their territories with them. Stuyvesant reported, "some *Esopus* . . . especially women and children are staying in and near the *Catskils* and have planted corn there." Hence, the Dutch looked suspiciously at the Catskill Indian group, as well as at other groups they believed harbored the Esopus Indians. Esopus Indians apparently continued to mingle with Catskill Indians after the war. This mingling probably resulted in a sense of shared ownership of some lands. In 1683 Wannachquatin, "an old Esopus Indian," sold "wood land" near the Hudson, including a portion "along the East side of the *Kaeterskil*, where it empties into the *Catskil*." Esopus Indians also received aid in the region of the Highland/Wappinger Indians. The Dutch wrote, "one of the *Esopus* Sachems, called *Caelcop*, with some friends are said to live and have a plantation among the *Highland*" peoples. In August 1663 it was reported, "the *Wappinghs* and *Esopus* . . . keep together," and the Dutch captives were "mostly hidden among the *Wappinghs* with the *Esopus*."[40]

Following a flexible strategy meant that sometimes the Esopus consolidated into a fort they had constructed, but many times they scattered with their captives throughout the region.[41] For the most part, however, the Esopus Indians did not remain together in these forts for lengthy periods. It was typical for the Esopus to "disperse in small detachments here and there among other tribes" or in isolated areas of their own territory. By the time the Dutch had destroyed one fort, most of the Esopus Indians had moved into nearby mountains. A former captive among the Esopus explained that the usual procedure was to take "all the prisoners out of the fort into the mountains during several nights," when they were "guarded together with their wives and children and old men, only the men, able to bear arms, remaining in the fort to guard it." At the time of the attack, the Esopus were "here and there in small bands."[42] In allying, or uniting, with other Native groups, the Esopus nevertheless retained an orientation around kin groups and small, dispersed communities. They and other Algonquians maintained this approach as they moved to places farther from their homelands and encountered a diverse range of peoples.

Exchanges, Economies, and Relations between Peoples

Many different types of exchange affected Algonquians' relationships and associations. These included gift giving at treaties and trade in furs, food, and various goods. Also important was the exchange of information along communication networks, which shaped relations among Algonquians and aided their survival. The Delaware Valley offers a particularly useful place for exploring the patterns of exchange as they intersected with and influenced intergroup dynamics. In this region various sorts of exchange had an impact on relations between Algonquians and Iroquoian Susquehannocks, among different groups of Algonquians, and between Algonquians and Europeans—including Swedish, Dutch, and English immigrants.

Indians whose homelands were outside of the Delaware Valley entered the region as competitors with local Algonquians for partnerships with European traders. These competitors were Susquehannocks—often called "Minquas" or sometimes "White Minquas"—and members of another group referred to as "Black Minquas" from beyond the Allegheny Mountains. In particular, contacts with the Susquehannocks had a significant impact on Delaware Valley Algonquians, resulting in relocations and new alliances.[43]

Competition between Algonquians and Susquehannocks became violent. One icy day in February 1633, "Minquas" from "north of the English of Virginia" met the Dutch onboard the *Squirrel* near Fort Nassau. There were "full fifty" of these Susquehannocks "on a warlike expedition," and the Dutch believed that "six hundred more" were on the way. Two days later three Armewanninge ("Armewamen") Indians appeared. They related "that the Minquas had killed some of their people" but that they themselves "had escaped." Further, the Armewanninges revealed, they had been left with little or no means of support: "they had been plundered of all their corn, their houses had been burnt," and "they were suffering great hunger." Other Indians from around the Falls of the Delaware ("Sankiekans") had lost "ninety men" in the Susquehannock assault. About a year and a half later, an Indian, presumably a Lenape, came aboard an English ship sailing along Delaware Bay. After some food, conversation, and gift giving, he abruptly "fell into a great passion of feare and trembling." Pointing to a canoe off in the distance, the man explained his sudden anxiety. On the way were "Minquaos," he said, who were "enimies to him, and to his Nation." They "had already killed many of them" and "would kill him also, if they saw him." The Lenape man reported "that the people of that River were at warre" with the Minquas and that much destruction of life and livelihood had occurred. Farther up the river a sachem or "king" meeting the English made a statement that suggested the fur trade was at issue in the war. Offering the ship's crew "two Otter skinnes, and some greene eares of corne," he apologized "that he had no better present . . . the Minquaos had lately harrowed his countrey, and carried much beaver from him and his subjects."[44]

In these accounts Algonquians *seem* stunned and overwhelmed by a superior enemy force; however, they survived and within a short time appeared to be on friendly and cooperative terms with the Susquehannocks. Sachems of two Algonquian groups—the Mantes and Armewanninges (or "Ermewormahi")—came together with Minquas on March 29, 1638, to seal an agreement that allowed the Swedes to establish themselves on the lower Delaware. In 1651 Minquas witnessed a land sale to the Dutch by several Delaware Valley sachems who may have been Armewanninges. Two of these sachems, Matthehoorn (or "Amattehoorn") and Sinquessen (or "Sinquees"), and one other named Pemenattha, claimed to be "great Chiefs and Proprietors" of certain lands on the west side of the Delaware "both by ownership and by descent and appointment of Minquaas and River Indians." This statement came at a time of heated disputes between the Swedes and the Dutch as they vied for control of lands and access to the fur trade. Although the evidence is difficult to decipher, it seems that some Algonquians had developed important ties with Susquehannocks, which they used to assert their own authority in this complicated situation. To speak as a representative of both the "Minquaas and River Indians" at such a time would have been seen as a powerful pronouncement.[45]

In this postwar period Algonquians appeared neither as defeated subjects nor as bitter enemies of the Susquehannocks. If they were as demoralized and badly beaten as the Dutch and English accounts seem to indicate, why then did they appear more as allies than subordinates of the Susquehannocks after the war? One answer may be that the damage done by the Susquehannocks, while extremely serious, was somewhat mitigated by the Algonquians' survival skills and tactics. If so, then the Algonquians could have emerged from the war years with their position in the valley reasonably intact, though considerable reorganization of groups may have occurred.

Indian peoples of the Delaware Valley apparently employed a wartime strategy similar to the one later used at Esopus. In order to protect and support their people, they moved to remote areas, possibly portions of their own hunting territories or those of a neighboring Algonquian group. Capt. Thomas Yong, the writer of the English account of the Susquehannock-Algonquian war, stated that the Indians on the west side of the Delaware "had wholy left that side of the River, which was next to their enimies, and had retired themselves on the other side farre up into the woods, the better to secure themselves from their enemies." De Vries explained that after the Susquehannocks had wreaked destruction, the Algonquians were "compelled to be content with what they could find in the woods . . . the main body of their people lying about five or six hours' distant, with their wives and children."[46]

Although a great number of Delaware Valley Indians were said to have withdrawn into the woods, their approach was more complicated than simply beating a safe retreat. At the time of the war with the Susquehannocks, Yong actually came across quite a few Indians remaining along the river. On one occasion he met with a sachem ("king") "who lived not farre of[f]" and came with "40 or 60 Indians," and on another occasion Yong arranged to meet with two other sachems (also called "kings") at the mouth of "a lesser River, which falleth into this great River." At one place he noted that for the first time women "came aboard our shippes." Heading upstream, he found "many Indians" who wanted to trade their food and some furs for English "commodities." Near the falls he anchored "neere to the dwelling of one of the principall kings of this Countrey" and met with this sachem and his brother. Thus these Indians had not completely withdrawn but rather were probably pursuing a policy of dispersing some of their group in the woods and mountains for security and food collection while others kept an eye on lands along the river.[47]

This technique of scattering in order to utilize different parts of the region would have brought various Algonquian groups into contact with one another, furthering the possibilities of exchange—both of resources and of information. Sharing the use of lands could be vital to survival in difficult times. There are hints that Delaware Valley Algonquians created networks during the seventeenth century, perhaps encouraged and enhanced by the need to regroup, reorganize, and reassess their position vis-à-vis the Susquehannocks. Evidence does not show that Algonquians formed themselves into a united tribe or single nation; however, different groups headed by different sachems communicated and worked with each other in important ways. During the war with the Susquehannocks, Algonquian groups quickly spread the word to other groups about the arrival of Yong's crew. Those Indians who had not retired to the woods were on the lookout for allies in the war against Susquehannocks. After Yong hid the frightened Indian from approaching Susquehannocks, Algonquians carried the hopeful message along the river that the English might fulfill this role. A sachem who met the English farther up the Delaware had learned of Yong's protection. This sachem "understood by an Indian that I was a good man," Yong wrote, "and that I had preserved him from the Minquaos, who would otherwise have slayne him." Peace agreements with various Native leaders along the river followed, aided by a communications network that sent favorable reports in advance of Yong's ship.[48]

During the seventeenth century, intergroup communication helped spread news not only about potential allies but also about impending threats. In addition to hearing about Yong's friendly deed, sachems along the Delaware would have learned of the arrival of the Susquehannocks who had struck fear in the Indian man on board the English ship. In the 1640s as the Swedes and Dutch competed for the fur trade, the Algonquian network apparently helped spread unfavorable and threatening reports about the designs of the New Netherlanders. Traveling upriver in the 1640s, Andreas Hudde, Dutch commissary on the Delaware, found he could not obtain access to the region of the falls, where he hoped to examine mineral resources. At "the first falls," he met the sachem Wirackehon, who knew of warnings issued by a sachem named Meer Kadt from near Tinicum Island below the Schuylkill. Having learned of a statement by Meer Kadt that the West India Company meant to send "250 men" to the falls as part of a plan to exterminate Indians, Wirackehon firmly halted Hudde's explorations. There was a hint that the Swedes had started the story to undermine New Netherland traders. If so, then the Swedish governor, Johan Printz, had capitalized on the Algonquian communication network to circulate the rumor.[49]

Relationships between Algonquians and Susquehannocks changed in part, it seems, because of ecological shifts linked with the fur trade. Within a fairly short space of time, Delaware Valley residents apparently saw a decline in fur-bearing animals. In 1634 Yong stated that the "River aboundeth with beavers, otters, and other meaner furrs, which are not only taken upon the bankes of the mayne River, but likewise in other lesser rivers which discharge themselves into the greater." By contrast, Printz said just ten years later that the Indians along the River had "no beaver trade," apparently indicating a local fur shortage. In the mid-1650s, Lindeström found "an abundance of various kinds of rare, wild animals" in the woods near the lower Delaware, but he noted that these animals "now begin to become somewhat diminished" by hunting. A Dutch report from the same period noted that "Thousands of Beavers can be bought" on the Delaware; however, no local source for these furs was given. Instead, it was stated that they were "brought down in great abundance from the Southern Indians (called Minquas) and the Black Indians," who would have come from inland. A reduction in furs obtainable in the Delaware Valley seemed to give these interior groups an edge in the local economy, and for their part, some Europeans did not refrain from denigrating Algonquians in comparison to other Native traders. Most strident was Printz who wanted the Swedes to possess the most fertile Algonquian lands and "then have the beaver trade with the black and white Minquas alone."[50]

Printz's statement hints that although declining numbers of the prized furbearers were apparently available in the Delaware Valley itself, Algonquians were still finding ways to play a role as traders—a role that the Swedish governor resented. A sachem told Yong that before the war with the Susquehannocks his people had hunted beyond the falls in "a mountainous countrey where there were great store of Elkes." It is possible that once the war ended, a certain amount of this hunting resumed, perhaps in the Kittatinny Mountains or in the Minisink. Even when Delaware Valley Algonquians could not obtain furs directly, they found a way to keep their hand in the trade, though sometimes they bypassed Europeans close to home in order to deal in the Hudson Valley. Another governor, Johan Rising, complained in 1655 about neighboring Indians who he said "threaten . . . to destroy" New Sweden's trade. His account, written in frustration in the final year of the Swedish colony, suggests that Algonquians were carving out a niche in the economy that allowed them a role in the fur trade even if their own hunting was reduced. Algonquians obtained Swedish goods, he claimed, sometimes by receiving friendship gifts and sometimes through purchases of commodities. The Swedes did not get the immediate benefit of these sales, he implied, because the Delaware Valley Indians "wish to get half on credit, and then pay with difficulty." Rising claimed that Algonquians' threats against the understaffed colony required the Swedes to accede to the demands of the Algonquians. Then "they run to the Minques," he wrote, "and there they buy beavers and elk-skins, etc., for our goods." With these pelts, Delaware Valley Algonquians proceeded to the Dutch at New Amsterdam ("Manathas"), "where the traders pay more for them than we do, because more ships and more goods arrive there."[51]

Besides sometimes acting as a type of intermediary in the fur trade, Algonquians also specialized in trading food, especially corn, for goods. Printz fumed that Swedes depended on the Indians for corn. "Nothing would be better than that a couple of hundred soldiers should be sent here and kept here until we broke the necks of all of them in the river," Printz wrote. He added that instead of beaver, the Indians offered "only the maize trade," and he wanted to sever even this economic link so that each colonist would "feed and nourish himself unmolested without" the Indians' corn. The Dutch used duffels to trade for corn and venison with local Indians. Hence, in 1658 when Jacob Alrichs, the Dutch director at New Amstel (present-day New Castle, Delaware), faced shortages with "many mouths" to feed and "few supplies," he worried that he was short on duffels to exchange for food. Algonquians, then, developed their own niche in the colonial economy in at least two ways. They built up a food trade that probably helped offset losses from the depletion of furs in their homelands. And they assumed a special role in the trade of rich inland furs by linking Swedes on the Delaware, Susquehannocks from the interior, and the Dutch at New Amsterdam, with themselves as intermediaries.[52]

The history of the food trade hints at how exchange helped create connections between Algonquians and Europeans in the seventeenth century. As a basic and daily necessity, food was a major and ongoing concern that brought Europeans and Algonquians together, probably with some frequency. Many early Europeans expected to make their fortunes in trade not in agriculture, and they found that their subsistence requirements could be met with the help of Indians. Algonquians came well supplied with food in their early encounters with Henry Hudson. In 1609, the crew of the *Half Moon* met Indians ready to trade food, especially maize, more often than furs in exchange for European-made goods. Other Europeans, especially later in the century, planned to farm but struggled initially to produce enough food for their families. Arriving too late in the year to plant crops, English Quakers who came to West Jersey in the 1670s needed the food trade to survive.

Burlington resident Thomas Budd mentioned a variety of foods among the items the Quakers obtained from their Algonquian neighbors: "The Indians have been very serviceable to us by selling us venison, Indian corn, pease and beans, fish and fowl, buck-skins, beaver, otter, and other skins and furrs." Mary Murfin Smith similarly remembered Indians who "brought corn and venison and sold the English for such things as they needed."[53]

Trading partnerships required a means of communication among peoples with different linguistic backgrounds. In the region below the Water Gap in the Delaware Valley, there may have been three different dialects of a language that linguists have called Unami. Above the Delaware Water Gap and into the lower Hudson Valley, Algonquians spoke a language later known as Munsee, which was distinct from the Mahican language to the north. Traders and travelers in the Hudson and Delaware Valleys used a pidgin based on Unami known as the "Delaware Jargon," which was undoubtedly a significant factor promoting trade and the exchange of information, especially in a culturally complex world where many different European and Native languages were spoken.[54]

Trade was more than an economic activity. Like land dealings, trade in goods involved the maintenance of relationships between peoples and included expectations of gift giving. Algonquians created both loose and formal alliances with their regular trading partners. Trade joined diplomacy to reinforce connections between Algonquians and Europeans; however, numerous cross-cultural conflicts—some violent—often prevented the formation of these alliances or split existing ones.

Aspects of the alcohol trade powerfully demonstrate ways in which certain exchanges were ultimately more destructive of relationships than they were constructive. Indians not only obtained liquor from colonists but also drank with them, suggesting that moments of sociability arose out of trade in alcohol. Jan Jeuriaens Becker, who had been a provisional commissary at Fort Altena (present-day Wilmington, Delaware), claimed in 1660 that Dutch and Swedes openly imbibed "at the tavern" with Meckeck Schinck, Wechenarent, Areweehingh, Hoppaming, and other sachems. One Saturday night in 1657 a party consisting of "five Indian men, two women, and a boy" drank from a "pail of beer" with young newlyweds Louwerens Piters and Catrine Jans at the couple's residence. Alcohol-related conflicts, however, typically overshadowed seeming camaraderie among drinkers. One Indian complained that "they had not received their measure" of beer from Piters, and Piters claimed that his guests became "drunk and insolent." Becker's experiences in the tavern may have suggested amiability and good times, but the former commissary's liquor sales were notorious. They were blamed for Dutch soldiers "brawling" and setting fire to "a small Indian canoe" and for "six Indians, totally drunk" producing "a great disturbance."[55]

As was the case at Esopus, Delaware Valley Algonquians worried about drunkenness and blamed colonists for its damage. When they suspected that Becker had caused the death of a man found lying in the woods next to an "almost empty" jug of brandy, they "threatened to kill" the New Netherlander, "saying that he had poisoned the Indian." Sachems on the east side of the Delaware explained how alcohol traders had harmed their people: "The strong liquor was first sold to us by the Dutch; and they were blind, they had no eyes, they did not see that it was for our hurt: The next people that came among us were the Swedes, who continued the sale of those strong liquors to us; they were also blind, . . . they did not see it to be hurtful to us to drink it . . . when we drink it, it makes us mad, we do not know what we do, we then abuse one another, we throw each other into the fire. Seven score of our people have been killed by reason of the drinking it, since the time it was first sold us." As the numbers of English immigrants began to increase around the Falls of the Delaware, the alcohol trade posed problems. One local dealer, Gilbert Wheeler, gained a bad reputation for selling "strong liquor to the Indians," causing them to "fight together" and threaten colonists.[56]

By the 1670s the region around the Falls of the Delaware had become the focal point of much resentment among Delaware Valley Algonquians. Tashiowycam's attack at Matinneconck Island occurred at this time. In the same period, Peter Jegou, who ran an inn at Leasy Point "lying and being over ag[ain]st" Matinneconck Island, was, in his words, "plundered by the Indians, & by them utterly Ruined." Feelings between Indians and colonists under the new English government were bitter. The expansionist ambitions of the English infuriated "the Sachems of the Indians," who explained the "reason of there warre that they threaten to make upon the Christians" was that "where the English come they drive them from there lands." This hostility had deepened in part through encounters with English Marylanders. Regarding their troubled relations with Maryland colonists, Indians succinctly stated, "the English have killed some of us and we some of them." One Dutch official at New Amstel wrote in 1661 that the "River chiefs do not trust the English." In a treaty with eleven sachems in 1670 the Indians offered "to remain brothers and friends" of the English; yet Tashiowycam's attack one year later and subsequent threats of all-out war suggested the limited impact of this agreement. Topping off this decade of turmoil came the barrage of disease that followed the Quaker immigrants to the western part of New Jersey in the late 1670s.[57]

How Delaware Valley Algonquians viewed the new colony of Pennsylvania would have been filtered through these recent events. Given the evidence for communication networks throughout the region, it is likely that animosities seething among Native residents of the falls area were known and felt among Algonquians in many parts of the Delaware Valley. Delaware Valley Algonquians were probably also well aware of the violence that had disrupted the Hudson and circum-Manhattan region. Reports of the Esopus wars reached the Delaware Valley, in part through Susquehannocks who were involved in peace negotiations.[58] Trade networks doubled as communication networks. Delaware Valley traders, both Indian and European, visited Manhattan and undoubtedly returned with information about the status of Hudson Valley Algonquians, whose conflicts with the Dutch had been so destructive. Painful memories would have competed with more positive memories of useful exchanges, friendly trading relationships, and sociable encounters between Algonquians and Europeans.

Trade and other forms of exchange between Europeans and Indians and among Indians depended on the many ceremonies and rituals of gift giving and alliance that had been repeated over and over throughout the seventeenth century. Alliance formation was a prominent feature of life in the Hudson and Delaware valleys, and it was an important approach to survival. Throughout the seventeenth century Algonquians forged multiple alliances, resulting in a world in which individuals moved among and within overlapping and crosscutting groups of varying sizes. Flexibility toward land use and ownership aided the formation of alliances, as Algonquians responded to the destructive consequences of war and disease.

"He knew the best how to order them"

"All . . . was done in much Calmness of Temper and in an amicable way"—such was a Quaker observer's impression of one of William Penn's final meetings with Indians in the Delaware Valley, presumably in 1701. On this solemn occasion one Indian man struck "his Hand three times on his Breast" to show that his people formed a "covenant" with Penn that was "made . . . in their Hearts." The number 3 was likely significant in his action. More than forty years earlier, a Lenape sachem meeting with Swedes had "stroked himself three times down his arm" as "a token of friendship." In the mid-eighteenth century, an Ohio Iroquois explained that "the Great Being . . . ordered us to send three Messages of Peace before we make War." Peacemaking deserved repeated efforts and extra emphasis. One attempt was not enough; three suggested completeness—a wholehearted endeavor.[1]

Concern with order and detail helped seal the agreement. Handling the distribution of Penn's gifts was the job of one of the Indian sachems or "Kings," who was so designated because "*he knew the best how to order them.*" This individual seemingly excelled in knowledge of the protocol necessary for recognizing each of the groups participating and their respective leaders. Penn offered "Match-Coats and some other Things," including "some Brandy or Rum." Despite the presence of alcohol, this was no drunken spree. The sachem receiving the gifts "poured out his Drams." Looking "to the Person which he intended to give the Dram to," he "made a Motion with his Finger, or sometimes with his Eye." Individuals "came quietly forward . . . and took their Drams" from the sachem who was seated "on the Ground or Floor." The Quaker reporter, obviously impressed with the solemnity of the event, wrote, "And withal I observed (and also heard the like by others) that they did not, nor I suppose never do speak, two at a time. . . . Their Eating and Drinking was in much Stillness and Quietness."[2]

After both sides "agreed that if any particular Differences did happen amongst any of their People, they should not be an Occasion of fomenting or creating any War . . . but Justice should be done in all such Cases," the Indians exited the building—Penn's country home, Pennsbury, near the falls—where the talks and gift giving had taken place. Euro-Americans on hand may have considered the main work completed; however, what happened next was perhaps just as important, if not more important, to the Indians. They moved "into an open Place" nearby "to perform their . . . *Worship.*" There they lit "a small Fire, and the Men without the Women sat down about it in a Ring." The Indians were riveted in their attention to their devotions as "they sang a very melodious Hymn" and "beat upon the Ground with little Sticks." The singing continued in a steady pattern. "One of the elder Sort sets forth his Hymn," the Quaker wrote, "and that being followed by the Company for a few Minutes, and then a Pause; and then the like was done by another, and so by a third, and followed by the Company, as at the first; which seemed exceedingly to affect them and others. Having done, they rose up and danced a little about the Fire, and parted with some Shouting like a Triumph or Rejoicing."[3]

There is much that remains unknown about this event. We cannot be certain of the backgrounds of all of the participants. Although the treaty occurred in the Delaware Valley, it seems to have been one in which Penn attempted to strengthen relations with Susquehannocks, Shawnees, and Conoys in 1701. Nevertheless, given the location at Pennsbury and the importance of multiple witnesses to treaties, it seems highly likely that at least some Lenapes attended. Minutes of the important 1701 meeting with the Susquehannocks, Shawnees, and Conoys listed the name of a "Passaquessay," who was likely the "Passakassy" listed in Pennsylvania records a few years later as "one of the Chiefs of the Delaware Indians" on the Susquehanna. We also do not know the extent to which Quaker biases shaped the narrative. Nevertheless, one thing that does emerge from the Pennsbury story is a sense of relationships among the Indian participants, who formed a type of unity combined with diversity. One sachem received gifts for the entire company and then, in the case of the drams, carefully made presentations to attenders one by one. And unity was represented around the fire ring, juxtaposed with examples of individual singers, who themselves elicited a musical refrain from the corporate body. This event, like the meeting in 1633 at Fort Nassau, emerged as more than a treaty binding Indians to Europeans; it also suggested a rich ceremonial life linking Indians to other Indians. As they divided up the gifts that confirmed their treaty with Penn, Indians—probably from a number of different communities—also confirmed their relationships with each other at a time of stress resulting from a burgeoning Euro-American population.[4]

Sharing Lands and Asserting Rights in the Face of Pennsylvania's Expansion, 1682–1742

With the growth in the number of Europeans entering the Delaware Valley in the late seventeenth and early eighteenth centuries, pressures on Lenapes' lands became increasingly intense. Some early arrangements in Pennsylvania suggested that Indians and Europeans might work out shared land use agreements; however, this possibility became more difficult to sustain against mounting demands from Pennsylvania colonists for farmland and from Pennsylvania's proprietors and other big purchasers for real estate. Under these pressures, some Lenapes moved up the Schuylkill in the Delaware Valley, and many headed westward toward the Susquehanna. When they settled in new regions, they brought along connections formed previously with other Indians, and they forged new relationships and shared lands with a culturally diverse range of Indian peoples. As they did so, Lenapes continued to consist of a variety of groups who shared territories with diverse Indian neighbors. Flexibility did not mean pliability, however. Lenapes bristled at Europeans' attempts to push them off their land and objected when they perceived payments for their lands were inadequate or absent. They were vocal in asserting their rights and in demanding that old promises and agreements be upheld.

Building on the Old and Forging New Connections

In the Delaware Valley, large-scale population pressure from Europeans did not come until fairly late in the seventeenth century. Neither the Dutch nor the Swedish settlements attracted sizable numbers of colonists. Early Dutch attempts to establish themselves, primarily as traders, were not very successful. Indians living in the area of present-day Lewes, Delaware, had attacked and destroyed the small Dutch post, called Swanendael, in the early 1630s. Just a few years before this incident, the Dutch had already decided to withdraw men from Fort Nassau on the Delaware and from a post near the falls in order to concentrate their forces at Manhattan. After Swedes arrived in the valley in 1638, their numbers were not impressive. By one estimate, only about three hundred Swedish colonists had arrived by 1644, and many of them took ill and died. Others left the colony. New Sweden saw a brief influx in 1654 with the arrival of about 250, mainly Finnish, colonists. After competing with the Swedes and then wresting control from them, the Dutch West India Company found their costs mounting on the Delaware. In 1656, the city of Amsterdam took charge of the southern portion of the Delaware colony, including Fort Casimir, which became New Amstel (later New Castle); however, the colonists struggled. It was during this period that the Dutch reported high numbers of deaths.[1]

Population pressures in the Delaware Valley significantly increased with the Quaker migration to West New Jersey starting in the late 1670s and after Pennsylvania was established as a proprietary colony in 1681. William Penn negotiated a sweeping policy of land purchases from Indians to try to set Pennsylvania on a firm footing. Penn's first acquisition occurred in 1682 and covered lands along the falls and southward to the Neshaminy Creek in present-day Bucks County. This purchase, handled by the proprietary agent William Markham, encompassed the area where Penn would set up his Pennsbury estate. Penn's subsequent purchases included the area within the present bounds of Philadelphia, around Chester (formerly the Swedish settlement, Upland), and within present northern Delaware State. Penn also sought to extend his holdings into the Susquehanna Valley. With Pennsylvania's territory expanding, Euro-American settlers poured into the colony. During the first fifty years of the eighteenth century, Pennsylvania's population reached 150,000. In July 1683 Penn estimated that in his new city, Philadelphia, in the vicinity of the Indian village Shackamaxon, there were "80 houses" and "300 farmers near it to help us with provisions." Seven years later he trumpeted the "good forwardness of Building" at Philadelphia and claimed the city now had "above One Thousand Houses finisht in it."[2]

As Philadelphia expanded, some Lenapes headed up the Schuylkill. Swanpees, one of the signers of the 1682 deed for lands near the falls had a "new Plantation ... about 35 miles From Philadelphia" in 1686. His settlement was possibly near a trading post recently opened on the Schuylkill by the Huguenot Le Tort family in the area of present-day Phoenixville. At this same time,

Indians were reported about a dozen miles from Philadelphia on the north side of the Schuylkill at Whitemarsh, where they were holding a ceremonial dance, or *cantico*. After an altercation with the Irish surveyor Nicholas Scull, these Indians "putt off their Cantico" and relocated to Swanpees's residence. Shakhuppo, a sachem who sold lands in 1685 between Pennypack and Chester creeks, including a portion of the Schuylkill above Conshohocken, was in the vicinity of the Le Tort post about nine years later. During the eighteenth century Sassoonan (also known as Allummapees), who as "a Little Lad" had been in the Perkasie area northwest of the falls, became a leader for Delawares who relocated to Tulpehocken (present-day Reading area) in the Schuylkill Valley.[3]

Lenapes also moved to the Susquehanna in the late seventeenth and early eighteenth centuries. Some were near present-day Millersville, Pennsylvania, at Conestoga ("Quanestaqua") by 1696. Other Lenapes relocated to Paxtang, a place within present-day Harrisburg near a creek flowing into the Susquehanna. In a region of ponds and springs, Paxtang lay several miles north of the "Washinta," an Iroquois name for the "great Falls" at the Conewago Creek's mouth. In July 1707 Pennsylvania's governor, John Evans, visited Paxtang ("Peixtan"), finding "only young People at home," along with an individual whom Evans approached as the "Chief Indian" and a trader named Nicole Godin, soon arrested for promoting French interests. Although the records for 1707 provide no identifying information for these Indians, there is better documentation for Indians in the area two years later. At that time it was reported that the "Chiefs of the Delaware Indians, settled at Peshtang . . . & other adjacent places," came to Philadelphia to meet with Governor Charles Gookin and the Provincial Council.[4]

Paxtang residents in 1709 included a complex mix of Lenapes, who did not come primarily from one small isolated portion of the Delaware Valley but rather from a range of areas between the falls and southward to New Castle. At least two of the Paxtang-area leaders were associated with Lenapes from the Schuylkill. One was Sassoonan, who through several subsequent decades had frequent contact with Pennsylvania officials. Sometimes they called him "King of the Delawares" or "Chief"; other times they used the Algonquian word "sachem" to refer to him. The second was Skalitchi, probably the same as the "Skalitzi," who appeared at a meeting with Swedes in 1654 as a representative of Lenapes living near the Falls of the Schuylkill.[5] Some of the Paxtang-area residents seem to have come from the Christina River, at least in the case of the sachem Owechela, located around Paxtang in 1709.[6] Sam, the interpreter for the Paxtang-area peoples, likely had ties to a range of areas from Philadelphia southward. His father, Essepenawick (or Essepe-naike), sold land to Penn between the Pennypack and the Neshaminy and farther south between the Duck and Chester creeks; in addition, Essepenaike signed as a witness to one of Penn's early purchases of Susquehanna lands.[7]

Delaware peoples with different backgrounds mingled around Paxtang; however, given the evidence of networks and exchange in the seventeenth-century Delaware Valley, it is likely that some of them had already con-structed relationships before migrating to the Susquehanna. As Delawares moved to areas such as Paxtang, they also came into contact with an increas-ing variety of non-Lenape peoples.

Of course, Lenapes had already had substantial contacts with Susquehan-nocks in the seventeenth century. Relationships between Lenapes and Susque-hannocks, or Conestogas as they were increasingly called, continued in the Susquehanna Valley during the next century. Lenapes and Susquehannocks also shared the valley with Shawnees, a people with an especially complicated history of migration. War with the Five Nations Iroquois between 1662 and 1673 had contributed to a scattering of Shawnees, who it is believed were located in the Ohio Valley at that time. Some joined the Minisinks in the Delaware Valley after a stay in Illinois. Other Shawnees settled along the Savannah River in Carolina. By 1692 Shawnees had entered the Susquehanna Valley, establishing themselves around the mouth of the river. Within a few years the Shawnees had constructed a settlement on Pequea Creek east of the Susquehanna. Here, they were not far from the Susquehannocks' main settlement, Conestoga.[8]

Other immigrants to the Susquehanna Valley were Conoys (sometimes called "Ganawese" or "Canawense"), who consisted of a number of affiliated Algonquian-speaking groups from southern Maryland, including the Piscat-aways. By the late seventeenth century Conoys had moved northward along the Potomac River where they skirmished with Euro-Americans. A treaty be-tween Maryland and the Piscataways in 1700 failed to achieve a lasting peace. In 1704 Col. Ninian Beale from Rock Creek complained that Potomac-area Indians had killed several colonists. Two years later Conoys protested their own mistreatment by Euro-Americans, stating that "the Virginians had much disturbed them, killed one of their men & abused several others." Disease de-pleted the Conoys at about this time. As pressures mounted, Conoys began migrating out of Maryland and Virginia. Already by 1701, some Conoys had apparently moved up to the "head of Patowmeck," and in 1706 Conoys were "settled some miles above Conestoga at a place called Connejaghera."[9]

In time, additional groups entered the Susquehanna Valley from the

South, including Algonquian-speaking Nanticokes from east of Chesapeake Bay, Siouan-speaking Tutelo and Saponi Indians originally from Virginia, and Iroquoian-speaking Tuscaroras from North Carolina. All of these groups had faced land pressures from Euro-American settlement, and in the case of the Tuscaroras, particularly violent events had precipitated their movement north. Angered that colonists were capturing and enslaving their people, the Tuscaroras engaged in a bloody war between 1711 and 1713 that ended with their defeat and migration toward the Susquehanna Valley.[10]

In this fluid situation, ownership of the Susquehanna Valley was a complex matter of crosscutting claims. As Penn set his sights on obtaining the valley, he encountered multiple claimants to the land. Native notions of land in terms of different usage rights likely contributed to a sense of overlapping ownership, as did habits of sharing territories with neighboring groups. The Susquehanna Valley, however, was not merely a place of territory sharing but also was a place of competition. Power relations and struggles for control involving the colonies of New York and Pennsylvania as well as various Indian peoples sparked controversies over land.

Kekelappan and Machaloha, two individuals from the lower Delaware, were among those who claimed lands in the Susquehanna Valley in early dealings with Penn. Both individuals appear to have been Lenapes. Kekelappan, thought to have been a sachem from White Clay Creek, ceded territory on the east side of the Susquehanna. Machaloha sold Penn land that included the area "between Delaware River the Bay of Cheasepeck bay and Susquahannah River." Penn hoped to use this acquisition to strengthen his claim to the mouth of the Susquehanna and to forestall Maryland controlling the area. Machaloha did not expect to vacate these lands but rather expected to share their use with Pennsylvania. Penn himself stated that he had "declared" in writing that Machaloha "should not be molested in his hunting in those parts" after Pennsylvania's purchase "in Delaware and Susquehanno." Maryland contested Penn's buying lands around the Chesapeake Bay from "Delaware Indians," apparently referring to the agreement with Machaloha. When Lenapes claimed a portion of the Susquehanna, it may have been partly because they saw it as their hunting territory.[11]

The Susquehannocks and the Five Nations also asserted rights over Susquehanna Valley lands. Susquehannocks, who had entered the valley by the sixteenth century, had briefly been residents of the Potomac area, and some of their number had recently moved north to Iroquoia. Five Nations Iroquois argued that they had conquered the Susquehannocks and assumed control of their territory. Colonial diplomatic relations were forged that strengthened the position of the Iroquois in asserting their claim to this oversight. With Governor Andros of New York, who had allied with the Mohawks against New England Indians during King Philip's War, the Iroquois created the Covenant Chain—a metaphor for the alliances that came to link colonial governments and Indian nations and to place New York and the Iroquois in the most prominent positions among the parties involved. Both New York and Pennsylvania turned to the Five Nations in attempts to gain control over the Susquehanna Valley. Anxious to open up a northern fur trade route for his colony, Penn sent commissioners in 1683 to negotiate with the Iroquois for purchase of the valley; however, "the people of Albany," said to be "Jealous of their Trade," had "much opposed" Penn's attempts. Thomas Dongan, the governor of New York by that time, stated that he had secured the region for his colony and for himself, writing that the Iroquois had "all of them agreed to Give Sesquehannah river to me and this Government." Over the next decades, New York's interests in much of the Susquehanna Valley would recede, while Pennsylvania continued to deal directly with the Iroquois for control of the Susquehanna.[12]

The grant to Governor Dongan of New York from the Iroquois may have been "neither a cession of territory nor a sale of real property, but rather a trust." Many years later the Iroquois argued that the deal with Dongan had been a flexible arrangement by which the Five Nations had "Charged him to keep the land safe for Our Use." "[Dongan] advised us," they said, "that we might always have Our Land when we should want it." Dongan, however, claimed much more. He assumed the entire Susquehanna Valley from its headwaters to the Chesapeake as his personal possession, which he then sold to Penn in 1697. Having made this purchase for £100 from Dongan, who was no longer governor of New York at the time of the sale, Penn no doubt hoped that he himself was now the legitimate owner of the valley.[13]

Nevertheless, ownership of the Susquehanna was far less fixed than this agreement may have implied. In 1683 Penn had sent his commissioners to Iroquoia while he remained unsure who could rightfully sell the Susquehanna Valley. Penn appeared uncertain whether he was sending his negotiators because the Five Nations had rights by "Claime of Conquest" or because "the remainder of the Susquahannahs, who are right Owners thereof, are amongst" the Five Nations. In other words, he seemed vague about whether these lands were the legitimate possession of the Five Nations or whether they belonged to the Susquehannocks, a portion of whom had recently moved into Iroquoia. After his purchase from Dongan, Penn saw that he needed to solidify his claim; thus he approached the Susquehannocks for

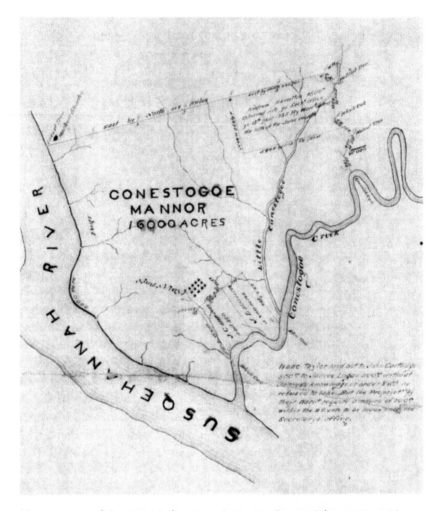

Figure 1. Area of Conestoga Indian town, Lancaster County, February 1718. Map #3698, Location 119-3698, RG-17, Records of the Office of Land Records, Land Office Map Collection, Pennsylvania State Archives, Harrisburg. Courtesy of the Pennsylvania Historical and Museum Commission, Bureau of Archives and History.

their approval, obtaining it first in 1700 and then confirming that treaty with a document called the "Articles of Agreement" in 1701.[14]

Pennsylvania's position in the Susquehanna Valley did not remain unchallenged, however. Even though Penn had obtained the signature of the Onondaga Ahookasoongh along with Susquehannocks on the 1701 Articles, there remained considerable controversy over the Susquehanna Valley lands. Iroquois continued to assert rights of ownership in the Susquehanna Valley. Speaking in 1710 at a meeting on the lower Susquehanna, an Onondaga man said, "That the Land belonged to the five Nations, and therefore Indians Might Settle wherever Corn could be made." Ten years later, the Susquehannock Taquatarensaly, also known as Civility, reported that "the Five Nations, especially the Cayoogoes, had at divers time expressed a Dissatisfaction at the large Settlements made by the English on Sasquehannah" and that the Iroquois "seemed to claim a Property or Right to those Lands." As late as 1736 there was a chance that Taquatarensaly might press his own claims to Susquehanna Valley lands—a possibility that led the Iroquois to try to prevent Pennsylvania from dealing with the Susquehannock leader. "Should he [Taquatarensaly] attempt to make a sale of any Lands," the Iroquois told government officials, "he hath no Power to do so, and if he does anything of the kind they, the Indians, will utterly disown him."[15]

Conestogas apparently believed that Penn's purchase of Susquehanna lands had not eliminated their usage rights in the valley. In 1722 Taquatarensaly remembered promises of sharing territory made at the time of the signing of the Articles of Agreement. "When the Conestogoes understood He [Penn] had bought their Land They were sorry," Taquatarensaly explained. "Upon which Wm. Penn took the Parchment and laid it down upon the Ground saying to them, that it should be in Common amongst them viz. the English and the Indians." Penn and the provincial secretary James Logan encouraged the Susquehannocks to expect to have a continuing place in the region. The Articles of Agreement of 1701 described a world in which Indians could "live Near or amongst the Christian Inhabitants" of Pennsylvania. Furthermore, a document addressed to the king of England and signed by Susquehannocks later that year depicted a vision of Indians sharing space with Euro-Americans. This document, a testimonial actually written by Logan, urged the king to "be good and kind" to Penn "and his children, and grant that they may always govern these parts." The Indian signers agreed to endorse Penn because his governance gave them "confidence, that we and our children and people *will . . . be encouraged to continue to live among the Christians* according to the agreement we have solemnly made for us and our posterity as long as the sun and moon shall endure, one head one mouth and one heart." The language of this testimonial as well as the Articles of Agreement may have offered some hope to Susquehannocks who sought an enduring stake in their homelands.[16]

Notions of land in terms of overlapping usage rights also would have shaped the way that Indian peoples related to one another. Flexible attitudes toward land use encouraged territory sharing that brought Delawares in contact with an increasing variety of Indian neighbors. In some cases they would have had prior knowledge of these Indians, and if so, old relationships would have been reshaped in changing surroundings.

Delawares and Susquehannocks continued to build on their long history of contact. The sachem Menanzes was a Delaware who had constructed relationships with Susquehannocks and knew their language. At a 1694 meeting responding to Iroquois calls to fight the French, Menanzes spoke for Kyanharro and Oriteo, "two Susquehanna Indians" who attended with the larger Delaware contingent in case these two "could not be understood." Menanzes relayed the Susquehannocks' request that Pennsylvania protect Indians who had recently "fought their way through" an attack by Miamis. Oriteo was Orettyagh (also known as Widaagh), one of the Susquehannock leaders who would sign the 1701 Articles of Agreement, which possibly included Delaware observers. Kyanharro may have spent time on the Schuylkill in the vicinity of the Le Tort trading post, where Delawares traded. In 1693 the wife of "Kyentarrah" (probably Kyanharro) had been at the Le Torts' with Shakhuppo, where they reported seeing movements of "strange Indians" called Shallnarooners (or Shawnees).[17]

This encounter and the use of the word "strange" suggest that Kyanharro's Susquehannocks and Shakhuppo's Delawares had little previous experience with the Shawnees. Shakhuppo said, "hee neither knew them, nor understood their Language." As Shawnees and Delawares gathered on the Susquehanna in the eighteenth century, they had an increasing number of opportunities to learn about each other. Sassoonan cooperated with the Shawnee leader Opessah. Both attended a meeting at Philadelphia in 1715, although Opessah had formally abdicated his sachemship since, as one Shawnee explained, his "People differed with him." After relinquishing his position, Opessah "lived at a great distance," but his location did not prevent contacts with Sassoonan's people. Instead, Sassoonan explained that during long journeys they came to depend on Opessah, who "entertained them with victuals & provision."[18]

The Delaware sachem Menanzes, who had links with the Susquehannocks, also constructed ties with the Conoys. Menanzes, as "the Indian Chief on Skuylkill," met with the governor of Pennsylvania in 1705 "in behalf" of the Conoys, "settled in this Province near the head of Potomock." These Conoys were "reduced by sickness to a small number" and were "Desirous to quitt their present habitation." They had approached the Schuylkill

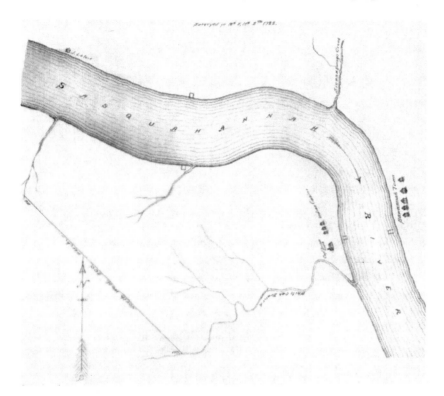

Figure 2. Area of lower Susquehanna, showing location of a Shawnee settlement, surveyed 1722, copied 1912. Copied surveys, book BB-3, p. 1, microfilm roll 28.12, RG-17, Land Records, Pennsylvania State Archives, Harrisburg. Courtesy of the Pennsylvania Historical and Museum Commission, Bureau of Archives and History.

Delawares with a request "that they might Settle amongst them" in the vicinity of Tulpehocken, a message that Menanzes relayed to the governor.[19]

As diverse Indians came together, they experienced many of the same problems and shared certain grievances, particularly concerning trade practices. On occasion, Susquehanna Delawares joined with other Indians to protest and seek redress. A meeting at Philadelphia in 1718 included Delaware, Susquehannock, Shawnee, and Conoy representatives disturbed by the alcohol trade. The Susquehannock Taquatarensaly protested Pennsylvania's failure to regulate the rum traffic, saying that "there have been such Quantities of that Liquor Carried of Late amongst them, by Loose persons who have no fixt settlements, that . . . mischief may arise from it." Sheeckokonichan, a Delaware formerly from the Brandywine, complained "that the young men about Pextan [Paxtang] had been lately so generally debaucht with Rum, carried amongst them by strangers, that they now want all manner of Clothing & necessarys to go a hunting." He urged the government to order that only "Traders who furnish them with all other necessarys" and who "Encourage them in their Hunting" be permitted to trade among his people.[20]

Some of the worst problems occurred when trading took place in hunting territories away from Conestoga, Paxtang, and other villages. Conestoga residents complained in 1710 that "several persons make it their business to waylay their young men returning from hunting, making them drunk with rum, & then Cheat them of their Skins." Attempts at government regulation, such as licensing traders who agreed to follow "certain Orders," failed again and again. Indians from Conestoga expressed outrage that "since Lycenses were granted they found themselves worse Dealt by than Ever, they received less for the Goods they sold The Traders; were worse Treated & suffered more Injouries." Underscoring Pennsylvania's inability to stop the rum sales in the woods, Governor John Evans shifted part of the burden for enforcement back to the Indians, warning them "to take Care among themselves that none of their people should sell anything to the Traders till they came home to their own Town."[21]

Susquehanna Valley Indians had other reasons for outrage at the behavior of Euro-American traders. Conestogans objected to "the Cattle the Traders kept," which "hurt & Destroyed their Corn." An "old Queen Conguegoes represented that" Ann Le Tort, one of the former Schuylkill Valley traders now at Conestoga, "did them great Damages by keeping of Hogs." The Susquehannocks also complained about traders' horses wandering about in Indian cornfields. "The Traders would Deny," the Indians maintained, "that those horses did belong to any of them that did it." In frustration, one Conestogan "Resolved to take a method to find to whom one particular horse belonged." After having removed this animal from the cornfield more than once, "he at last shott him, that the owner meeting with that Loss might be discovered by his complaints."[22] How traders priced goods aroused more discontent. The Delaware Sassoonan complained of changeable prices, saying that "formerly they exactly knew the prices both of our Goods and theirs, but now they varied so there was no understanding them." Fluctuating and declining prices, excessive emphasis on the rum trade, uncontrolled livestock, and unsuccessful or unenforced trade regulations created bitterness among Indians along the lower Susquehanna. Although they constructed friendships with Euro-American traders, Indians of the Susquehanna Valley expressed their resentment when confronted with what they perceived as unjust treatment.[23]

Given their common circumstances, it is not surprising that diverse groups of Susquehanna Valley Indians sometimes acted jointly, as was the case at the 1718 Philadelphia meeting as well as at the Articles of Agreement signing. Another attempt at a broadly coordinated response occurred in 1717 as a result of Susquehanna Indians' fears of "some Considerable Forces arm'd against" their people hunting "beyond the Furthermost Branch of Potomack." On this occasion the death of the son of the sachem Owechela aroused the concern not just of Delawares but also of Susquehannocks, Shawnees, and Conoys. Together they sent a letter to Governor William Keith "to know of the Govermt. what Christians were settled Back in the Woods behind Virginia & Carolina," and subsequently representatives from all four groups appeared at Philadelphia for a meeting.[24]

Yet Susquehanna-area Indians were far from being solidly united. Warfare, for example, tended to be organized around specific goals, probably involving limited numbers of warriors. In the eighteenth century, Susquehanna Valley Indians, sometimes joining members of the Five (later Six) Nations, participated in sporadic warfare against Indians of the Carolinas and Virginia. A Delaware leader named Depaakhossi, it was said, "had particularly distinguished himself" in this warfare. Retaliation for a previous attack was a likely motive for many raids, such as when Susquehannocks sent forty warriors against South Carolina Indians who had struck Susquehannocks near the Potomac in 1729. Warfare also allowed young men to demonstrate and test their abilities, as in the case of a joint Shawnee-Iroquois assault on southern Indians in 1720, which ended in the deaths of ten Iroquois and two Shawnees. A Shawnee sachem explained the origin of this particular raid: "A Dispute arising among some of their young men" about "Who was the best man," so in order "to end it they resolved to make the Tryal by going out to War."[25]

Delawares' relationships with their neighbors were no doubt complex and variable because the Delawares themselves were a highly diverse group and would have included individuals who had differing ties with Susquehannocks, Shawnees, Conoys, and other Indians on the Susquehanna. One account hints at the wide variety of groups among the Delawares. At a meeting with Pennsylvania officials at Whitemarsh in 1712, Sassoonan, Skalitchi, and other Delawares displayed thirty-two wampum belts, which they were taking to the Five Nations. These belts likely included groups of matrilineally related kin. One belt was said to be from "a woman" who "desires peace & ease from the rising of the sun to his going down," one from "a woman, that a long time ago they made a peace and Desired that it may always be strong & Firm," and one from a woman who sent her belt so "that she may plant & reap in quiet." Yet another belt arrived with the message that "the principal of the Family that sends it" had died. Even as they connected and reconnected with a variety of peoples, Delawares maintained fundamental kin group associations.[26]

Contesting for Lands along the Schuylkill and Brandywine

After Delawares migrated northwest to the upper Schuylkill, they lived among and increasingly struggled with Euro-Americans in this region, which included the valleys of the French and Manatawny creeks—an area roughly between modern-day Phoenixville and Pottstown.[27] These Euro-Americans came from a variety of backgrounds. Already by about 1700 Swedes had moved onto the Manatawny, settling at Molatton at present-day Douglassville. The Manatawny and French creeks especially attracted individuals who were early developers of the iron industry in Pennsylvania, including the smith Thomas Rutter, who left the area around Germantown to set up an ironworks on the Manatawny about 1716. Soon after, Samuel Nutt, originally from Coventry, England, obtained an iron mine and established a furnace on French Creek. On the northwest side of the Manatawny lay Oley, a place that became a destination for French Huguenots, such as Isaac De Turck, who arrived there perhaps as early as 1709, after having lived in the Hudson Valley at Esopus. Germans also settled in the Oley area, including Johannes Keim from Speier, who with his wife Katarina moved in 1706 to the vicinity of present-day Pikeville. Matthias Baumann, former resident of the lower Palatinate and founder of the perfectionist "New Born" sect, appeared at Oley about 1717. Inspired by powerful religious visions, Baumann gathered followers from around the area, such as Maria De Turck, who wrote ecstatically to her relatives back in Germany that regeneration through Christ had made her unable to "sin any more." In addition, English Quakers such as Arthur Lee and George Boone were among Oley's early residents.[28]

As these diverse peoples moved up the Schuylkill, Delawares, led by Sassoonan, complained that his people "had not been fully paid for their lands," challenging the growing Euro-American presence. At a treaty in Philadelphia in 1718, James Logan "produced to those Indians a great number of Deeds" in order to convince them that "their Ancestors had fully conveyed, & were fully paid for all their Lands from Duck Creek [below New Castle, Delaware] to near the Forks of Delaware [in the Lehigh Valley]." Sassoonan, along with six other Delaware Valley leaders, received a small number of goods, as "a free Gift," not a payment, and signed a confirmation of the previous deeds, releasing "all the said Lands situate between the said two Rivers of Delaware & Sasquehannah," naming Duck Creek as the southern boundary and "the Mountains on this side Lechay [Lehigh]" as the northern boundary. Subsequent events showed that Sassoonan considered Oley and the Manatawny as part of the region covered by the confirmation but that he believed the area north of the range of hills surrounding Oley was excluded from it.[29]

Over the next decade Sassoonan and other Delawares struggled to hold on to their remaining lands lying within a portion of the fertile "Great Valley" between the Kittatinny Mountains on the north and the Oley Hills and surrounding piedmont on the south. The Oley Hills were part of the range, sometimes labeled simply South Mountain, stretching from below the Lehigh and across to the west side of the Susquehanna. A late-eighteenth-century writer described South Mountain as consisting "not in ridges" but instead in "small, broken, steep, stony hills." "In some places," he added, "it gradually diminishes to nothing, not appearing again for some miles; and, in others, it spreads several miles in breadth." This area included what was sometimes called the "Lechay Hills." Sassoonan considered the broken South Mountain range to be "the Mountains on this side of Lechay" mentioned in the 1718 confirmation.[30]

After 1718 the pace of new settlements on the upper Schuylkill did not slacken. As long as Euro-American immigrants stayed south of the "Lechay Hills" it could be argued that they were not in violation of land agreements; however, any Euro-American settlers above the broken heights of South Mountain, particularly along the Tulpehocken Creek where some of Sassoonan's people were living, contravened the 1718 treaty as it was apparently understood by Native residents. Thus after 1722, when thirty-three families of Palatine Germans left New York to settle on the Tulpehocken, with the encouragement of Governor Keith, Delawares protested. At Philadelphia in 1728, Sassoonan, accompanied by the sachem Opekasset, registered his people's complaints about encroachment on the Tulpehocken lands. Sassoonan asserted that the Indians' grant to Pennsylvania "reached no further than a few miles beyond Oley" and that any lands settled by Euro-Americans north of that region "had never been paid for."[31]

Euro-Americans on the upper Schuylkill by the 1720s were no doubt aware of the outrage that their presence provoked among the local Indians.

Possibly there were dissenters among Sassoonan's people who objected to the 1718 confirmation.[32] Despite a lack of solid evidence about how Delawares viewed Sassoonan's negotiations, it is clear that animosities with Euro-Americans worsened in the 1720s and came to a head in 1728. The winter of 1727–28 was "long" and "hard," so that by spring many Indians faced starvation. From his vantage point near the Susquehanna, John Wright observed Indians "in a destracted Condition, the hardness of the Winter Sweeping away there corne." Although their lands were covered by the 1718 confirmation, Euro-Americans on the Manatawny must have sensed that they were not welcome among upper-Schuylkill Indians living through such trying conditions. In May 1728, when a group of armed Shawnees appeared in the vicinity of one of the ironworks, Manatawny residents immediately assumed the worst. Although they did not recognize any of these Indians, the colonists may have feared they were allies of local Delawares. Such alliances probably seemed quite possible to the fearful colonists, because there were rumors that Manawkyhickon, a "Delaware" Indian on "the upper parts of the River Susquehannah," was rallying the Iroquois and the Miamis to attack Pennsylvania. Aware of these stories and "so Alarmed by a Nois of Indians," the "Frontier Inhabitants of the County of Philadelphia"—a county that then included Manatawny—were fleeing their "Plantations with what Effects they Could Possibly Carry away; Women in Child bed being forced to Expose themselves to Coldness of the air, where by Their Lives are in Danger." When the Shawnees arrived at Manatawny, the residents must have already been in a state of panic. They wondered whether these Indians, who seemed "strange" and "foreign," could have come from French or Spanish enemies, perhaps harboring the frightening thought that they came as allies of aggrieved Delawares. The Manatawny residents' imaginations must have run rampant when they saw that the Indians were armed and seemed to be speaking in Spanish. Shots were fired and colonists wounded, though later the Shawnees said that they had not meant to get into a fight; instead, the Shawnees explained, they had exhausted their supplies while on their way to defend against a possible raid from southern Indians and had merely stopped for provisions at Manatawny.[33]

If local Indians felt resentment toward the Manatawny residents in 1728, they no doubt felt even more bitterness toward the Tulpehocken immigrants who lived in the region still claimed by Sassoonan. Some of this dissatisfaction was likely directed at the Welsh living along the Cacoosing Creek, a tributary of the Tulpehocken. Among the neighbors to the Tulpehocken Indians were Walter and John Winter, two Welsh brothers at "Cucussea" (or Cacoosing) within Cumru Township, at that time part of Chester County. Like the Manatawny residents, the Winters panicked at the thought of an Indian attack in 1728. As residents of the Tulpehocken Valley, the brothers probably knew all too well of the unrest among Indians disputing encroachments in this region.[34]

Hearing rumors of an Indian attack, the Winters responded to an urgent call from a neighbor's son to help defend against "Indians at his father's house." As he arrived at the home of the neighbor, named John Roberts, the Winters came upon "an Indian man, some Women and some Girls, sitting on a wood pile" in front of the house. After the Indian man, named Taka-Collie, "took his Bow & stepping backwards took an arrow from his back, putting it to the string of the Bow," Walter reported that he "presented his gun and shot at the Indian." His brother John then "shott one of the Indian Women, and then run up and knocked another Indian Woman's Brains out." Later it was discovered that one of the Indian girls was wounded. Both incidents, the one at the ironworks and the other at Roberts's house, should be understood within the context of the ongoing land disputes on the upper Schuylkill. Panic flourished in an environment fraught with tensions over land claims.[35]

Seemingly on the verge of a war, at least a certain segment of the Delawares, led by Sassoonan, joined with Pennsylvania officials in trying to repair damaged relationships. Especially since the Winters had killed "persons ... all related ... to some of our Indian Chiefs," as Governor Patrick Gordon explained, "we cannot expect but that so barbarous a fact must be resented." Taka-Collie may have been a relative of one of the sachems who met in Philadelphia that year to discuss the status of the upper-Schuylkill lands. In June, Sassoonan, himself now a resident neither of Tulpehocken nor of Paxtang but rather of Shamokin on the Susquehanna, traveled to Molatton on the Manatawny. From here, he and several other leaders proceeded to Philadelphia, along with "some of the Relations of those Indians that were lately Killed by the Winters," whom he had presumably joined around Molatton. After giving such items as blankets, duffels, shirts, powder, lead, flints, knives, and looking glasses for "the general Present" to Sassoonan's people, Governor Gordon and his council provided "three Strowds, three Blankets, three Duffells, three Shirts, and Six Handkerchiefs for the Relations of the Dead." Eventually the Winter brothers were sentenced to hang for their crimes. The gift giving and especially the stern judgment against the Winters demonstrated how much was at stake for Pennsylvania as the government tried to ease panic among its citizens and prevent an Indian war.[36]

Besides getting satisfaction for Taka-Collie's kin, Sassoonan realized the need for resolving the issue of the Tulpehocken lands, as did Pennsylvania officials. Both the Indians and colonial leaders could see that Tulpehocken was a tinderbox. To Indian leaders, the killing of Taka-Collie probably suggested that more of their people would suffer unless they made concessions. In 1732 Sassoonan and several others agreed to resolve the dispute by selling the lands between the Lechay Hills and the Kittatinny Mountains, which encompassed Tulpehocken. In doing so, they no doubt recognized that the Palatines and other immigrants were not likely to leave the area anytime soon and hoped that Tulpehocken Indians could find safer locations on the Susquehanna and farther west. The payment for these lands fell short of Sassoonan's expectations, however, and he expressed dismay over the quality of the goods that the Indians actually received from the sale.[37]

At about this same time Delawares raised other land concerns along the Brandywine, which flows through Chester County, Pennsylvania, to the area of present-day Wilmington, Delaware, where it meets the Christina River. A seventeenth-century leader of this group was Seketarius, who had significant dealings with Penn. The proprietor mentioned Seketarius (or "secatareus") in a letter promoting his new colony in 1683. By the end of that year Penn had convinced Seketarius and several others to promise that "in the Spring next" they would sell their lands between the Christina and the Chester—an area through which the Brandywine flowed. In spring 1685, Penn may have been still trying to gather the resources to pay Seketarius and others for their land. At this time Seketarius was among those listed as a potential recipient of Penn's variously decorated caps, gifts perhaps meant to reassure the Indians that they could expect future payment.[38]

Like the Indians who signed the 1701 Articles of Agreement, the Brandywine Indians believed that Penn had promised them a continuing place in the region. "When William Penn first came to this country," they said, "he settled a perpetual Friendship with us; and after we sold him our Country, he reconveyed back a certain Tract of land upon Brandy-wine, for a Mile on each Side of said Creek. . . . [He] promised that we should not be molested whilst one Indian lived, grew old and blind, and died; so another, to the third Generation, that is . . . from Generation to Generation." This strip of land ran from the Brandywine's mouth up to the head of the creek's West Branch.[39]

In 1725–26, when the matter was under investigation, no one came forward with documents substantiating Penn's agreements with the Brandywine group. The Indians remembered some sort of paperwork. A Thomas Chandler also recalled that "Meeloch, an old Indian of Brandywine" had "above twenty years Since" shown him "a paper" that the Indian told him "was a Grant from the Govern[ment]" for the reserved Brandywine lands. The document "had a piece of a Seal to it and the name Markham" on it, but the paper "was so defaced" that only "a word here & there" could be read. At any rate, by 1725, the Indians' written proof, which over the decades must have gotten tattered and smudged from being handed around among the local populace, no longer existed. It had been "destroy'd," the Indians explained, "by the Burning of a Cabin." Speaking for the Commissioners of Property, James Logan reported that he had located no copy of a document showing Penn had reconveyed the Brandywine land to the Indians.[40]

Even without documentation, Logan and the other commissioners apparently recognized that some Brandywine lands still belonged to the Indians. In 1706, Logan wrote to Penn "about a very troublesome claim of the Indians to the land on Brandywine, *reserved* at their great sale." The commissioners seemed to accept the idea that certain lands had been set aside for the Indians when, in 1706, they decided that Pennsylvania could only obtain these lands by negotiating another purchase. This sale covered the lands from the mouth of the Brandywine "up to a certain Rock by Abraham Marshall's Line." Marshall's property was on the eastern side of present Newlin Township, Chester County, along the Brandywine's West Branch. Negotiations were contentious, and from the Native perspective possibly inconclusive because, as Logan indicated, the Indians received a "promise" of £100, but this amount was "a third only of what they insisted on" for the land. After 1706, the Indians, who had a town on the creek's north side, continued to claim the strip along the West Branch starting at Marshall's—an area that had not been included in the purchase.[41]

Complaints from Brandywine Indians about encroachment on these remaining lands led to the 1725–26 investigation by the Commissioners of Property at the request of the Provincial Assembly. "We are molested," Brandywine Lenapes said, "and our Lands surveyed out, and settled, before we can reap our corn off." Their criticisms were aimed especially at Nathaniel Newlin, who had purchased lands on the West Branch in 1724 and had begun to sell off lots that included the creek-front area still claimed by the Indians. The Indians considered it "very unkind that N. Newlin . . . never came to see them at their Town" to explain his actions. Instead, Newlin secretively "marked the Trees with small nicks & not large Notches," so that his surveying was visible to the Lenapes only "afterwards." Euro-American encroachment had caused Lenapes other troubles. Even though Indians selling Brandywine lands had reserved the right to the creek itself, dams constructed downstream had "so obstructed" its flow that, as the Lenapes complained, "the Fish cannot come up to our Habitation. . . . We are a poor people, and want the benefit of the Fish." Cheekapeenas (possibly Sheeckokonichan), Peequaneechen, and other Brandywine Lenapes explained to the commissioners that the dams "prevent the Rock & Shad fish from coming up as formerly," resulting in "very great Injury & the Suffering of their Families whose dependance was on these fish for food during a considerable part of the year."[42]

Fearing a disruption to the peace of the province and knowing that the Brandywine Lenapes were adamant about their claims, both the House of Representatives and the Commissioners of Property sought to calm the Indians. With a promise to compensate for losses, the House and commissioners convinced Newlin to agree in writing "that he will not give them [the Indians] any manner of Disturbance or Uneasiness in their Possessions and Claims." Nevertheless, this agreement did not settle matters. The Indians' lands on the Brandywine continued to tempt Newlin. In 1729 the sachem Sheeckokonichan ("Checochinican") protested that, despite his signed statement, Newlin had gone forward with the sale of a portion of the Indians' lands and barred the Indians from using timber in areas they claimed. Even their "town at the head of the Brandywine" had been "surveyed to one James Gibbons," who supposedly had "an assurance of a conveyance" from the commissioners themselves. As late as 1762 the dispute still rankled. By that time some of the former Brandywine Lenapes had relocated to the Ohio Country. One of these was Neemakcollen, son of Sheeckokonichan ("Chick-og-nick-an"). From his home in the Muskingum Valley, Neemakcollen "set off" for Pennsylvania to "see the Governor" about the West Branch Brandywine lands "Sold by Old Newlin." A man named John Langdale had "Encouraged him much to go down to be paid for his Lands." Neemakcollen did not get far on this occasion because he "was taken Sick" before he could reach the governor.[43]

While making a spirited defense of their lands, the Brandywine Lenapes, like the Tulpehocken group, were also turning toward the Susquehanna Valley. Some of those who appeared as "Brandywine Indians" or "Delaware Indians on Brandywine" in provincial records were probably at least part-time residents of the Susquehanna by the 1720s. They may have returned to the Brandywine at various times to stay with kin. Although Sheeckokonichan, referred to in the minutes as "a Chief of the Delawares, formerly on Brandywine," was associated with Paxtang Indians in 1718, he also maintained ties with people in the Brandywine area. As his protest against Newlin indicated, he defended claims to lands on the Brandywine and represented the area's Indians as late as 1729, though he may have been residing primarily on the Susquehanna by that time. During the 1720s or earlier, some of the Indians from the Brandywine were possibly living in or around Conestoga. Three of their sachems—Oholykon, Peyeashickon, and Wikimikyona—attended a council held at Conestoga in 1728 in response to the disturbances on the Manatawny. Wikimikyona ("Wiggoneeheenah") possibly had once lived "In a Turn" of Conestoga River on a "plantation" that he sold to the trader Edmund Cartlidge in 1725.[44]

Some Indians remained in Chester County in or near the Brandywine Valley after the 1720s. They eked out a living in various ways. A longtime resident of Chester County, the Indian Hannah Freeman (c. 1731 to 1802) remembered that when she was a child, her family spent summers growing corn at Newlin—probably on the West Branch lands above Marshall's that were swallowed up into Newlin Township. Winters were spent in Kennett Township, where wage work may have been available. This pattern did not last because "the Country becoming more settled[,] the Indians were not allowed to Plant Corn any longer." As land pressures mounted, Hannah's father moved to Shamokin on the Susquehanna and "never returned." After he left, Hannah remained with her mother and other female relatives—her "Granny Jane" and "Aunts Betty & Nanny." Hannah supported herself by sewing, collecting herbs, and selling baskets. According to one account, she also had a husband named Andrew, with whom she lived on the east side of the Brandywine "in a hut or wigwam on the high ground" in the area of Birmingham Township. Through life's vicissitudes, Hannah struggled to maintain ties to places along the Brandywine. It was said that Hannah and Andrew "always made claim" to the lands on the "high ground" in Birmingham Township. And, although Hannah was laid to rest in a pauper's grave, she had hoped instead for interment in what must have been a significant ancestral place—"a certain Indian burying-ground which she designated."[45]

Defending Rights in the Forks of the Delaware

Like Indians along the Schuylkill and Brandywine, those living in the Lehigh Valley faced pressures from Euro-American encroachment that sparked Native resentment and struggles to hold onto lands. Central to these struggles was the triangle of land west of the Delaware and east of the Lehigh within an area known as the Forks of the Delaware or "Lechay." Competition for these lands came to a head in the late 1730s and early 1740s. The process of trying to advance land claims was probably a highly significant factor in strengthening associations among Delawares in disputed areas. In addition, as disputants failed to win desirable outcomes for their cases, they also would have come to share something else—the frustration and resentment that accompanied dispossession.[46]

Along with that of the nearby Minisink, the early history of the Lehigh Valley is largely shrouded from view. The Falls of the Delaware prevented ships from traveling upriver. Far from being a huge cataract, the falls consisted of an approximately two-mile area, described in the seventeenth century as a place "where the river is full of stones, almost across it, which are not very large, but in consequence of the shallowness, the water runs rapidly and breaks against them, causing some noise." Although not a dramatic spectacle, the falls caused major problems for navigators. A seventeenth-century sailor from an English crew failed twice in one year to traverse them, finding this portion of the river "impassable with any great boate."[47]

Some early European traders, however, did manage to travel beyond the Delaware falls. The Dutch wrote of a Michiel Karman who may have been one of these, perhaps traveling through the Forks as far as Minisink. In 1660 he brought news to Fort Altena "from above where he had been trading with the Indians" about the death of Minisinks fighting alongside Esopus Indians. By 1701, and probably earlier, Indians in the Forks had encountered the debilitating rum trade. In that year the leader "Oppemenyhook at Lechay" was expected to consult with the Pennsylvania government and other Native principals on "a Law for Prohibiting all use of Rum to the Indians of their Nations." The trader James Le Tort obtained access to Indians at Pechoquealing near the Delaware Water Gap. Oppemenyhook ("Ohpimnomhook" or "Oppimemock") and his son-in-law were among those in debt in 1704 to Le Tort when he listed accounts from his trade at "Pachoqualmah" and Conestoga.[48]

By the late 1720s European immigrants were settling in the Forks, even though the land had not been cleared of Indian title. William Penn had died in 1718, leaving a tangle of issues involving mortgaged property and disputes over inheritance. During the years after his death, Pennsylvania's land affairs were handled haphazardly, and lax arrangements allowed immigrants to move onto lands without official permission. Not surprisingly, the turmoil on the Manatawny and the disputes along the Brandywine arose in this chaotic period. In the Forks, Scots-Irish immigrants took advantage of the fluid situation and in 1728 moved near the Hockendauqua and Catasauqua

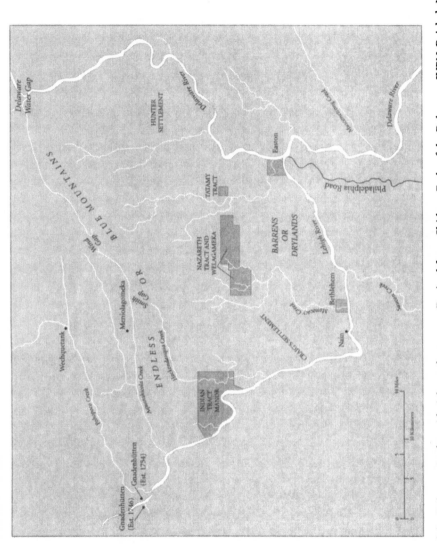

Map 3. The forks of the Delaware in the mid-eighteenth century. Derived from Chidsey, *Forks of the Delaware*; *IVPN*; Reichel, *Memorials*, 34n-35n; Paul A. W. Wallace, "Historic Indian Paths of Pennsylvania," *PMHB* 76 (Oct. 1952): 411-39 and accompanying map.

creeks, two tributaries of the Lehigh. This area became known as the Irish or Craig's Settlement. Within a short time another Scots-Irish community, called Hunter Settlement, emerged in the Forks. Northeast of Craig's, Hunter Settlement was situated along the Delaware at Martin's Creek and in the area of present Lower and Upper Mount Bethel townships. Because of easy access to water sources, the Scots-Irish chose these areas rather than the "dry lands" in the south-central part of the Forks.[49]

After 1732—by which time the proprietorship lay with William Penn's sons John, Thomas, and Richard—irregular land practices and illegal settlements continued in the Lehigh Valley. Thomas Penn set about reorganizing the province's land policy so that he and his brothers could maximize profits from their holdings. Like their father before them, the Penn brothers struggled under heavy debts. It had always been difficult to convince Pennsylvanians to pay quitrents—an annual payment on patented lands—which William Penn had hoped would serve as a regular source of revenue for the proprietary. Facing financial distress, Thomas now planned to collect back payments and to increase quitrent rates. The Penns also expected to shore up their fortunes by encouraging immigration and opening up new lands for sale and settlement. These initiatives, however, could only raise a sizable income for the proprietors if they had a substantial amount of land to sell. With an eye to potential real estate revenues, the Penns thus turned their attention toward unsold lands in and near the Forks of the Delaware. They began selling speculators thousands of acres, to which Indians still claimed title. One of these major purchasers in the late 1720s and early 1730s was William Allen, future chief justice of Pennsylvania's supreme court, who obtained acreage in the Saucon Creek valley, just south of the Lehigh. His acquisitions also extended into the Forks, where he bought lands that he then resold, some to the Scots-Irish already squatting at Craig's Settlement.[50]

Indians raised strong objections as the Lehigh Valley lands were being sold and surveyed by Euro-Americans. The Indians resisted pressure from the proprietors, who with James Logan tried to work out a bargain advantageous to themselves. One of the vocal opponents of proprietary plans was Nutimus, who owned lands north of Tohickon Creek. About 1726, Logan had entered into an agreement with Nutimus in order to obtain land for an iron mine in the region, though his purchase was not legally secure until the proprietors cleared the area of Indian title. After Thomas Penn arrived in Pennsylvania in 1732, he pressed Nutimus and other Indians to agree to a major cession of lands north of the Tohickon. Such an agreement would enable the proprietors to eliminate Native challenges to the sales they had already negotiated with speculators and would free up additional lands. Another opponent to the proprietors' land ambitions was Manawkyhickon, who resented that one of his relatives Wequeala had been hanged in New Jersey. In 1728 during the Manatawny dispute, rumors of Manawkyhickon's preparations for war circulated, and as we have seen, heightened tensions at that time. According to Sassoonan, an outraged Manawkyhickon threatened "that If he Did want wear [war] he could make a handel to his Hatsheat [hatchet] Seventey ffaddom Long" and then Sassoonan "should Se what that would Do." As Logan pressed for trans-Tohickon lands, he described a still discontented Manawkyhickon, "endeavouring to raise War between the Indians and English."[51]

Nutimus and other Indians voiced their concerns at meetings with Thomas Penn, now joined by his brother John, at Durham below the Forks in 1734 and at the family estate, Pennsbury, in spring 1735. At the Durham conference, Nutimus and another leader, Tisheekunk, protested Euro-American encroachment on unsold land in the Forks. Although these conferences gave Indians a chance to air complaints, the proprietors saw the meetings as an opportunity to convince them to part with their lands above the Tohickon. Delawares portrayed Thomas Penn as particularly desperate for their property. He resorted to "begging & plagueing us to Give him some Land," they reported, "till he Wearies us Out of Our Lives." Despite high-pressure tactics, the proprietors failed to secure the Indians' consent at either Durham or Pennsbury. In July 1736, John Penn, now back in England, indicated that the land in question remained unpurchased, though he seemed optimistic that Pennsylvania would expand into the Forks and beyond. "There is a very Large Quantity of Land to be disposed of Between the forks," he wrote to his brother Thomas, "& if it is fill'd it would be well to Purchase of the Indians a day or two's Journey above the Mountains, for I doubt not Settling [a] Great part of that Land Soon."[52]

Meanwhile, the Penns did not let the lack of clear title stop the surveying of lands. Surveys were a crucial stage in Native dispossession, and as had been true on the Brandywine, in the trans-Tohickon region Lenapes probably observed surveyors and their telltale marks with great distrust. Early surveys were done along the Hockendauqua and Catasauqua creeks in the vicinity of the Irish or Craig's Settlement. Surveying in this area occurred just months after the inconclusive Pennsbury meeting. Furthermore, soon after this meeting, the Penns had 6,500 acres surveyed as their own property, called the "Indian Tract Manor," in the area of modern-day Lehigh Township,

Northampton County. This proprietary acquisition, said to have been "Survey'd for the use of the Indians," lay just north of Craig's Settlement and included an upper branch of the Hockendauqua. It appears that the Penns incorporated this reserved tract, such as the one created earlier on the Brandywine, as part of their negotiations over a larger region—in this case, above the Tohickon. Some vague, probably unwritten promises to leave untouched Native homes in the Indian Tract Manor were likely meant to smooth relations and lead to Delawares' relinquishment of claims to the trans-Tohickon region. In addition, any Indians remaining in the area of Craig's Settlement or on other Forks lands would be expected to relocate to the reserved tract, making way for increasing Euro-American settlement and serving the Penns' own interests.[53]

As part of Pennsylvania's attempt to gain territory, Logan began to construct a precedent for Iroquois authority in the Delaware Valley. Unable to convince the Delawares to relinquish their lands, Logan pursued a plan by which the Iroquois would assume rights over the area above the Tohickon, trumping the claims of the defiant Delawares. Logan's efforts were designed to undermine Iroquois support for the Delawares and to leave them in an isolated and weakened position.[54]

In October 1736, Pennsylvania negotiated an agreement with the Six Nations concerning lower Susquehanna Valley lands. The Iroquois deeded to Pennsylvania all the lands from the mouth of the Susquehanna up to the Kittatinny (or Endless) Mountains along both sides of the river. With this sale Logan and the proprietors expected to put to rest the complaints of Iroquois who had long maintained that Penn's claim to having purchased the Susquehanna through New York's governor, Dongan, was not legitimate. Logan also seized on these negotiations as an opportunity to obtain a release from the Six Nations of their rights to "the Land lying within the Bounds & Limits of the Government of Pennsylvania, Beginning Eastward on the River Delaware" and "as far Northward" as the "Endless Mountains." This declaration served Logan's purposes by implying that the Iroquois had previously held jurisdiction over the disposition of Delaware lands and hence over the Delawares living there. Seeking compensation for Maryland and Virginia lands that they claimed by right of conquest over southern tribes, the Six Nations bargained for Pennsylvania's assistance in obtaining this payment. As part of these negotiations, several Iroquois leaders agreed to sign a statement that the Delawares had "no Land remaining to them"—a document that

Pennsylvania officials would later show as they made their case against Delaware claims.[55]

All the surveying in the Forks no doubt aroused Delawares' suspicions, and the Penns and Logan failed to gain the land by an outright purchase. Instead they employed the tactic of arguing that the Indians had agreed to sell these lands at a treaty with William Penn long ago. Nutimus, Lappawinzoe, and other Delawares concerned with Forks lands would have known this claim was false. According to one Indian's account, Nutimus had made it clear during earlier negotiations with William Penn that the Indians had not sold lands north of the Tohickon, and Penn apparently had accepted Nutimus's position. Penn's sons, in contrast, refused to acknowledge that the trans-Tohickon lands were off-limits. They produced paperwork supposedly showing that their father had made a purchase from near the Neshaminy back into the woods as far as a person could walk in one day and a half. This vague wording, however, by no means proved their claims to the northern lands they coveted; hence, in order to accomplish a major expansion of their holdings, they stretched, manipulated, and distorted the meaning of this sketchy documentary evidence.[56]

In August 1737, Nutimus, Lappawinzoe, Tisheekunk, and Manawkyhickon came to Philadelphia where they were persuaded to sign a paper crucial to the proprietors' schemes. With this document, the Indians confirmed the old agreement supposedly made with William Penn; they approved a walk lasting one day and a half in order to clarify the boundaries described in this agreement; and they relinquished any claims to lands measured off by the walk. The Indians assumed the proprietors' walkers would follow the Delaware to the Tohickon and then travel along that creek at a moderate rate. Instead the walkers traveled at a fast and exhausting pace along a much more direct route that had been freed from obstacles and carefully checked in advance. The walkers reached far beyond the Tohickon and marked off a line at an angle over to the Delaware River so that this "Walking Purchase," as it came to be called, covered an area far beyond the bounds of the sale that the Indians thought they were confirming and included the Forks of the Delaware.[57]

Threats and occasional violence surfaced during the tense 1730s and 1740s. As early as 1733, Nutimus, Tisheekunk, and another leader called Captain John had joined a number of other Delawares in objecting to "a white Man's having struck" an Indian "with a piece of Iron." Nutimus and the others granted that the wounded Indian had been guilty of "break[ing] the Man's Windows which was not good," but they thought the white man had

Figure 3. Portrait of Tishcohan, 1734, by G. Hesselius (1834.1). Courtesy of the Atwater Kent Museum of Philadelphia, The Historical Society of Pennsylvania Collection. Tishcohan (or Tisheekunk) was a signer of the Walking Purchase document of 1737.

gone too far by wielding the iron instead of striking with "his Arm only." Within a few years after the Walking Purchase, Delawares complained vehemently about "100 families Settled" on their lands illegally. This "*We think must be Very Strange,*" the Delawares protested, "*that T. Penn Should Sell . . . that which was never his for We never Sold him this land.*" These Indians were not in an accommodating mood, and they put the proprietors on notice with the warning "*We Desire Thomas Penn Would take these People off . . . that we May not be at the trouble to drive them off.*" Finding Pennsylvania authorities unresponsive, the Delawares restated their complaint: "We are Very much Wronged & Abused of having Our Lands taken & Settled & We know not how nor What for."[58]

Besides issuing complaints and warnings, Delawares attempted yet another tactic to defend their rights to the trans-Tohickon lands. They sought the support of non-Delaware Indians, especially the Iroquois. Just as large numbers of Native witnesses and participants had helped validate land agreements in the seventeenth century, in the 1740s the Delawares called upon their Indian neighbors to serve as witnesses to lend force to their claims in and around the Forks. They stated, "*The Land We Will hold fast With both Our hands not in privately but in Open View of all the Countrey & all Our Friends & Relations.*" These friends and relations were "the Eastern Indians & Our Uncles the five Nations [Iroquois] & the Mohikkons" as well as the Miamis ("twitways"); the Shawnees, including their division called the Sewickley ("Shawekelou"); Tuscaroras (listed separately from the other Iroquois nations); and a group called "Takkesaw" (thought to be the Conoys or Nanticokes). This long list was surely meant to impress the Pennsylvania authorities, but it also suggests that the Delawares were seeking Indian allies to reinforce their claims.[59]

The Delawares' continuing resistance to Euro-American expansion above the Tohickon led Pennsylvania to go further in pushing the notion of Iroquois dominance over the Delawares. At a treaty in Philadelphia in July 1742, Pennsylvania officials met with representatives from five of the six Iroquois nations, as well as with Delawares, including Sassoonan and Nutimus. Pennsylvania paid the remainder of the goods still owed from the 1736 release agreement. The Onondaga spokesman Canasatego pressed for an enlargement of the gift, and Governor George Thomas agreed. Thomas then laid papers before the Iroquois, which he argued showed that the Delawares had previously sold the land, and he urged the Iroquois to "cause these *Indians* to remove from the Lands in the Forks of *Delaware*, and not give any further

Disturbance to the Persons who are now in Possession." Three days later Canasatego openly declared support for Pennsylvania's position and told the Delawares, "You ought to be taken by the Hair of the Head and shaked severely, till you recover your Senses and become sober. You don't know what Ground you stand on, nor what you are doing." Referring to Pennsylvania's documentary evidence of previous Delaware land dealings, the Onondaga leader stated, "how come you to take upon you to sell Land at all: We conquered you; we made Women of you; you know you are Women, and can no more sell Land than Women. . . . This Land that you claim is gone through your Guts; you have been furnish'd with Cloaths, Meat and Drink, by the Goods paid you for it, and now you want it again, like Children as you are." Finally, he instructed the Delawares, "to remove instantly; we don't give you the Liberty to think about it."[60]

This speech raises questions about the nature of the relationship between the Iroquois and the Delawares at midcentury. Canasatego's words appeared to define Delaware-Iroquois relations in a strikingly clear way—that is, Delawares were subordinates of the Iroquois, who had conquered them. At a time when the Iroquois themselves were struggling to survive, Canasatego sought to ensure access to the colony's support. Further, he seems to have represented a faction among the Iroquois that turned to Pennsylvania as "a counterbalance to the predominance of New France and New York in the Iroquois' economic and diplomatic life." Still hoping for Iroquois support against Pennsylvania's claims, Nutimus and other Forks-area Delawares would have received Canasatego's speech as a painful blow and would have seen it as driving a wedge between themselves and the Iroquois. Despite the seeming forcefulness of Canasatego's language, however, there were ambiguities in the Delaware-Iroquois relationship.[61]

The term "women" as applied to the Delawares to characterize their relationship with others, including the Six Nations, would have raised a question: What did Canasatego mean when he said, "you know you are Women, and can no more sell Land than Women"? As one scholar writes, "He invoked specific European concepts of the female gender, in which women could not own or sell land, to delineate Delawares' subordinate position in terms that Euramericans would clearly understand." To Euro-Americans, Canasatego's comment undoubtedly was a clear statement of Delaware inferiority; however, his equating women with the inability to sell land concealed an ambiguity that would have been more apparent to the Delawares than to Pennsylvania officials. Land possession was not the exclusive domain of males among the Delawares, de-

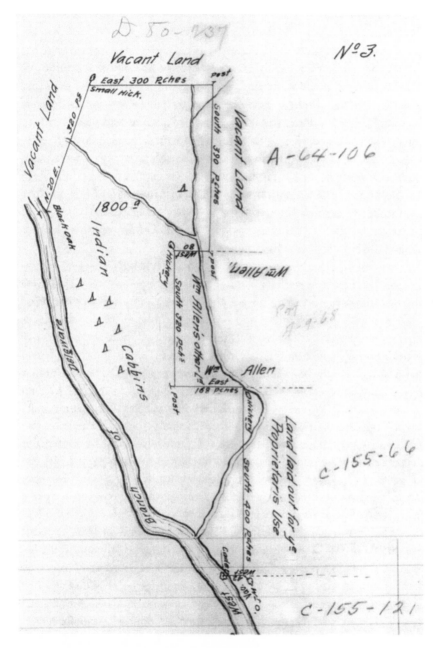

Figure 4. Area of "Indian Cabbins" in the northwest part of the Forks of the
Delaware, surveyed 1735, copied 1910. Copied surveys, book D-89, p. 232, microfilm
roll 28.253, RG-17, Land Records, Pennsylvania State Archives, Harrisburg. The
"West Branch of Delaware" refers to the Lehigh River. Courtesy of the Pennsylvania
Historical and Museum Commission, Bureau of Archives and History.

spite Canasatego's assertion to the contrary, and Algonquian women were not traditionally barred from participating in land sales. As the primary cultivators of fields, women would have had users' ownership rights to their plots and would have played a role in group decisions to sell tracts. A woman named Anameackhiskaman, for example, claimed ownership of Forks lands in 1733. Canasatego's later actions, in spite of his earlier words, revealed this ambiguity when in 1749 he joined with Delawares, including Nutimus, to sell to Pennsylvania lands north of the Kittatinny Mountains. Given that, in 1742, Canasatego had prohibited the Delawares from "medling in Land-Affairs," this development surprised Thomas Penn, who wrote, "When I consider the behaviour of the six Nations to the Delawares, I admire they should consent that Nutimus should have any of the purchase money."[62]

In addition, female terminology used to describe the Delawares in relation to the Six Nations was ambiguous because the Iroquois "might very well call the Delawares women both when they were pleased and when they were displeased with them." Context and audience would have shaped the meaning behind the word. It appears that this terminology could appear positive or negative depending on one's position in society. A missionary explained that a warrior might be "ashamed" by a female designation; however, other men might not object to this label as an acceptable way to indicate a friend or noncombatant. Women were associated with practices of mediation; warfare was typically men's domain. When male leaders worked out alliances and held treaties, they might have been seen as figuratively becoming women. For Delawares, the term "sister" could smooth relations between groups. "My sister! listen to what I say!" declared one Delaware leader trying to involve other Indians in peace negotiations later in the century. Another referred to a peace envoy from Ohio as "my Sister of Allegany."[63]

What also made the Iroquois-Delaware relationship far from clear-cut was that the Iroquois were not monolithic, and different portions of the Six Nations would have related in different ways to various Delawares, who themselves consisted of many groups. Many *relationships* as opposed to one *relationship* between the Iroquois and the Delawares operated at any given time, and these relationships shifted over time in response to rapidly changing circumstances. Delawares' relationships with the Iroquois were far more complex than Canasatego's words implied. Delawares did not consider themselves "conquered" by the Iroquois, and they did not quickly clear off from the lands included in the Walking Purchase. Not only did they later join the Iroquois in selling land, but several months *after* the Philadelphia treaty some Delawares still believed "the Six Nations were pledged to sustain them" in their struggle to maintain their homes in the Forks. Nonetheless, it is difficult to escape the conclusion that Iroquois-Delaware relations suffered serious damage in 1742.[64]

Out of the multitude of small "nations" mentioned in seventeenth-century records, new corporate entities were emerging among Delawares in the eighteenth century. Struggles over land revealed groups that were asserting themselves through collective action. Three of these were associated with the Forks, the upper Schuylkill, and the Brandywine. But Delawares in these places were not isolated from Delawares in other areas. They were part of a network of communication and connection that stretched into the Susquehanna Valley. Substantial mixing of Lenapes from different parts of the Delaware Valley occurred as they maintained a flexible approach to land that involved sharing territories with multiple groups, including non-Lenape peoples. The approach and language of William Penn may have left some Delawares with hope in the possibility that they could form "one heart" with him and with the colonists of Pennsylvania. Again and again, however, alliance building with Euro-Americans met formidable setbacks.

Chapter 4

Networks, Alliances, and Power, 1742–65

In the mid-eighteenth century, the story of the Delawares remained one of movement and reorganization. Even as they shared territories with a variety of Indians, Delawares also constructed ties with Euro-Americans. Nevertheless, Indians' interactions with the expanding English colonies had long been fraught with tension, and by midcentury the outbreak of the Seven Years' War marked a sharp deterioration in Anglo-Native relations. Although the war was part of an imperial struggle between England and France, it was much more; it involved a complex array of Indian peoples, including the Delawares, whose grievances were many. Even after France's surrender, Indians continued their struggles against the English in the brief but bloody Pontiac's War. Alliances and attempts at forming alliances were striking aspects of the war years. Consisting of many groups themselves, Delawares continued to maintain a variety of relationships with other Delawares along a network that linked communities and kin across wide distances. Delawares were not politically unified during this era; however, by the mid-1760s, some Delawares were attempting to come together to map out a specific role for their people within regional politics and diplomacy. As they did so, they constructed definitions about what it meant to be Delaware, emphasizing the Delawares' leadership role in alliance building among many peoples.

Negotiating Space and Forming Communities in the East

By midcentury Delawares in the east were struggling to survive on small pieces of land amid a growing number of Euro-Americans. New Jersey Indian communities were described as very small, with "not more than two or three families in a place." In 1744, Sakhauwotung, a settlement in the Forks, had just a few Indian inhabitants; the rest had "dispersed, and removed to places farther back in the country." Delawares remaining in the Forks were typically scattered in tiny enclaves "several miles distant from others." Some of those who had moved "farther back in the country" were probably living along the Blue Mountains in "little Indian towns," such as Chestnut Hill, Pohopoco, and Meniolagomeka.[1]

Delawares, however, utilized not merely the resources available within the boundaries of these small settlements in order to survive. They attempted to use various resources from a range of areas, thus continuing a method dating back to previous generations of flexibly using different territories; nevertheless, with Euro-American expansion and demands for absolute possession of land, it became increasingly difficult for Delawares to pursue this mode of subsistence. A Minisink message, conveyed by the Oneida Thomas King in 1758, revealed that Indians struggled to maintain usage rights in New Jersey. "When they sold the Land," King said, the Minisinks had not meant "to deprive themselves of hunting the Wild Deer or using a Stick of Wood when they should have Occasion." The Minisinks objected to the Euro-Americans' occupation of lands that had "never been sold," but were apparently even more outraged that Euro-Americans had denied them access to resources on these lands. "You claim all the Wild Creatures, and will not let us come on your Land to hunt for them," was their complaint. For Delawares, it was outrageous that Euro-Americans had placed off-limits even the bark of the trees, which had a variety of uses. "You will not so much as let us peel a Single Tree," the Indians protested. "This is hard, and has given us great offence."[2]

Struggling with shrinking access to lands and with increasing indebtedness, Indians developed wage-work arrangements with Euro-Americans. Two female Indian residents of the upper Lehigh Valley were employed in "pulling turnips" on the farm of their Euro-American neighbor George Custer. "An Indian family" from Pohopoco moved about the Forks in order "to help the white people with their harvesting." Other sources of income might come from the sale of Indian-made baskets and brooms. In short, the socioeconomic situation of these Indians was probably similar to that of Hannah Freeman and her family on the Brandywine.[3]

Over and over Delawares grappled with the question of how they might hold onto a share of lands in eastern regions. They had not forgotten William Penn's promises, and they were not quick to leave the Forks. Time and again, they and other Indians had agreed to be as "one People," "one Body," "one Head," and "one Heart" with the proprietors and their colonists and had received numerous assurances of friendship from Pennsylvania. Embedded in the physicalness of the language of alliance was a sense of sharing physical space.

Allied peoples were thought of as being from the same flesh and blood, even the offspring of the same body. Sassoonan characterized this relationship as that of two peoples coming "from one Woman." When Delawares remembered the promises of being "one Body" with Pennsylvanians, they may have visualized this alliance in terms of sharing physical space, which would have entailed sharing a territory's resources. Against this background, some Delawares continued to try to find ways that they could remain in the Forks and nearby areas.[4]

With decreasing options, it appears that some Delawares looked to the notion of reserved lands as one way of ensuring space for their people in Pennsylvania. Used at an early date on the Brandywine and later on the Susquehanna, the designation of reserved Indian lands became a tool for Pennsylvania to ensure its control over large swaths of territory and the dispossession of Native inhabitants. Reserved areas included the Conestoga Indian town (southwest of present-day Millersville) and a Conoy town between present-day Washington Boro and Harrisburg (near Bainbridge in Lancaster County). This reserved-land policy *seemed* to echo Penn's Articles of Agreement and the promises of maintaining space for Indian friends. In practice, though, living in the reserved areas was likely not an attractive option for most Indians—space was limited and Indians were subject to conflicts with their Euro-American neighbors. Departing from the Bainbridge-area reserve, the Conoy leader Old Sack explained, "now the Lands all around them being settled by white People, their hunting is spoiled." Nevertheless, some Delawares in the Forks may have thought they would be able to turn the idea of reserved lands to their advantage.[5]

The notion of reserved space was possibly on the mind of the Delaware Tunda Tatamy when, in 1733, he succeeded in convincing the proprietors to grant him land in the Forks that amounted to 315 acres after being surveyed. Tatamy had made his request around the time when the Penns were eager to convince the Delawares to sell the lands above the Tohickon. Furthermore, the proprietors probably agreed to the grant because they saw that Tatamy's knowledge of English made him useful as an ally and interpreter. Likely drawing upon the examples of this earlier grant and of the reserved Indian Tract Manor in the Forks, Captain John and other Delawares, including Tatamy, sent a petition to Governor Thomas several months after the 1742 Philadelphia treaty had called for Delaware removal from the area. "Having embraced the Christian Religion and attained some small degree of Knowledge therein," they requested permission to dwell "under the same Laws with the English." The Delawares wished that "some place might be allotted them

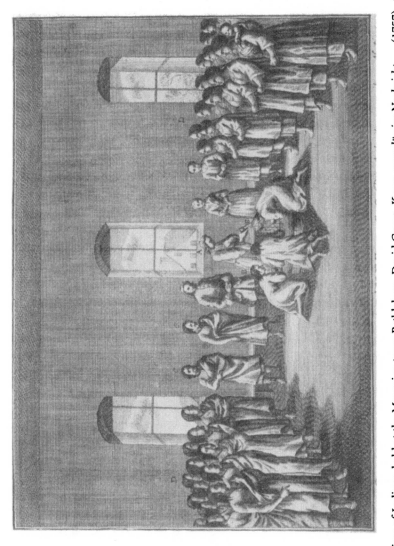

Figure 5. Baptism of Indians, held at the Moravian town Bethlehem. David Cranz, *Kurze, zuverlässige Nachricht . . .* (1757). Courtesy of Moravian Archives, Bethlehem, Pennsylvania.

where they may live in the Enjoyment of the same Religion & Laws" as the other inhabitants. Unfortunately for Captain John, by the time he made his appeal in the post–Walking Purchase era, Pennsylvania officials were far from accommodating.[6]

When, in 1741, German pietist Moravians settled in the Forks with hopes of Christianizing local Indians, Delawares no doubt viewed the newcomers in light of their own ongoing struggle to claim space in eastern regions and in light of past negotiations with Pennsylvania. The long-standing language of Indians' becoming "one people" with Pennsylvania colonists, the repeated rhetoric of both groups living as friendly neighbors, and the earlier promises of setting aside lands for Indian peoples probably had an impact on how Delawares responded to the Moravians.

The Moravians purchased from William Allen five hundred acres at the intersection of the Monocacy Creek and the Lehigh, which became the site for their town, Bethlehem. In an area northeast of Bethlehem, they bought a much larger "Nazareth Tract"—the location of the Delaware town We-lagameka, where Captain John lived. To many Delawares, the Moravians probably appeared to be just another example of Euro-American dispossessors entering the Forks. Beneficiaries of the Walking Purchase, the Moravians occupied lands where Captain John and his people had a peach orchard, a substantial amount of cultivated land, and a graveyard.[7]

Yet, surprisingly, substantial numbers of Delawares eventually participated in Moravian missions and constructed friendly relations with various missionaries. One factor, among many, may be that the Delawares came to see ways in which the Moravians' approaches seemed to overlap with Indians' approaches to land as shared space and resource. Listening to Moravians, some Delawares may have heard echoes of Penn's earlier promises that Indians and Euro-Americans could "live together as Neighbours and freinds." Trying to smooth over differences with Captain John, the Moravians offered "that he enjoy the Use of all the Land he has hitherto cleared" and continue residence "as our Tenant, but without any Payment of Rent to us, because the said Place has been a Settlement of his Forefathers." Although Captain John does not appear to have taken them up on this offer, other Delawares did live among the Moravians. In 1745 the Moravians decided "to build a hut to provide lodgings for the Indians" who were calling at Nazareth. At about the same time, "seventeen Indians," presumably from the small Delaware settlements beyond the Blue Mountains, had "arrived and settled in a hut near" Bethlehem's "brick kiln."[8]

The practice of sharing the use of lands and resources with nearby groups

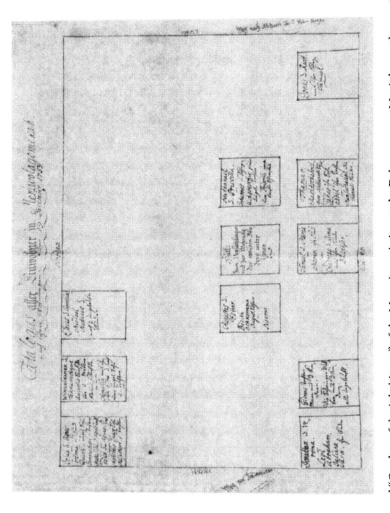

Figure 6. Diagram and "Catalog of the inhabitants" of the Moravian mission at the Delaware town Meniolagomeka, north of Bethlehem. 1/4/122, *RMM.* Courtesy of Moravian Archives, Bethlehem, Pennsylvania.

was not just a friendly gesture; it had been a basic aspect of Delaware and Hudson Valley Indians' survival for a long time. Undergoing difficult conditions at midcentury, Delawares continued to utilize this approach. In Moravian settlements, Delawares in "great need" received food and medicine. Some of these Delawares apparently came from the Susquehanna, as they tried to escape sickness rampant at Wyoming (present-day Wilkes-Barre, Pennsylvania, area) in the winter of 1745. "We visited the Indians who had built a hut for themselves near our brickshed," the Moravians wrote. "We also sent each of them a roll" and "took care of their sick." On another occasion, the Moravians gave a group of Indians "a large loaf of bread for supper and two knives as a present." Despite the neediness of the Delawares, there were signs of reciprocity in the Moravian-Delaware relationship, because the Moravians were using the area around the Delawares' Pohopoco settlement to obtain timber.[9]

But the Forks-area Delawares did not survive merely by building relations with Euro-Americans such as the Moravians; they also depended greatly on alliances with other Algonquians from the Hudson Valley and New England. These included Indians who had previously joined the Moravians. Most of the Moravians' first Algonquian converts were Mahicans or belonged to a group known as Wompanosch, a term that probably meant "easterner" but also may have applied more specifically to Housatonic peoples such as the Paugussetts. Other early Moravian converts were Esopus, Highlands, and Minisinks. Increasingly in the eighteenth century, an alternate name for the Minisinks—"Monsys" or "Munseys"—came into use in written records of Moravians and others. This term, today typically written as "Munsee," also developed as a linguistic label for the peoples—including the Minisinks—who spoke the northern Delaware language. Moravians preached to Algonquians in such areas as Shekomeko (near Pine Plains, New York), Pachgatgoch or Scaticook (near Kent, Connecticut), and Wedquadnach (near Sharon, Connecticut).[10]

When Delawares visited Moravian communities, they met some of these Indians from the Hudson and Connecticut regions. For example, they encountered Otapawanemen, a Wompanosch man renamed Isaac at his baptism, and two Mahicans—Wilpey (or Nathanael) and Nanhun (or Joshua). At Nazareth these three men spoke with Delawares "until late at night with deep feeling in their hearts concerning redemption through the blood of Jesus." Two other converts—an Esopus Indian, Pechtawapeht (or Thomas), and his Wompanosch wife, Esther—also communicated their understanding of Moravian Christianity. In 1743, Thomas, Esther, and their two children had left Shekomeko and had come to live at Bethlehem, where the Moravians "commenced to build a house"

for the family. This couple had numerous contacts with visiting Delawares during the hard winter months of 1745. Thomas and Esther brought an Indian
mother with a sick child "into their house to take care of them." A week later "all
the visiting Indians gathered in the house of Thomas," and "he gave them a
friendly evening meal in love." When a Delaware couple decided to request baptism, they turned to Thomas in order to make their wish known.[11]

Certain Delawares, however, were not eager to embrace Moravian
Christianity. A man from Tunkhannock on the Susquehanna's North Branch
was "frank" in telling the Moravians that "he did not want to have anything
to do with" their "teachings. For he saw that many Indians and white people,
even though they observed Sunday, were just as wicked as others." This man
had two children buried in the Indian graveyard that had become part of
Nazareth, and his hostility could have been deepened by the Moravians' occupation of this sacred site. Some Delawares may have seen the Moravians'
plan to "erect a nice fence around the Indian graveyard" as needed protection
for this space; however, others may have seen it as yet another example of
Euro-Americans trying to limit and control access to lands—not unlike the
boundary lines drawn by surveyors.[12]

Mobility was important to Delaware survival, and it was an important factor promoting the mixing of peoples. It encouraged the flexible use of land and
the development of a variety of alliances. The family of a woman named Awialschashuak, who became a Moravian convert, exemplified the ways that
Delawares moved about and adapted to varying situations. Awialschashuak and
her first husband, Abraham, were Indians from Long Island, who migrated
southward along the New Jersey coast. They had a daughter, Awach-
schauschqua, who was born in spring 1727 "in the Jerseys at the sea side, in a
place called good Luck," and a son, Nahnquei, born in about 1733 at Little Egg
Harbor in the southern portion of New Jersey. Approximately two years later
the family had apparently moved inland to Salem on the Delaware River, where
another daughter was born. From there the family seems to have headed northward to the Burlington area, where Abraham died in 1738. During at least part
of the 1740s, Awialschashuak and her kin lived in the Forks of the Delaware.[13]

Over the years as they made a circuit from Long Island, down along the
Jersey coast, across southern New Jersey to the Delaware, northward toward
the falls, and then over to the west side of the river, Awialschashuak and her
family would have tied their fortunes to quite a number of different communities and individuals. Not only did Awialschashuak join the Moravians but
her husband Abraham also had ties to Euro-Americans. Referred to as "a

famous Doctor," Abraham was known for his "good understanding of herbs, roots, and the like medications." His healing arts were not limited to the Native population but extended to the English. On one occasion, he was "called" to aid "one of the sick wealthy English women" of Salem.[14]

Delawares frequently moved between New Jersey and the west side of the river as they struggled to survive in the eighteenth-century Delaware Valley. There is ample evidence that an important contingent of Moravian converts in the Lehigh Valley came from a network of Delaware communities lying roughly between the falls and the Raritan River Valley. Some may have included descendants of the Raritans and nearby Algonquian groups. The family of Tammekappei or Keposch, a sachem who attended the Philadelphia treaty of 1742 ("Toweghkappy"), came from this area. Born in 1672, just a year after Tashiowycam's attack at Matinneconck Island, Tammekappei and his parents had lived at "Pennytown," which was probably Pennington, New Jersey, just north of the falls. Tammekappei also resided in the Raritan Valley, and he was born at Rocky Hill near the Millstone. In 1749, he still had a brother and sister living in New Jersey, although he himself was known as "the Delaware King in the Forks." Delawares living at Meniolagomeka above the Blue Mountains had a similar background. Their sachem, whom the Moravians called "George Rex," was born in 1716 at Kingston, New Jersey, very close to Tammekappei's birthplace at Rocky Hill. Teedyuscung, son of an Indian called "Old Captain Harris" at Pohopoco in the 1740s, was born east of Trenton in about 1700. Teedyuscung would later play an important role in charging Pennsylvania with defrauding the Delawares of lands in the Forks.[15]

At least one of the Delawares in the Moravian missions during the 1740s came from the lower Delaware. The sachem Depaakhossi was born in 1689 in the southern part of the Delaware Valley "during the wheat harvest at Christina Bridge in New Castle County." He spent enough time among Euro-Americans to forge a bond with the Pennsylvania lawyer, Joseph Growden. As a sign of this friendship, Depaakhossi himself sometimes took Growden's name. Depaakhossi eventually settled with the Moravian converts at Meniolagomeka, after having lived in the upper Schuylkill Valley at Oley and on the Susquehanna at Conestoga. In 1748 he had a number of relatives residing at Shamokin.[16]

Depaakhossi's migrations from New Castle County (present-day Delaware State), up the Schuylkill, to the Susquehanna, and back toward the Delaware River offer yet more evidence of the mobility and adaptability of Delawares who mixed with other Algonquians in Moravian communities. These various examples no doubt only begin to show the complex interactions in this region, which

also included African Americans—as indicated, for example, in the marriage
of two Bethlehem residents, a Shawnee named Anna Charitas and an African
American named Joseph. When the Moravians established a new mission
town, Gnadenhütten, farther up the Lehigh beyond the Forks, another complex community emerged, including Mahicans, Wompanosch, Minisinks,
Esopus, Highlands, and Delawares primarily from the Forks-New Jersey region. Evidence suggests that Algonquians remaining in the east had an extensive range of contacts that would continue to shape their experiences in the
coming decades as Pennsylvania moved toward war.[17]

Forging Bonds and Fighting Back

Other Delawares who had migrated to the Ohio Valley also lived in a complex and shifting world of alliances involving many Indian peoples. They
constructed alliances formed in part around shared needs, common grievances, and overlapping territories. Ohio Delawares were not cut off from Indians living farther east. During the Seven Years' War, communications and
movements across a broad region linked Delaware communities on the
Susquehanna and the Delaware to those in the Ohio Valley. Although
Delawares were not politically united during the war, they kept in contact
with far-flung friends and relatives.

Nevertheless, topography and transportation challenges probably
helped create, at least temporarily, a sense of separation from the east and its
burgeoning European settlements. Accounts from Euro-Americans suggest
that they found travel to Ohio far from an easy jaunt. Following the
Frankstown Path along the Juniata River, the Presbyterian minister Charles
Beatty found the road "bad." At "a place called the Narrows," near present-day
Lewistown, Pennsylvania, the way was treacherous "where a rocky mountain
bounds so close upon the river as to leave only a small path along the bank
for the most part." "For about ten miles" the way was "very uneven" and
"greatly encumbered by trees fallen across it"—the remains of a recent wind
storm. A portion of another road, the Raystown Path, was reportedly "very
winding and crooked in many places, to avoid creeks and swamps; and very
uneven, as it passes through a mountainous country." Even after this path
had been turned into a wagon road—that is, Forbes Road—for the British
army, Moravian Frederick Post called a portion of it "one of the worst roads
that ever was traveled." Yet another entryway to the Ohio Country lay farther

north along the Shamokin Path, near the West Branch of the Susquehanna. One commentator appreciated the "beautiful and fertile region" on the eastern portion of this path, but his impression soured as his party headed farther west. There he complained about passage "over precipitous and ugly mountains" and "through two nasty, rocky streams."[18]

In the Ohio Country, Indians whose homelands had once been in the Hudson or Delaware valleys continued to orient their lives around rivers and creeks as they established communities along the watershed of the upper Ohio Valley and its sizable tributaries, particularly the Allegheny, the Muskingum, and the Scioto. These rivers, as well as the Monongahela, helped delineate the region. The Allegheny Mountains created a natural boundary on the Ohio Country's east side. West of the region lay the Scioto River and the elliptically shaped Scioto Plains. To the north was the Lake Erie Plateau. Feeder rivers of the Monongahela served as loose markers of the southern reach of the Ohio Country. These landscape features, however, only suggest general outlines, for the Ohio Country was an "ill-defined region."[19]

Delawares were well established in the Ohio Country by the early 1730s. In 1731 the Indian trader Jonah Davenport, "lately come from Allegeny," observed "Indian Settlements consisting of about three hundred Delawares" in that region. Many of these Delawares were probably living in settlements within the Allegheny River Valley. One of these places, "Connumach" or (Conemaugh) in the present-day Johnstown area, had twenty families including about sixty men. Other Allegheny Valley settlements of Delawares that existed in 1731 were Shannopin's Town, within present-day Pittsburgh, and Kittanning, at the site of the town with this name today. Kittanning was an especially large and important settlement of Delawares, with a population of fifty families, including one hundred and fifty men.[20]

It is difficult to trace the backgrounds of the earliest known Delaware residents of the Ohio Country, although available records offer hints. Sometimes town names suggest leaders' locations. Shannopin, a Delaware whose town bore his name, had links with the Schuylkill group; it appears that in 1748 he was one of the sachems who received a gift from the Shawnees as part of a condolence ceremony after Sassoonan's death. The brothers Shingas, Tamaqua (or Beaver), and Pisquitomen—all in the Ohio Country by the 1750s—were relatives of Sassoonan. Another brother, John Hickman, was living at Shamokin in 1745, but had moved to the Allegheny region by 1758. Netawatwees (or Newcomer) was an important Delaware leader in Ohio. Despite the significance of Netawatwees, we know little about his origins. He

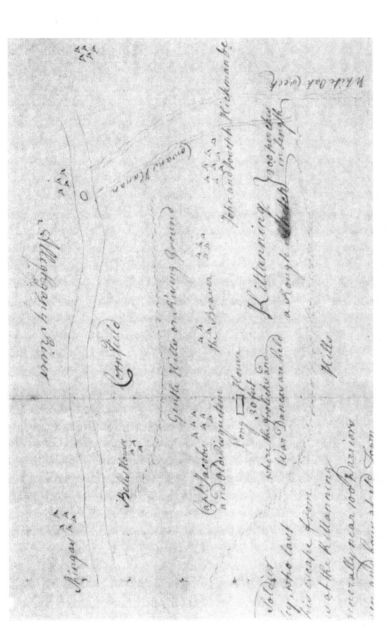

Figure 7. John Armstrong's map of the Delaware town Kittanning. Plan of Expedition to Kittanning, neg. 1023. Courtesy of the American Philosophical Society, Philadelphia, Pennsylvania.

may have been the "Nedawaway or Oliver," who witnessed the 1718 confirmation of the sale of lands below Tulpehocken by Sassoonan's group. Possibly
he was the "Nectotaylemet," named as witness to the signing of the Walking
Purchase document in 1737. Yet another major figure was Custaloga, considered one of the "heads of the Delawares" of Ohio in 1758. Custaloga was half
Iroquoian (perhaps Seneca). During the 1750s he lived on the upper Allegheny, placing him in the vicinity of the western Senecas.[21]

Like the Delawares, many of the Ohio Country's residents were relative
newcomers to the area. By the late seventeenth century, war had scattered
most of the area's Indian inhabitants, and diseases that followed trade routes
may have depleted populations as well. Intent on obtaining furs as a means
for acquiring European trade goods and on gathering captives as their own
population was decimated by epidemics, the Iroquois struck Indian peoples
at increasingly farther distances from Iroquoia. Those affected by this warfare
included not only the Shawnees but also the Eries, who had shifted inland
from lands along Lake Erie by 1644 and were defeated and dispersed by the
Iroquois ten years later. Although Native hunters continued to pursue the
Ohio Country's game, Indians made few attempts to resettle the region until
the early to mid-eighteenth century. The Delawares were among those who
came to find new opportunities in the Ohio Valley as animal populations declined in the east and Euro-American settlements expanded.[22]

During the mid-eighteenth century, the Ohio Country and its Indian residents became enmeshed in territorial contests between England and France.
The French understood that the Ohio River system offered an important water
route between Canada and their other settlements in the Illinois Country and
Louisiana. The English also sought to control the area, realizing the value of
commerce with the Ohio Indians and the potential for gain in eventually opening up the region for colonial settlements. An English enterprise out of Virginia
called the Ohio Company tried to claim a westward extension of Virginia's
boundaries through the Ohio Valley by using an agreement with the Iroquois
made at the Lancaster treaty of 1744. Around the same time that the Ohio Company land speculators were laying their plans, Pennsylvania traders in the west
began offering goods at attractive rates. Pennsylvania trading operations
opened on the south side of Lake Erie and at Pickawillany, a Miami town at
present-day Piqua, Ohio, on the Great Miami River. In these circumstances, the
French took a series of steps to stop English advances in the Ohio Country and
to halt the breakdown of their own relations with Native trading partners and
allies. In 1752, the French attacked English-allied Miamis at Pickawillany, and in

1753 they strengthened their position in the Ohio Country with the construction of Fort Presque Isle (present-day Erie, Pennsylvania) and Fort Le Boeuf (Waterford, Pennsylvania). They also began the establishment of Fort Machault at Venango (present-day Franklin, Pennsylvania).[23]

Indian peoples had various reasons for opposing the British in the ensuing conflict known as the Seven Years' War, but for eastern Indians such as the Delawares, an important factor was their experience of land loss and their suspicions of further British encroachment. Several developments only served to deepen their anxieties and those of other Ohio Indians. Virginia's expansionist interpretation of the 1744 Lancaster treaty clearly signaled English designs on the Ohio Country. At the multiethnic Ohio River settlement Logstown in 1752, Virginia pressed its claims, telling the Indians "that they must . . . consent to the Settlement of the Lands on the Branches of Ohio." These remarks got a negative reception from Indians, who "expressed much Anxiety and much Unwillingness at the Proposal." Their own reading of the Lancaster treaty was that they had not ceded territory beyond the Allegheny Mountains. At Logstown, the Iroquois granted Virginia permission to build a fort in the Ohio Country, but Indians continued to oppose expanded British settlement.[24]

Indians also recognized the persistent British interest in the Ohio lands with the Albany treaty of 1754, when Pennsylvania tried to secure the Ohio Valley for itself through an agreement with the Six Nations. Although Pennsylvania claimed that the Albany Purchase gave the colony lands beyond the Alleghenies, Indians again disputed a transfer of the Ohio Country into British hands. In marking the Albany Purchase boundary, Pennsylvania's negotiator, Conrad Weiser, encountered opposition from Indians who believed that "the Purchase must only include the Land then settled by the white-People." In 1756, after war had broken out, Pennsylvania knew that the Ohio Indians were unhappy with Pennsylvania's Albany Purchase claims. They "would have been better pleased," it was said, "had the Boundary Westward, been the <u>Allegany Hills</u>," for "the Land on the River Ohio" was viewed as "a very good hunting Country."[25]

In addition, the blusterings of British general Edward Braddock in 1755 helped convince Delawares of English designs on the Ohio Valley. A conversation between Braddock and Shingas heightened Ohio Indians' animosity toward the British. Shingas asked Braddock "what he intended to do with the Land if he Could drive the French and their Indians away." Braddock's reply, "the English Shoud Inhabit & Inherit the Land," was far from reassuring. Echoing the rhetoric of coexistence from the early days of Pennsylvania, Shingas wondered "whether the Indians that were Friends to the English might not be Permitted to Live and Trade Among the English and have Hunting Ground sufficient To Support themselves and Familys." With the curt reply that "No Savage Shoud Inherit the Land," Braddock did not even pretend to support the old vision of Delawares and English sharing lands as friendly neighbors.[26]

Delawares had reasons to suspect French designs on the Ohio lands as well. Indians distrusted a 1749 expedition by Capt. Pierre-Joseph Céloron de Blainville into the Ohio Valley. Along the way, Céloron buried lead plates inscribed with the declaration that the French had "re-taken possession of the said River Ohio and of those that fall into the same, and of all the lands on both sides as far as the sources of the said rivers." The French had suffered setbacks in their relationships with Ohio Indians during King George's War, which had ended in 1748. Indians became dissatisfied with the French inability in wartime to offer sufficient and reasonably priced goods. However, the building of the new French forts in 1753, with the addition of Fort Duquesne in 1754 at the Forks of the Ohio, offered Indians centers for obtaining goods and new focal points for constructing potentially useful alliances at a time when the British command seemed particularly backward in diplomacy.[27]

With reason to question the motives of both the British and the French, Ohio Delawares initially avoided active support for either side. Early Indian military allies of the British came primarily from a few Ohio Iroquois under the leadership of the Seneca Tanaghrisson. He and his warriors joined troops under George Washington—at the time, a young officer barely in his twenties—in a fateful skirmish with the French under Joseph Coulon de Villiers de Jumonville in May 1754. This small, though bloody, affair sparked the larger conflagration of the Seven Years' War. In July some Delawares fought as allies of the French at the Battle of Fort Necessity, but most did not turn against the British until Braddock suffered a devastating blow at the Battle of the Monongahela where he and hundreds of his men lost their lives. Scarouady, an Oneida leader in Ohio, laid great blame for the defeat on Braddock, complaining of "the pride and ignorance of that great General that came from England." "He is now dead," Scarouady added, "but he was a bad man when he was alive; he looked upon us as dogs, and would never hear any thing what was said to him." The Indians tried "to advise" Braddock "and to tell him of the danger he was in with his Soldiers"; however, Scarouady noted, "he never appeared pleased with us, & that was the reason that a great many of our Warriors left him & would not be under his Command."[28]

Braddock's words and his defeat showed Delawares and other Ohio Indians that the British were arrogant *and* vulnerable—two qualities making them unappealing allies. One Indian man named Lamullock, an associate of Shingas, described the British as "a Parcel of old Women." "They could not travel without loaded Horses and Waggons full of Provisions and a great deal of Baggage," he said, and "they did not know the Way to their Towns without Pilots and for these they must be oblidged to take Indians with them." "We Indians," Lamullock continued, "are all one as Wolves[;] we can lay in Ambuscade and take you English all one as in a Trap." To those Ohio Indians wishing to oppose the French, the British now looked too weak to help them. In a message directed at the British, Ohio Indians relayed why they decided to support the French: "The French . . . came and became our Neighbours," but "you [English] neither coming yourselves, nor assisting as with Warlike Stores, our People, of necessity, were obliged to Trade with them for what we Wanted." Meanwhile, the English traders "left the Country," and "the Governor of Virginia took care to settle on our Lands for his own Benefit."[29]

The war led to new alliances, but it was also built upon already existing ones. Particularly important to the Ohio Delawares were the relationships they had created with Shawnees. Not only had Delawares and Shawnees lived as neighbors in the Susquehanna Valley, but they had also resided near each other in the Scioto area, where a small settlement headed by the Delaware Windaughalah lay not far from the more sizable Lower Shawnee Town. In 1754, as fears mounted about how the Anglo-French conflict would affect them, Shawnees called upon Delawares to remain close by them, saying, "let Us live and die together and let our Bones rest together." When Delawares decided to wage war against the British, they did so in close alliance with Shawnees. Some Delawares and Shawnees were suspected of being responsible for the attack on Euro-American settlers around Fort Cumberland on Wills Creek at the end of June 1755. In October 1755 a Pennsylvania official reported that the "Chiefs of the Shawonese with other Delawares and Shawonese have most unmercifully fallen upon the Frontiers of Virginia and Murdered all before them." Soon thereafter about one hundred Delawares and Shawnees were blamed for attacks on Euro-Americans at the Big Cove, which lay just west of the Tuscarora Mountain in the area of present McConnellsburg, Pennsylvania, and along the Tonoloway Creek area bordering Maryland.[30]

The Delawares' decision to fight the British also involved alliances with Wyandots, descendants of the Wendats (known to the French as Hurons) and Khionontateronons (also called Petuns). Wendats and Khionontateronons were Iroquoian-speaking peoples who had battled in seventeenth-century

wars against the Five Nations. The Wyandots moved about considerably before some of them established communities in the Ohio Valley. From home
areas north and west of Lake Ontario, they had traveled as far as the western
end of Lake Superior before returning east to areas more accessible to both
French and English traders. They were located at the French trading center
Detroit by 1704, but in the 1730s Wyandots under the leaders Orontony
(Nicolas) and Angouriot moved near Sandusky Bay on the southwest shore
of Lake Erie. By the late 1740s, Wyandots from Sandusky had moved to the
Ohio Valley, where they had an opportunity for increased contacts with
Delawares. One of their settlements was in the vicinity of the Beaver River in
present western Pennsylvania, and another called Conchaké (near present
Coshocton, Ohio) was close to the mouth of the Tuscarawas River. By 1752,
disease and probably starvation had weakened the Wyandots as crops failed
and smallpox appeared along the Ohio. The deteriorating situation pushed
the Wyandots back toward the French at Detroit; however, it appears some
Wyandots remained along the Beaver River for a few years longer, possibly
until the fall of Fort Duquesne to the British in 1758.[31]

In the years after Braddock's defeat, Ohio Delawares fought alongside
Wyandots, Miamis, and other Indians, including Ottawas, Ojibwas, and
Mesquakies (or Fox) from the Great Lakes region. A few Mesquakies had come
to the Allegheny by 1749, and a small number of them were still there in 1768.
The Ottawas and Ojibwas—peoples who referred to themselves as "Anishin-
abeg"—also migrated, at least in small numbers, to the eastern Ohio Valley during the eighteenth century. Ottawas had homes on the Tuscarawas in the early
1750s, and some were reported living at Logstown before the Seven Years' War.
A small population of forty Ojibwa warriors and their families reportedly
resided in the Ohio Valley in 1748. Various peoples who shared residence of the
Ohio Country with Delawares would have had opportunities to forge friendships with them in the years prior to the war. Ironically, some of these relationships had probably been forged out of anti-French sentiments during King
George's War (1744–48). In the changed circumstances of the mid-1750s, many
of these same alliance partners turned their animosity against the British.[32]

As the presence of Tanaghrisson and Scarouady attested, Iroquois also
joined Delawares in migrating from the east into Ohio. Referring to this
movement, Governor James Hamilton of Pennsylvania stated in 1750 "that
Numbers of the Six Nations have late left their old Habitations and settled on
the Branches of mississippi, and are become more numerous there than in
the Countries they left." He believed these Iroquois, along with western

Delawares, Shawnees, and "their new Allies" the Wyandots and Miamis comprised "a Body of Fifteen Hundred if not Two Thousand Men." Relations between the Iroquois and Ohio Delawares at midcentury were especially complicated, as were Delaware-Iroquois relationships in the east. Ohio Delawares had much in common with their Ohio Iroquois neighbors, but they also lived in tension with the Iroquois leadership centered at Onondaga. When Ohio Delawares began launching attacks against Euro-American settlements in 1755, they acted independently of that leadership.[33]

Shared family life and residential proximity no doubt created close relations between Delawares and Iroquois within the Ohio Valley. There were likely various instances of Delawares marrying Iroquois, as was apparently the case with Custaloga's parents. In 1757, when a call went out to Delawares to meet in peace negotiations, the response of Custaloga, that the Delawares "must first go and Consult their Uncles the Senekas who lived further up the River," underscored his connection with Allegheny-area Senecas. On the Beaver River in 1748 one "Indian Town" consisted "chiefly" of "Delawares," and "the rest Mohocks." Iroquois were apparently living near both Delawares and Shawnees in the Scioto region in 1751 when "Southward Indians" attacked the Lower Shawnee Town. Delawares, Iroquois, and Shawnees all had experience with this long-running warfare with southern Indians, such as Cherokees and Catawbas. Ohio Indians, "much affraid of the Southern Indians" after "having been struck three times by them," in the spring of 1757 were said to be moving "fast up the Ohio towards the Senecas."[34]

Just as they had claimed rights of possession in the Susquehanna Valley, Iroquois leaders asserted ownership of the Ohio Country and authority over Indians there; nevertheless, Delawares and other Ohio Indians resisted this view of the Six Nations' position. Delawares and Shawnees probably fueled each other's dissatisfactions with the Grand Council at Onondaga. In 1744, Governor Thomas stated that the Iroquois and Shawnees were "far from being on Good Terms" with each other, and he worried that Shawnees were "endeavouring to draw the Delawares from Shamokin to Ohio." In 1748 at Logstown, the Pennsylvania government dealt directly with Ohio Indians instead of working through Onondaga, eroding Iroquois claims of oversight and bolstering the increasingly independent stance of Ohio Indians. About this time, the Iroquois Council attempted to maintain its authority by making Tanaghrisson a "Half King," a role in which he was to represent the Six Nations' interests while serving as a leader for Ohio Indians. Scarouady also came to hold a supervisory role. It was said that he was "deputed by the Six

Nations to look after" the Shawnees. After France and Britain came to blows in the Seven Years' War, many Delawares, both in Ohio and farther east, did not accept the preference for neutrality among Iroquois leaders during the first part of the war. When, in January 1756, "the Six Nations . . . sent a Message to the delawares to order them to desist from Killing the people of pensilvania, . . . the delawares paid no regard to it."[35]

Despite the distinctive associations that developed among Indians in the Ohio Country, it would be a mistake to think of western Delawares and eastern Delawares as part of two separate groups that never overlapped. Sassoonan's associates, for whom we have some of the best documentation, spanned both regions in the 1750s. The Delaware Lapapeton, who was in line to succeed Sassoonan but who declined the position, remained on the Susquehanna after Sassoonan's kinsmen Shingas, Tamaqua, and Pisquitomen had removed to Ohio. Lapapeton lived in at least two Susquehanna North Branch settlements—Oskohary at the mouth of Catawissa Creek in 1754 and Secaughkung in the Chemung River Valley in 1758. According to the New Jersey/Forks Delaware Teedyuscung, Sassoonan's people were called "Unami," at least by 1757. "Unami," the term also used to distinguish the southern language from the northern "Munsee" language of the Delawares, meant "downriver people." The use of "Unami" by Teedyuscung probably indicates that in relation to Teedyuscung's people, Sassoonan's came from lower parts of the Delaware River Valley, especially the Schuylkill. The example of Sassoonan's associates suggests that a network of Unamis stretched over a considerable area.[36]

As war broke out, western and eastern Delawares were in contact and influenced each other. When Ohio Indians associated with Shingas attacked Euro-Americans settled at Penn's Creek in October 1755, and when Pisquitomen and others killed members of a reconnaissance party under the Euro-American trader John Harris, the conflict reached the Susquehanna. Harboring some of the same grievances as western groups and knowing that they were seen as suspects anyway after the recent attacks, certain eastern Delawares began to assault Euro-American settlements. "An Indian from Ohio" reported that Indians in the west were trying to "draw all the Indians out of the Province and off Susquehanna." The Ohio Indians did not succeed in concentrating their forces in the west. Nevertheless, western and eastern Delawares communicated with each other and came to take some joint actions. In January 1756 Susquehanna Valley Delawares "settled at Wyoming" and "at and about" Tioga (present-day Athens, Pennsylvania) had gone "with a Party from Ohio" to attack the frontiers. The following summer the Tioga Indians had left for Allegheny "to hold a Confer-

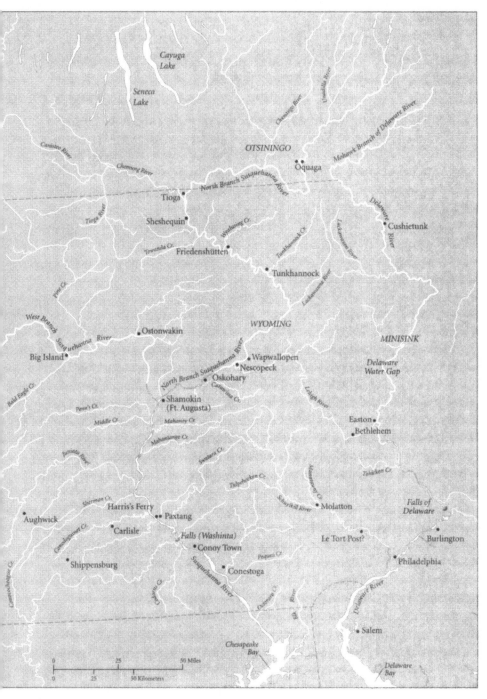

Map 4. The Susquehanna and Delaware valleys in the eighteenth century. Derived from Hanna, *Wilderness Trail*, vol. 1, fold-out map; *IVPN*; map in Wallace, "Historic Indian Paths"; Rupp, *Berks and Lebanon*, 125; Jennings, *Ambiguous*, 231.

ence," which was expected to result "in a Large Body" coming to attack Pennsylvania "in Harvest time & in the fall of the year."[37]

The experience of Euro-American encroachment was one that western and eastern Delawares shared. For the Forks Delawares, the Walking Purchase was a particularly sore point. Some of the sharpest charges of fraud came from the Forks/New Jersey Delaware Teedyuscung, who got support from Quakers in putting forth his complaints against the Walking Purchase, citing "the Land" as "the Cause" of Delawares' conflict with the English. The Albany Purchase not only had affected western Delawares but had also affected Delawares farther east. In 1750, an area of the Juniata that lay "twenty-five miles from the mouth thereof and about ten Miles North from the Blue Hills" was described as "a Place much esteemed by the Indians for some of their best hunting Ground." The prized Juniata hunting grounds fell within the Albany Purchase, and Susquehanna-area Delawares would have keenly felt the loss of these lands. Many Indian attacks occurred in areas where there had been land disputes, including the Albany Purchase lands beyond the Blue Mountains, the Forks, Tulpehocken, and the Minisink.[38]

Delawares, however, were not united in violent opposition to the English colonists during the Seven Years' War. The relationships some Delawares had constructed with Euro-Americans over the past decades conflicted with those forged among Delawares, Shawnees, and other Indians fighting the British. Moravian-affiliated Indians made up a core group of those who remained friendly toward Pennsylvania. "The Christian Indians . . . fled with Precipitation" to Bethlehem after a Delaware war party attacked the mission town Gnadenhütten and killed a number of missionaries in November 1755. "It is now a great many Years," Moravian Indians said, "that we have liv'd in Quiet & Peace under the Protection of the Government of this Province," and "none of us have any hand in the abominable Murders lately committed by the Indians but abhor & detest them."[39]

Alliance and Power

Delawares lived within a world in which notions of alliance and power were closely connected and had been for a long time. Generations earlier, the Iroquois had created a league linking their original five nations. This league represented power—that is, a "spiritual and temporal force marshaled by alliances among the people, kin groups, and villages of the League." Many years later, the Delawares demonstrated a similar understanding that power was acquired through alliance building among many groups. Just as Delawares during the 1740s had claimed to have Iroquois, Mahicans, Miamis, Shawnees, and other Indians backing them in their opposition to the Walking Purchase, Delawares in the 1750s and 1760s continued to seek strength through alliances. As Delawares sought to define themselves as a people, they advanced a notion of themselves as alliance builders. This notion reflected their opposition to Six Nations' claims of authority over the Ohio Country and its peoples. It also reflected a sense that Delawares were specially equipped to be mediators able to marshal allies.[40]

One individual who helped construct a definition of Delawares as mediators was Teedyuscung. By the summer of 1756 eastern Delawares were suffering greatly, and a group of them led by Teedyuscung came to see advantages in holding peace talks. In July 1756 Susquehanna-area Indians were "in want of provisions," and later in the year it was said that "some Indians on the Sasquehanna was starved to Death for want of Victuals." The dangers of the conflict had kept Euro-American traders away from the Susquehanna towns, and Native agricultural production was especially low in the wartime conditions. Susquehanna-area Indians were probably still weak from the food shortages of the previous year. At Ostonwakin ("Otstuacky"), a "Town about 45 miles above Shamokin" on the West Branch, Indians had "lost all their corn" because of a "great Frost," which hit "in the Night" of May 29–30, 1755. That had been "the second Frost" on the Susquehanna "since their Corn was up," and it had "entirely killed it." A trip to Niagara revealed to Teedyuscung that the French could not offer the eastern Delawares much help. Though the French had "middling plenty" of bread, their "Meat was very scarce, and that little they had was spoiled." For the time being, "Goods were scarce with them." In these circumstances, Teedyuscung saw advantages in negotiating with the English at Easton in 1756, obtaining a substantial present and the expectation that a trading house would open at Shamokin.[41]

Teedyuscung indicated that strength came from building and tending alliances, a process that had been essential to Delaware survival for a long time. Expressing urgency, Teedyuscung used the term "Whish Shicksy." Teedyuscung's interpreter explained its meaning: "The times are Dangerous, they will not Admit of Delay, Whish Shiksy, do it Effectually, and do it with all Possible Dispatch." This effort required a combination of many people: "Suppose you want to Remove A large Logg of Wood that Requires many Hands, You must take pains to gett as many together as will do the Business;

if you fall short of one, tho' ever so weak, all the Rest are to no purpose." The missing helper may seem "in itself nothing, yet if you Cannot move the Logg without it, you must spare no pains to gett it." "Whish Shicksy," Teedyuscung urged, asking the English to help the Delawares obtain this power. "Look round you," he said, "Enable us to get every Indian nation we can."[42]

In part, the message seemed to say that Delawares needed English goods for alliance gifts and wampum for official messages, otherwise they would never obtain the strength needed to make peace among nations. Intertribal alliances had to be constructed and bolstered with such items to achieve peace. But Teedyuscung's statement was more than a statement of practical needs; he underscored that his request was about alliance as *power*. Whish Shiksy was not spoken lightly, for Teedyuscung laid his "hand to his heart" and explained that his words came from there. He voiced them "with great Earnestness and in a very Pathetick Tone." Conrad Weiser recognized that *Whish Shiksy* had "a very extensive & forcible sense." Far removed in time, we cannot know the full meaning of the Delaware leader's words; however, he implied something more than a useful strategy of urging people to work together. His words seemed to call upon a sacred force attained through a mighty alliance of many peoples.[43] Teedyuscung stated that he brought together "ten nations" through his peace negotiations. Claims to an alliance with many nations were so important to Teedyuscung that he stated these claims many times. Not only did he probably expect to impress the English with the force of his connections, but he also may have hoped to persuade a Native audience that he could attract the extraordinary power needed to end bitterness and violence.[44]

An alliance among Indian nations was one thing, but an alliance between Indians and British colonists was quite another. Although they disagreed among themselves, Indian peoples continued to share territories and absorb members from other Native groups in the eighteenth century. In fact, war probably encouraged this tendency, as refugees from battle zones sought help from neighbors. Mainly with the exception of individuals in Moravian communities, however, Indians and Pennsylvania colonists had moved farther apart. War had destroyed the already fragile "one Heart" alliances. "The Great Being who created us made our Hearts alike at first," said Teedyuscung, "but of late they are divided, and have leaned different Ways."[45]

After so much blood had been spilt, an alliance between Indians and English increasingly involved, ironically, finding ways to keep the parties separate. The old notion of reserved lands could be adapted to this approach to alliance. In 1757, at another Easton treaty, Teedyuscung told Pennsylvania's governor,

William Denny, "We intend to settle at Wyoming," on the Susquehanna's North Branch, "and we want to have certain Boundaries fixed between you and us, and a Certain Tract of Land fixed, which it shall not be lawful for us or our Children ever to sell, nor for you or any of your Children ever to buy." Whereas once the idea of reserved Indian space had at least hinted at the possibility of Indians and Euro-Americans sharing territories as neighbors, Teedyuscung now stressed that reserved space meant keeping these peoples apart—for the better security of the Delawares. "We would have the Boundaries fixed all round, agreeable to the Draught we give you," he said, "that we may not be pressed on any side, but have a Certain Country fixed for our own use & the use of our Children for ever." Teedyuscung called for Indians and English to "unite . . . as firmly as in the days of our Forefathers"; however, given what he had seen of English treatment of the Delawares, Teedyuscung indicated an alliance with the English was best achieved through separation.[46]

The first several years of the Seven Years' War went badly for the British, and they greatly needed an alliance with the Delawares to convince Ohio Indians to abandon the French. But even after Teedyuscung's negotiations at Easton in 1756 and 1757, Ohio Delawares continued to suspect British intentions. Several told a British representative, "We have great reason to believe you intend to drive us away, and settle the country; or else, why do you come to fight in the land that God has given us?" Ohio Indians' relations with the British improved midway through the war, though, and the tide of events began to turn against the French. In October 1758, Pennsylvania hosted a large meeting, again at Easton, at which the colony's negotiators offered important concessions, freeing the way for a peace agreement with the western Delawares. Pennsylvania removed one major roadblock to good relations with Ohio Country Indians by revising the Albany Purchase so that it no longer included the lands beyond the Alleghenies. In addition, the council fire dating back to William Penn's early dealings with the Delawares was to be rekindled at Philadelphia—a concession that appealed to Delawares who sought to act on their own authority rather than depend on Six Nations' intervention. Meanwhile, the British had set up a naval blockade of the St. Lawrence and disrupted French-Indian relations by capturing Fort Frontenac on Lake Ontario, a place vital to supplying western posts with goods for trade and gift giving. Finally, the British takeover of Fort Duquesne in late 1758 dealt a serious blow to France's ability to hold onto Ohio Indian allies.[47]

The Ohio Delaware Tamaqua exemplified the movement of his people toward better relations with the British at this time. Furthermore, Tamaqua's activities helped shape the image of the Delawares as a people who led through mediation. Like Teedyuscung, Tamaqua placed hope in alliances among many nations as a force capable of achieving peace. In the months after the fall of Fort Duquesne and the renaming of the area as Pittsburgh, Tamaqua was reportedly busy trying to convince Indians to make peace with the British. In March 1759, he arrived at Pittsburgh with two Ottawas "from over Lake Erie" who wanted to learn about the possibility of peace negotiations. Soon after he had arrived, Tamaqua was off again, heading another peace mission to "the Nations inhabiting on the other Side the Lake." At Pittsburgh in August, Tamaqua met with "Eighty Indians" and leaders of the Wyandots, Miamis, Ottawas, Ojibwas, and others. He and the rest counseled together "in order to take the French Hatchett out of the hands of some few of their People" still supporting the French.[48]

Even though the Seven Years' War had essentially ended in Ohio by 1760, Delawares and other Indians were dissatisfied with their situation. Once again, the old issue of an insufficient supply of goods, so vital to maintaining alliances, became a reason for Indians' discontent. British policy, under Gen. Jeffrey Amherst, ended the custom of periodical gift giving and stifled Indian trade with strict regulations. Other developments also aroused Indians' concerns. British fort building began to look especially domineering as Fort Pitt took on massive proportions relative to the former Fort Duquesne. Meanwhile, the growing numbers of Euro-American hunters and eager squatters in the Ohio Country worried local Indians struggling to survive. By one count there were "above one Hundred Houses" in the vicinity of Fort Pitt by 1761. At about the same time, a hard winter and epidemic disease added to the misery of Indians in the west. At the Lower Shawnee Town in fall 1762, more than one hundred were reported dead from a terrible "Ague." Farther east, Indians charged that Euro-Americans continued to attack them even after British victory and the peace settlement of 1763. "The English have killed more of us since the Peace has been made than they did in the first War" was an Indian complaint heard along the Susquehanna.[49]

In these circumstances, Tamaqua's message faded to the background, and more militant voices sounded forth. Bill Hickman, a Delaware, told Euro-Americans living "about Juniata" in early 1763 to expect Indians "to break out in a War" in the spring. The Seven Years' War had scarcely ended when renewed fighting began in the conflict known as Pontiac's War. Pontiac, the Ottawa man who led the opposition to the British, developed a diverse Indian following. Indians first attacked in the Great Lakes region with Ottawas, Potawatomis, Mississaugas and other Ojibwas, Shawnees, and

Delawares besieging Detroit. Eventually thirteen additional British posts were affected, including eight that were seized by the Indians. Forts Pitt, Ligonier, and Bedford were particular targets of the Delawares, though all three places withstood assaults. Once again, parties of Delawares and Shawnees began attacking Euro-American settlements in Pennsylvania.[50]

In April 1763 Teedyuscung was burned to death when arsonists set fire to dwellings of the Delawares at Wyoming. Teedyuscung had never received a guarantee of a fixed Delaware reserve at Wyoming, although Pennsylvania and the Quakers had assisted in constructing some houses for the Delawares there. Teedyuscung's death and the fire contributed to Delaware outrage during Pontiac's War. New England settlers had moved in to occupy the area where the Delawares had been burned out. The settlers' sponsor, the Susquehanna Company of Connecticut, claimed—in opposition to Pennsylvania— to have purchased Wyoming at Albany in 1754. It appears likely that the Susquehanna Company was involved in the arson that led to Teedyuscung's death. Taking his revenge against the interlopers, Captain Bull, a son of Teedyuscung, wiped out the New Englanders' recently established settlement at Wyoming, killing or capturing its inhabitants.[51]

Pontiac's mission to defeat the British received inspiration from a Delaware prophet named Neolin. As part of his effort to create a broad Indian alliance, Pontiac told the story of this prophet at a meeting of Ottawas, Potawatomis, and Wyandots. Neolin's vision involved a difficult trip to heaven to meet the "Master of Life," who explained how the Indians should live in order to become prosperous. About 1762, amid famine and disease, Neolin moved around the region near Lake Erie, where he preached new hope to Indians seeking an end to their afflictions. To reveal these teachings, he utilized a diagram portrayed on a deerskin, showing a "country given to the Indians to hunt, fish, and dwell in" but which Indians had "lost by neglect and disobedience." This diagram portrayed the "vices which the Indians have learned from the White people" and which acted as a roadblock to a happier state. The Master of Life gave the Indians a prayer to be recited "every morning and night." He attacked overindulgence in alcohol and urged the Indians to "drive off" the British—"those dogs clothed in red."[52]

Neolin spread a message that placed him, in one sense, in the tradition of Teedyuscung and Tamaqua as a mediator among Indian peoples, although he rejected accommodationist approaches toward the British. The Delaware prophet's message assisted Pontiac in building a diverse Indian coalition. Neolin taught that the Master of Life called for peace among Indians. "Do not fight among yourselves" was one of the Master's admonitions. The vision revealed how Indians should mark their unity. "When ye meet one another," the Master of Life said, "exchange greetings and proffer the left hand which is nearest the heart." The heart—that symbol of wholeness so frequently invoked in treaties between Indians and Euro-Americans—represented the bond being forged among Indians against the British aggressors. Underscoring the power behind this vision of alliance was the name of the visionary himself. "Neolin" meant "four"—"a sacred number" linked "with the spirits of the four cardinal directions and also with the winds, sacred to the Delawares as well as to the Ottawas." Neolin's very name probably suggested that this prophet could summon the extraordinary spiritual power that emerged from the forces of nature and that flowed from the combination of many peoples.[53]

Neolin's Delaware background may have held special meaning for his Indian audience. In their struggles with the Six Nations and in their dealings with Pennsylvania, Delawares had sought to demonstrate that they could bring Indian peoples together. Furthermore, Delawares stood out in the mid-eighteenth century as a special source of visionaries who offered guidance to Indians in times of trouble. In 1745, a prophet on the Susquehanna, thought to have been a Delaware, informed the missionary David Brainerd that "God had taught him his religion, and that he never would turn from it; but wanted to find some who would join heartily with him in it; for the Indians, he said, were grown very degenerate and corrupt." Brainerd learned that this man "opposed" Indians "drinking strong liquor," and "if at any time he could not dissuade them from it by all he could say, he would leave them, and go crying into the woods." A few years later at Wyoming, a Delaware woman explained that she had received a vision, which explained the cause of illness among the Indians. Two prophets who arose among Munsee-speakers were Papunhank (or Papoonan), who converted to Moravianism, and Wangomen, who, in contrast to Papunhank, opposed the Moravians vigorously. Given this strain of prophecy among the Delawares, Neolin may have subtly used the reputation of his people to lend authority to his message. Delaware, he indicated, was spoken in his vision. "A woman . . . whose garments dimmed the whiteness of the snow," Neolin recalled, told him "in his own tongue" how to find the "Master of Life." Living in a polyglot world, Neolin could have understood more than one language, but he noted that the woman in white chose to communicate in the Delawares' "own tongue." Given the role Delawares had been constructing for themselves, Neolin's remark seems more than incidental.[54]

Indians' desires to unite with other Indians probably grew as British colonists increasingly lumped all Native peoples together as equally worthy of opprobrium. A divide constructed more and more in the racial terms of "whites" versus "Indians" deepened during this troubled time. "Back inhabitants," as Euro-Americans beyond Philadelphia were called, had "got it into their heads that one Indian should not be suffered to live among us," wrote Governor John Penn. An Indian strike in the Forks of the Delaware "enraged & provoked" whites so much that they set off "in revenge . . . into the Indian Country." Other Indian war parties attacked above the Blue Mountains on the upper Schuylkill and along the Juniata. Reports of Indians on the Conodoguinet just a few miles from Shippensburg raised alarms, and soon the town was bursting with "distressed Back Inhabitants" sleeping in "Barns, Stables, Cellars, and under old Leaky Sheds." Much anger became focused on the Indians living at the Great Island on the West Branch of the Susquehanna. It seemed that even the elderly Delaware Nutimus, who had "acted a friendly part" toward Pennsylvania in recent years, might "fall a sacrifice . . . to the unbridled rage of the people of Cumberland [County] in their expedition to the great [or Big] Island."[55]

Other Indians who had constructed relationships with Euro-Americans were not spared from the hatred of the "Back Inhabitants." Among these were Indians at Conestoga, who apparently included Six Nations Iroquois and who had been living as neighbors with Euro-Americans of Lancaster County. In December 1763, "a number" of these whites, "armed & mounted on Horseback," entered the Conestoga Indian town and "killed Six of the Indians settled there, and burnt & destroyed all their Houses & Effects." Fourteen Conestoga Indians who survived the attack were placed in the county workhouse, where they suffered the same fate after "fifty or Sixty" white vigilantes "armed with Rifles" and "Tomahawks" murdered them "at Noon-Day" and "in the Presence of many spectators." Next, some Euro-American "Inhabitants of the Townships of Lebanon, Paxton, and Hanover," all within Lancaster County at that time, targeted a group of "about 140 other friendly Indians," including Delawares, said to "have for the most part, lived several Years at Bethlehem and Nazareth." After the Pennsylvania government moved these Moravian-affiliated Indians to Province Island in the Schuylkill, militant whites "threatened to come down and destroy" them. A plan to relocate the Indians "to the heads of the Susquehanna," where they would be near their relations, failed when New York refused them entry into the colony. Instead, they spent more than a year within military barracks in Philadelphia, escaping an assault by "a very considerable number of armed men . . . from the Frontiers."[56]

After the British army, with more than one thousand troops, marched into Ohio Indians' towns in 1764, negotiations moved toward peace, but it was a peace that left unresolved problems between Indians and the colonies. By the end of the war, a variety of relationships complicated the era's tendency toward "Indian" and "white" groupings. Delawares built on and extended the many relationships they had already created with a great variety of Indians of different nations, especially from the Great Lakes, the Finger Lakes, the Susquehanna Valley, and New England. For some, ties that linked them with other Indians reflected a deepening of differences with the English, but left open possibilities of allying with the French. These Delawares were reluctant to agree to peace terms as the war ended in 1765, and they believed that with help from the French and the Indians on the Wabash and in the Illinois Country they would "be able to drive" the English "out of this Country in less than two Years."[57] Wartime stresses led other Delawares to strengthen or reforge links with England's colonists. Some western Delawares, such as Tamaqua, tried to help their people survive by reconstructing connections with the English. In the east, certain Delawares remained friendly toward Pennsylvania. Indians at Wyalusing on the North Branch of the Susquehanna attempted to prove their peaceful intentions in 1763. They stated, "we cannot see that there is the least Reason that there should be any Difference between our Brethren, the English, & ourselves." All portions of their community, "Men, Women, & Children," they said, had worked together to prevent the "Relations" of a slain Delaware from taking revenge against "White Folks." These North Branch Indians had "joined in a Collection of Wampum . . . to pacify" the dead person's kin and to prevent an attack. For their part, a few Euro-Americans, such as some Quakers and Moravians, tried to bridge the gap between Indians and whites.[58]

Delawares remained diverse, differing among themselves in their degree and type of connection with Euro-Americans and representing many different communities, kin groups, and leaders. Amid this diversity, some Delawares suggested that history and precedent distinguished the Delawares from other peoples, declaring at a Fort Pitt meeting in 1765 that they were "the first Nation that met the Quakers when first they came to Philadelphia." This statement renewed claims of the Delawares to speak for themselves in treaties with the English rather than to depend on Six Nations' negotiators. It echoed the promises made at Easton in 1758 to rekindle the council fire at Philadelphia. The Delawares referred to their historic connections with the Quakers as a sign of their nation's ability to take a lead in alliance building. By working with Quakers, Delawares said, they "would make a peace & bring all other Nations into it." Their work had legitimacy, they explained, because it had a sacred source, having been revealed by the "great Spirit."[59]

This vision of the Delawares and their role had links to the notion that Delawares as "women" were mediators. The Six Nations would continue to claim authority over Delawares as well as other Ohio Indians; however, certain Delawares worked to position themselves at the center of peacemaking for their region. In agreeing to terms at the end of Pontiac's War, Ohio Delawares at the Johnson Hall treaty referred to themselves as "women" and urged reconciliation. "We are determined to act for the future better, and to walk in the Road of our Ancestors," they said, and they recommended to Senecas attending the meeting that they "do the same." "You know you made us Women," they told the Senecas. This statement, however, did not assume quiet submissiveness. Instead the Delawares took the lead in urging the Senecas to return their English captives. In so doing, Delawares linked their female status with the authority to "strongly recommend" actions and to shape policy. "We expect that Men will not refuse what we earnestly desire," they said as they pressed the Senecas to make peace.[60]

Both war and calls for peace stimulated alliances and reorganizations in the mid-eighteenth century, as had been the case in the seventeenth century. Tending to communications and ties across a sizable region was not a new experience for Delawares by the time of the Seven Years' War. Delawares would have been able to draw upon established practices as they maintained relationships among peoples across the Delaware, Susquehanna, and Ohio valleys. In the tumultuous 1750s and 1760s, Delawares utilized their experience with alliances, formulating ways in which they could lead mediation efforts. Although Delawares such as Tamaqua and Neolin might hold opposing viewpoints about the British, they had something in common—they participated in a process of linking Delawares with alliance building and the ability to attract sacred power. The Delawares' words at the Johnson Hall treaty, "To walk in the Road of our Ancestors," could have meant a variety of things. It likely invoked memories and oral traditions of numerous treaties, including those with William Penn and more recently with Pennsylvania's negotiators at Easton. When Delawares constructed meanings about themselves as a people, they highlighted a view of their history that recalled such moments.

"All the people which inhabit this Continent"

During the preliminaries to the Pittsburgh treaty of 1765, "four Delawares" arrived "from one of their Towns where two of their Tribes" had been meeting. These "two Tribes" were not ready to come to the treaty, the Delawares reported, because "one of their Men" had "been called up to Heaven by the Great Spirit of Life, who . . . had told this man several things of great Consequence" in order to "make a lasting peace." The Delawares requested that Alexander McKee, an assistant agent for Indian affairs, come to hear what the man had learned and to "commit it all to writing." In addition, Quakers must be contacted, the messengers urged, for the Great Spirit had said that the Philadelphia Friends (no longer colonial government insiders) would give instructions for peacemaking.[1]

The British negotiators considered the message a preposterous delaying tactic. "We are surprized at the Message you delivered us," they told the Delawares. "[T]he man you mentioned who says he spoke to the Great Spirit, you may be assured is deceiving your people, as we are persuaded he never spoke to him." Referring to a recent treaty with Col. Henry Bouquet in the Muskingum Valley, the British added, "Your Nation agreed to terms of accommodation last Fall" and "begged . . . for peace. . . . We have received Messages from the Senecas, Shawanese, and Sandusky Indians, that they are now on their way here" and had expected "your Nation would be the first to come here." "Return to your Chiefs," they pressed, "& let them know that no People whatever, in this Country, can give you Peace but the King's Commander-in-Chief; and we desire them to come here with the other Nations . . . & not suffer themselves to be amused by Idle Dreams or Stories that may be told them by any body."[2]

Nearly a month after this rebuff, leading Delawares brought their visionary speaker directly to Pittsburgh, where he tried once again to transmit his message from the Great Spirit. This man told the British agent George Croghan that his vision had occurred "one hundred & fifteen days since"—that is, near the beginning of February 1765—and it had led him to "know every thing on Earth, and good from bad." Reiterating what he perceived as a divine directive, he stated, "I have . . . been informed . . . in what manner we ought to proceed in order to make a firm and lasting Friendship between one another, and the persons amongst the White people to whom we are to Speak to on this head . . . are the Quakers." A message had been revealed to him, the visionary explained, "concerning all the people which inhabit this Continent" and what "method we ought to pursue to live."[3]

In keeping with the viewpoint from the era of Pontiac's War, this man delineated differences between Indians and Euro-Americans. "We are people of different Colours," he stated. Nevertheless, unlike the prophesying that had inspired Pontiac's War, at Pittsburgh the visionary was using language of reconciliation toward the colonists. "We ought to be as one people," he said, returning to words heard repeatedly in years past. His call for unity spanned Indian nations as well as alliances with English neighbors. Furthermore, within this plan for "all the people which inhabit this Continent" was a special place for the Delawares. It was on this occasion that the Delawares explicitly outlined their leadership role as a unifier of peoples. The Great Spirit had taught, they declared, that the Delawares "ought to be the first apply'd to in making a lasting peace for all other Nations in this Country."[4]

Chapter 5
Defining Delawares, 1765–74

Euro-American encroachment was still a source of great insecurity after Pontiac's War. Instead of improving Anglo-Indian relations in the Ohio Country, a treaty held in 1768 at Fort Stanwix in the Mohawk Valley deepened resentments among many Indians, whose homes and hunting grounds fell within areas newly claimed by the British. With frustrations mounting, Delawares participated in intertribal councils, and some Delaware leaders expanded on the idea that the Delawares had a special role to play in ensuring security and peace. Residential patterns had long supported associations formed among Indian peoples. Delawares continued, with a few exceptions, to live in small, dispersed settlements often organized around clusters of kin. At the same time, however, Delawares participated in deeply rooted processes of alliance that helped link multiple groups of kin and community. Gaining strength by sharing territories with neighbors and working out overlapping usages of lands were strategies with staying power. As Ohio Delaware leaders sought to halt further land loss after Pontiac's War, they pursued these approaches with urgency. In particular, they pressed friends and relatives, mainly Delawares who were still living in the Susquehanna Valley and in New Jersey, to relocate to Ohio. In doing so, they reflected the notion that bringing peoples together, both diplomatically and physically, promised access to the power needed for difficult times. Through the processes of gathering in the Ohio Country and asserting their authority as alliance builders, Delawares constructed definitions of themselves as a people.

Settlements, Kin, and Relocations

Following Pontiac's War some Delawares remained in the Susquehanna Valley, even though Indian settlements there, on or near the Chemung branch, had been devastated in 1764. In the spring of that year Indians of Oquaga (near present-day Windsor, New York) and of a "new Oneida Village" called Canowaroghere had agreed, apparently with reluctance, to join "several Woodsmen" and attack Shawnees, Delawares, and Senecas, who were blamed for attacks on British settlers. Enlisting the support of a métis man, Andrew Montour, and the Oneida leader, Thomas King, British official Sir William Johnson urged this assault, which resulted in the temporary captivity of Captain Bull as well as a number of Bull's associates. Immediate loss of life from this campaign was minimal; however, the damage to the Susquehanna settlements of the Delawares and their allies was substantial. Montour and his men "destroyed two large towns of well-built square loghouses with chimnies, and a large quantity of Indian corn, and other provisions." The war party then burned the town Canestio (or "Kanestio"), which was said to have consisted of "sixty good houses" and to have been "composed cheifly of Senecas, Shawanese, & a few Delawares."[1]

Despite accounts that emphasize the large size of these towns, it is likely that most Indian settlements in the region were unconsolidated and that dispersed residential patterns were common. Even one account that reports the destruction of the "three Lar[ge] Towns" in 1764 suggests a scattered population, indicating that "all there [sic] little out Villages" were also demolished. By the eighteenth century, some larger Susquehanna Valley towns actually consisted of several dispersed settlements. At or near Otsiningo (vicinity of present-day Binghamton, New York), for example, there appeared to be at least four different sites in 1766—one thought of as a Mahican town, one as Nanticoke, one as Conoy, and another as Onondaga. The Mahican town was as much as ten or twelve miles from the Onondaga town (at present-day Chenango Forks, New York).[2]

Like the New Jersey and Forks Indians, Susquehanna Valley Delawares had typically lived in small, dispersed locations for some time. In 1750, above Wyoming, the great fertile plain also called Skehantowa, Moravian travelers entered the part of the Susquehanna where the river "makes great curves." There they noticed "seven or eight huts, in a very fertile tract of land, beyond which rise very high rocks." Farther along, they saw that Native residents had established tiny communities, consisting of "two Indian huts" in one place and "several huts" in another, both near the mouths of creeks running into the Susquehanna. Only somewhat larger was the settlement of Wapwallopen (also Opeholhaupung or Wombhallobank) below Wyoming, where in 1744 Brainerd had found "twelve Indian houses, and . . . about seventy souls, old and young, belonging to them."[3]

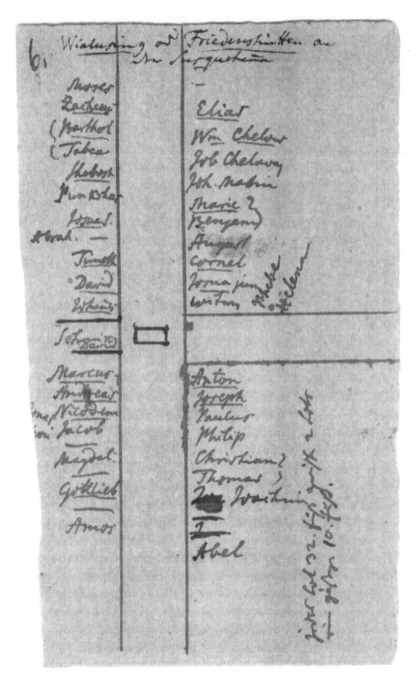

Figure 8. Location of the lots of the inhabitants of the Moravian mission Wyalusing (or Friedenshütten) on the North Branch of the Susquehanna. 6/10/131, *RMM*. Courtesy of Moravian Archives, Bethlehem, Pennsylvania.

After Pontiac's War many of the Delawares who remained on the upper Susquehanna were Munsees. With all the years of moving, mixing, and reorganizing, it is likely that the Munsees of the mid to late eighteenth century consisted of peoples whose ancestors came from various parts of the upper Delaware and lower Hudson valleys. As Munsees moved to the Susquehanna as well as to the Ohio Valley, they brought along their own language, distinct from that of the Unami peoples. Munsees lived at Wapwallopen, where there was a "Mennissinger Chief." Farther up the North Branch at Sheshequin (present-day Ulster, Pennsylvania) lived the Munsee sachem Achcohunt. A number of Munsees resided at Chemung (or "Shammungk"), considered a "new town above Tioga" in 1768. The approximately three-hundred-acre "Great Island" on the West Branch was the home of the Munsee sachem Newollike, who left there about 1771. After suffering through an epidemic with other Moravian-affiliated Indians in the Philadelphia barracks, the Delawares from Wyalusing, led by the Munsee Papunhank, returned after the war to their North Branch town, where the Moravian mission Friedenshütten was established. Growing rapidly to a population of more than 170, Friedenshütten was probably the area's main exception to the typical pattern of small, unconsolidated settlements.[4]

Farther west in the Allegheny Valley, Delawares adhered to the familiar dispersed approach. The Munsee community Goschgoschunk, near where the Tionesta Creek flows into the Allegheny River (present-day Forest County), consisted of at least three small settlements in 1767. The lowermost hamlet, called Damascus (meaning "Muskrat"), lay about four miles downriver from one hamlet and six miles below another. At the middle community lived Allemewi, an elderly blind sachem, who later joined the Moravians, and at Damascus resided Allemewi's likely successor, a nephew named Gendaskund. The prophet Wangomen resided at the uppermost settlement, where his house stood out as larger than the fourteen or so other dwellings in the place. Goschgoschunk residents included those who had fled to the Allegheny after the destruction of their homes in the Susquehanna Valley in 1764.[5]

In the Beaver River Valley to the southeast of Goschgoschunk, Delawares also settled in many small communities. Along the Beaver and its tributaries the Shenango and the Mahoning River were numerous settlements seemingly organized around kin, some of which may have been as small as nuclear family units. "The Indians have settled always in a scattered fashion . . . up the [Beaver] creek," Zeisberger explained, "and where still here and there a space remained, Indians live now in a family group [*Familien weise*]." At a village called "Shenenge" (or Shenango) about twenty miles from the mouth of the

Mahoning River, near present-day Sharon, Pennsylvania, the Munsee sachem Laweloochwalend lived apparently with "his entire family" in 1773. New Kaskaskunk on the Shenango (present-day Newcastle, Pennsylvania), the headquarters of the sachem Custaloga, had only about twenty houses in 1770.[6]

Numerous small settlements hinted at the kin and community groups that continued to be a fundamental part of Delaware life; although physically separate, these communities were not disconnected from each other. Associations among kin extended across the miles, linking place to place. Within the Susquehanna Valley, Friedenshütten Delawares had relatives at Chemung, Otsiningo, Sheshequin, and Wapwallopen. Living in his Allegheny Valley town, the sachem Allemewi not only had a nephew in the nearby settlement Damascus but also had relatives at Kawunschannek (or Cowanshannock, a stream flowing into the Allegheny in present-day Armstrong County). There were also strong family links between Susquehanna and Allegheny communities. One of Allemewi's daughters, Rebecca, lived at Friedenshütten, and Tschechquoapesch (later called Jeremias), a leader at Goschgoschunk, had a sister, Johanna, from the Susquehanna mission. Allegheny Munsees also had kin (*Freunde*) living at Chemung and Wapwallopen.[7]

In the years following Pontiac's War, peace and security were elusive. Delawares and their Indian neighbors complained that the killing of their people had not stopped. At Fort Pitt in early 1767, "a great number of Six Nations, Shawanese, Delawares, and Hurons [Wyandots] from Sanduskey" complained of the "Murder of some of their people" in border areas, including "on the River Ohio." A focal point of tensions was Redstone Creek, a tributary of the Monongahela, where Euro-Americans had been settling on lands still claimed by Indians. Captain Peters, a Delaware, was shot and killed at Redstone in a "Scuffle" with a "White Man by the name of Ryan." About 1766, "Three Delaware Chiefs were Robbed and Murdered near Fort Pitt by two Inhabitants" of Pennsylvania. A year or so earlier, "a Chief of the Six Nations" had been "murdered near Bedford." Tensions were high, as Euro-Americans issued their own complaints that "the Indians . . . have . . . killed a considerable Number of Pennsylvanians, at different Times and Places."[8]

In early 1768, a particularly brutal incident occurred. Two Germans, Frederick Stump and his servant John Ironcutter killed ten Indians, including Mahicans, Shawnees, Delawares, and a Seneca along Middle Creek, a stream entering the Susquehanna from the west, south of Shamokin. Among the dead were "One Woman, two Girls and one Child," whom Stump and Ironcutter had "killed, in order to prevent their carrying intelligence of the

Death of the other Indians." Stump burned some of his victim's bodies in their cabins; others he dumped in the creek through a hole in the ice. The murderers' deeds were discovered, and they were captured and jailed at Carlisle as officials sought to defuse the situation. Soon, however, Euro-American hatred of Indians fueled mob action. "A large body of Armed Men," sympathetic toward Stump and Ironcutter, "seized" the jail and freed the prisoners, who escaped, apparently to some isolated location.[9]

Delawares and other Indians responded in different ways to these ongoing troubles; however, one frequent response of Delaware leaders was to try to gather their people from far-flung locations. Hoping to bolster their position on threatened territory, Delawares approached the defense of their land and people with plans to encourage migrations of their friends and relatives to a shared area. This approach fit with the notion that connections among many people were a source of power. A possible location for this convergence was Cuyahoga near Lake Erie, which had already been the home of Delawares, including the sachem Netawatwees. The Presbyterian missionary Charles Beatty learned in 1766 that the Delawares "intended to goe up next Spring to *quiahaga* [Cuyahoga] & there make a large Town." A few years later Delaware leaders unsuccessfully tried to convince the Friedenshütten Indians to relocate to Cuyahoga, a region described as "a large plain, where many Indians can live."[10]

At about this same time, New Kaskaskunk, Custaloga's headquarters in the Beaver River Valley, became the centerpiece of another drive to bring together Delawares, in this case primarily Munsees, in the Ohio Valley. In 1769 leaders on the Beaver sent out a call to Indians living on the Susquehanna and at Goschgoschunk to settle near them. Soon it seemed that "nearly all the Indians from Goschgoschunk" would come to settle at Old Kaskaskunk (near the intersection of the Shenango and the Mahoning). The residents of Kawunschannek and nearby Mahony also relocated from the Allegheny to the Beaver Valley around this time. Furthermore, Munsees living in the Moravian mission on the Allegheny joined the general trend and relocated to a spot below New Kaskaskunk in May 1770. Their new mission community, known as Langundo-Utenünk or Friedensstadt, was located upon a "somewhat steep" bank on the west side of the Beaver. With an initial population of twenty-three adults and nineteen children, it lay about eight or nine miles below Custaloga's town.[11]

Meanwhile, many Delawares were gathering around a portion of the Ohio Valley west of the Beaver River. There were numerous, probably fairly

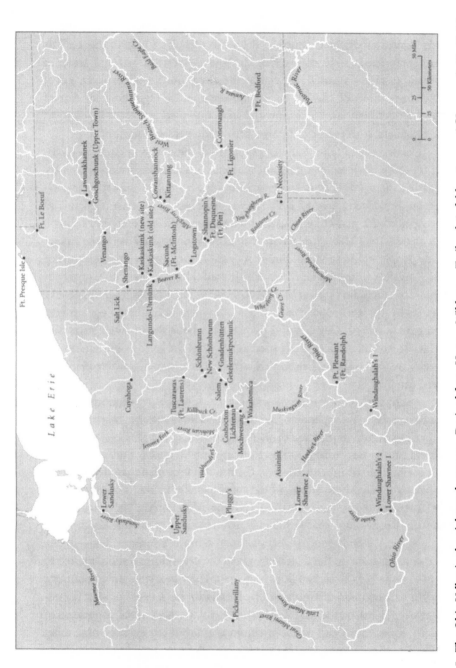

Map 5. The Ohio Valley in the eighteenth century. Derived from Hanna, *Wilderness Trail*, vol. 1, fold-out map; *AGL*, maps 9, 11, 14, 15, and 16; *IVPN*; map in Wallace, "Historic Indian Paths."

small, communities throughout the area, but two places were prominent because of each one's link with a major Delaware leader. Assinink or "Standing Stone" on the Hocking River was the residence of Tamaqua, who had moved there after having lived during the war years on the Tuscarawas near its intersection with the Big Sandy Creek in the Muskingum Valley. Gekelemukpechunk (present-day Newcomerstown, Ohio) on the west side of the Tuscarawas was the home of Netawatwees. This place also stood out because of the relatively large number of Indians settled there. According to one account from 1766, Gekelemukpechunk, which spread over half a mile, contained approximately "200 men besides women & Children." A report from five years later indicated that Gekelemukpechunk had "about 100 houses," of which "most" were of log construction.[12]

According to a Moravian record from 1771, "most of the Indians" in the Muskingum area were "from the Unami Nation." It appears that "Unami," perhaps once mainly a location marker ("downriver"), increased in significance as an ethnic/political designation after 1757. In that year Pennsylvania colonial records first included the term, noting that Teedyuscung mentioned the "Wename" nation. A smaller number of other Delawares also lived on the Muskingum at this time, including Munsees and a poorly documented group called Unalachtigos. These names do not reflect known seventeenth-century named groupings. A variation on the word "Unalachtigo" appeared in Moravian records beginning in 1769 but only in rare instances. These records hint that the Unalachtigos may have included Delawares who originally came from New Jersey. Zeisberger called the Unamis, Unalachtigos (or Wunalachtico), and Munsees (or Monsys) separate "nations" of Delawares. For Zeisberger, these "nations" were, at least in part, linguistic groupings. "Of the three," Zeisberger explained, "the language of the Unamis sounds the most pleasant and differs only very little from Wunalachtico. The Monsy language, however, differs markedly, although all three are basically one language."[13]

The emphasis on these three groups may partially reflect a Moravian bias, especially because the term "Unalachtigo" has not been found in contemporaneous New Jersey or Pennsylvania government records. Moravians favored sorting and organizing people within their communities and emphasized Indian languages in preaching and teaching. Thus it would not be surprising if they sought a way to understand Delaware subdivisions along clear-cut linguistic lines, when the reality was more complex. Yet we should not dismiss their testimony because their informants were Delawares themselves and because Moravians were firsthand observers. It seems likely that, as Indians originally from the Hudson and Delaware valleys moved about, mixed, and merged populations, similarity in language may have become increasingly important as a shared point of connection among peoples reestablishing themselves in new places.[14]

Some of the Delawares in the Muskingum Valley had once lived in and around the Forks. Welapachtschiechen, leader at Assinink after Tamaqua's death in 1769, had been born about 1716 on land later within the Nazareth tract. Tepisscowahang or Samuel, who was living at Gekelemukpechunk in 1766, had formerly been at Meniolagomeka north of Bethlehem. By 1768 Tepisscowahang was dead, but his sister Sarah and niece Elisabeth were living "a little above Tuscarawi," the site of Tamaqua's former town. Elisabeth was the widow of Zacharias, the son of Joe Evans (baptized Nicodemus). Through this relationship, she was connected to the Harris-Evans family of "Old Captain Harris" from Pohopoco, which had included Teedyuscung. Other individuals from the Harris-Evans group had relocated to the Muskingum watershed. A son, a daughter, and a son-in-law of Teedyuscung also lived in the area, where they became affiliated with the Moravians. Relatives of Nutimus, who had been involved in the Walking Purchase, were living at Gekelemukpechunk in the 1770s. These included Isaac Nutumer, apparently the son of "old Nutimus," and Isaac's daughter, the wife of a trader named Thompson.[15]

After Pontiac's War, Netawatwees, assisted by the leaders Killbuck and Quequedegatha (or White Eyes, also Grey Eyes), organized an effort to convince Indians from the east to move to Ohio. These included New Jersey Delawares, such as those at Brotherton, a reserved tract in Burlington County set aside in 1758 as part of a land claim settlement between Indians and the New Jersey government. Ohio Indians sent messengers to encourage the migrations of New Jersey Delawares, a number of whom were affiliated with the Presbyterian minister John Brainerd. Netawatwees undoubtedly hoped that Delawares from New Jersey would come and bolster the numbers of his supporters around Gekelemukpechunk. He also urged Indians on the Beaver River at Langundo-Utenünk and on the Susquehanna to come live near him. To attract Moravian-affiliated Indians to the Muskingum Valley, he promised them "a large, beautiful piece of land" for their town. By inviting people from other regions to live among them, Netawatwees, Custaloga, and other Delaware leaders pursued a familiar strategy of surviving difficult times by sharing territories with allies. As neighbors, Delawares could strengthen bonds with one another and gain the power derived from gathered peoples.[16]

Delawares' Relationships with Their Neighbors

Delawares' alliances were not just with other Delawares; they also continued to include a range of non-Delaware peoples. All eastern Delawares did not immediately accept invitations to relocate to the Ohio Valley. Susquehanna Valley Delawares had numerous ties with other Indians living along the river, and these alliances may have been a major factor when Delawares hesitated to relocate to Ohio. Intermarriage and shared residences suggested complex loyalties and obligations among diverse neighbors on the Susquehanna. When Netawatwees and other Ohio leaders called for relocation, some Susquehanna Delawares hesitated, probably because of their commitments closer to home. Invoking loyalties to the Iroquois, Indians from the Chemung tried to dissuade Friedenshütteners from moving west: "It is not good that you go to Ohio," they said, "it is contrary to the wish of the Six Nations and, especially, to the Chief of Cajuga that the Indians should move away from the Susquehannah to the Ohio." For Delawares remaining on the Susquehanna, local family ties were undoubtedly a consideration in their choice of residence. Kin connections with the Cayugas, who assumed authority over the upper Susquehanna for the Six Nations, may have been particularly important. The Cayuga sachem Gagohunt, a resident of Wapwallopen, had married a Delaware and had learned the Munsee ("Mennissinger"), and apparently the Unami ("Dellawarisch") languages. Marital ties likely reinforced connections between Delawares and Shawnees on the Susquehanna. The wife of Achcohunt, a Munsee sachem at Sheshequin, had at least one Shawnee parent. Some Delawares may have also developed family ties with non-Delawares at Otsiningo, perhaps in the case of a Munsee woman and her twelve-year-old son, who lived among the multiethnic population there in 1768.[17]

Details about those killed by Stump and Ironcutter in the little settlement on Middle Creek hint at the mix of peoples along the Susquehanna and the bonds that formed between Delawares and their neighbors. "Women . . . said to be of the Delaware and Shawanese Tribes" were among the dead. Although their names were not recorded, colonial records indicate that one of these women was married to a Seneca, who came from the Genesee. Two of them were believed to be wives of slain Mahicans, one named Cornelius, who came from a place six miles downriver from Tioga, and another called John Campbell. Within this small Middle Creek group, there also lived a man named Jonas Griffy, who was either from Stockbridge or New Jersey.[18]

Some of the Delawares had roots in the Susquehanna Valley as residents of Friedenshütten and a smaller Moravian mission established nearby at Sheshequin. Involvement with the missions probably was a factor in some Delawares' decisions to live on the Susquehanna. The migration of a few Delawares from Friedenshütten to Goschgoschunk in 1768 did not result in the immediate exodus of the rest. Loyalties to the Susquehanna mission may have conflicted with ties to relatives already in Ohio, as in the case of a Munsee woman named Lydia. When the prophet Wangomen arrived at Friedenshütten to try to encourage Moravian Indians to emigrate to Ohio, he brought an invitation to Lydia from her "kin [Freunde]." Lydia responded, "I love my Freunde, but I cannot go to them," and she added, "I am here in the congregation [Gemeine] and live blessedly and desire nothing more than the Savior."[19]

Friedenshütten offered advantages at a time of great distress following Pontiac's War. As they sought divine favor that would relieve their troubles, some Indians probably saw hopeful signs at Friedenshütten. At the close of 1766, a missionary there reported that an "epidemic disease raging among the Indians on the Susquehanna has affected few in this place, and those who have had the fever are recovered." The following spring, many at Wapwallopen and Otsiningo were sick with a fever; however, Friedenshütteners experienced only a limited outbreak of disease (smallpox) in this same period.[20]

Furthermore, food shortages were apparently less frequent and less severe among Friedenshütteners than among many of their neighbors. The Friedenshütten Indians both traded and gave away food to starving visitors. During 1766 and 1767 they fed large numbers of Nanticokes and Tuscaroras who were passing along the North Branch. In September 1767, for example, "57 needy and hungry Nanticokes, among whom were two chiefs, arrived with their wives and children." Moravian Indians, often referred to in the missionary records as "Brothers" and "Sisters," held a large feast for the newcomers, for which "several Brothers bought oxen so that all might have meat since they had not had meat for many days," and "the Sisters baked breads." "Toward evening all the inhabitants sat in a circle and so did the Nanticokes." At this meal, which must have fed well over one hundred, "attendants distributed the meat and the bread," and "all were pleased and thankful for it." In spring 1769, the Cayuga Gagohunt reported that the inhabitants of Oquaga (Anahochquage), Wapwallopen, Owego, and Otsiningo were starving. At Otsiningo "many" had been reduced to eating "only once a day" and had to eat "wild potatoes" in order to survive. Nanticokes from Otsiningo brought blankets and cloth that they had received at the Fort Stanwix treaty to trade with Friedenshütteners for corn.[21]

The missions on the Susquehanna lasted until 1772, at which time Euro-American encroachment on the North Branch and persistent entreaties from Ohio Indians resulted in Moravian Indians relocating to the Beaver River town Langundo-Utenünk and to the Muskingum Valley communities Gnadenhütten and Schönbrunn (or Weelhik Thuppeek). The Fort Stanwix treaty in fall 1768, which aided the expansion of Euro-American settlement, was a factor in Susquehanna Indians' migrations. This treaty resulted in a large cession of Native land, extending beyond the boundaries of the Albany Purchase. On the North Branch, lands on both sides of the river below the Awandae (or Towanda) Creek fell within the 1768 purchase, including the towns Friedenshütten and Wapwallopen and hunting grounds around Wyoming, Tunkhannock, and Shamokin. The Fort Stanwix line also ran along the West Branch, putting the Great Island and nearby Bald Eagle Creek within the cession. Not surprisingly, within months after the treaty, Friedenshütteners encountered surveyors and Euro-American immigrants passing through their area. These included "an entire family of white people" from Schoharie in the Mohawk Valley, who planned to settle at Wyoming. By summer 1770, new landholders had constructed fences on the Great Island and were encroaching around Friedenshütten. The Pennsylvania governor's promise of a five-mile reserved tract for their town did not entice most Friedenshütteners to stay. No doubt many had lost hope in such promises after the infamous treatment of the Conestoga Indians and of the Delawares at Wyoming.[22]

The Fort Stanwix treaty not only affected migrations but also influenced Susquehanna Delawares' relationships with their neighbors, particularly with the Six Nations. Although there were Delawares and Shawnees present at the treaty, the land cession was determined ultimately by Sir William Johnson and Iroquois leaders, who were the only Indian signers of the deed. Once Indians living in the ceded areas understood the terms of the deed, some openly criticized the Iroquois. "You know that you sold to your white brothers the Wyalusing land, upon which you placed us seven years ago," the Munsee Papunhank (or Johannes) and the Mahican Nanhun (or Joshua) from Friedenshütten complained to Cayuga and Mohawk leaders.[23]

Indeed, the Friedenshütteners had heard hopeful words from the Iroquois, which, even if sincerely expressed, now probably seemed misleading. In the spring after the treaty, an old relative of the Cayuga Gagohunt had said that the Iroquois had not sold the land at Friedenshütten and that "the boundary line of the land sale had not yet been correctly and firmly established." Furthermore, this Cayuga seemed to invoke the old notion of land in terms of usage rights, which promised Susquehanna Indians continued access to areas within the purchase. He said that the Iroquois had told Johnson: "You require only land for your people to live and make money upon," but "the Indians need deer, bears, beaver, and other animals that dwell in the woods and water." Euro-Americans should not encroach upon Native hunting areas, they said, nor should they assume that their purchase extended to any precious minerals found on the land. Nevertheless, as Euro-Americans advanced into the area, Friedenshütteners felt their homes were far from secure, and they contrasted the Six Nations' treatment with that of their "*Freunde*" on the Allegheny, suggesting that the Iroquois seemed to neglect them while the Ohio Indians eagerly sought them as neighbors. Iroquois leaders tried to repair their relations with Indians living at Friedenshütten, Wapwallopen, and elsewhere on the Susquehanna by offering them "land on the Tioga"; however, departing Friedenshütteners told them the offer came "too late."[24]

Nevertheless, there were a few Delawares who apparently approached the sale more amicably or at least did not mount a vigorous protest at the proceedings. If so, then these would have included Ohio Delawares, most notably Killbuck, an associate of Netawatwees on the Muskingum, and another Delaware, Turtleheart. They were joined at the Fort Stanwix treaty by the Ohio Shawnee Benevissica. Sir William Johnson portrayed his dealings with Delaware and Shawnee leaders as generally successful. "Every thing that could possibly occurr to me was said to [the] Shawanese and Delawares . . . and it appeared to have made a good impression on [them]," he reported. "And I gave them at their return Some additional [prese]nts, & sent them away as well Satisfied with the Whole of [the] Transactions as was in my power." Of course, it is questionable whether the Delawares and Shawnees left "well Satisfied," but a few apparently calculated that it was worthwhile participating in the treaty.[25]

We can make informed guesses about how Killbuck, Turtleheart, and other Delawares who attended the Fort Stanwix treaty perceived the proceedings. Although the Fort Stanwix line ran past the Allegheny Mountains into the Ohio Country, important Delaware territories, including the Beaver River, the Allegheny River above Kittanning, and the Muskingum Valley, lay outside of the purchase. These exclusions may have offered some consolation for the loss of western lands. Delawares probably saw this treaty line as similar to an earlier British attempt at boundary drawing—the 1763 proclamation that had declared lands beyond the Appalachians off-limits to British colonists. Despite the failure of this earlier plan, a few Ohio Delawares, as well as Iroquois negotiators, may have hoped that a new boundary line between Indians and Euro-

Americans would hinder "intrusions & encroachments" on Native homes. Furthermore, it appears that the Ohio Indians represented by Killbuck had decided to make the best of the situation by using the Stanwix cession to help convince Susquehanna Indians that it was time to move to the Ohio Country. Soon after the treaty, Killbuck arrived at Friedenshütten, where he visited his mother's sister and her sons, that is, some of his matrilineal kin. Killbuck spent about three weeks at the mission before returning to Ohio, during which time he was probably urging Friedenshütten residents, including his kin, to head west. According to one report, Killbuck "related much about" the Ohio Indians' "beautiful country and their hunting." He explained to one missionary that in Ohio there were "many good people . . . who wish to hear God's Word." His picture of Ohio seemed designed to attract members of the mission community at a time when the Fort Stanwix treaty left them uncertain about the status of their own land.[26]

Various private conversations were probably key in shaping how Delawares viewed the Fort Stanwix negotiations. Although these were generally unrecorded, a few scraps of information remain. The treaty reportedly included discussions of Delawares gathering in the west. "It was settled by Sir William Johnson at last year's treaty that the Delawares should not live so close to the Six Nations," Zeisberger wrote in June 1769, apparently having learned this information from Munsees on the Allegheny. Ohio Delawares seemed to believe that the treaty endorsed their plan that Delawares live "far off" from the Iroquois. Johnson knew that Killbuck and other Ohio Indians had a keen interest in convincing their people to relocate, and he could have argued that the sale of Susquehanna lands would advance their project. As Johnson had remarked about his Fort Stanwix negotiations, "Every thing that could possibly occurr to me was said to [the] Shawanese and Delawares." This broad-ranging conversation probably included scenarios of Delaware kin uniting in Ohio as a way of making the cession more palatable to Killbuck and his associates. Apparently, in other private conversations with Susquehanna Delawares, and perhaps Cayugas who hoped Delawares would remain nearby, Johnson left open the possibility of some communities within the cession remaining undisturbed. The Delaware Billy Chelloway returned from the treaty with the information for Friedenshütten "that he had spoken himself with Sir William Johnson," who told him that he, Johnson, was "much contented with our Indian town and its inhabitants and wants to have many such Indian towns."[27]

Whatever Killbuck's and Turtleheart's approach, Ohio Indians reacted negatively to the treaty. Only a small number of Ohio Delawares had actually participated in the proceedings. Out of more than three thousand Indians attending, there were apparently fewer than thirty in Killbuck's and Turtleheart's group at Fort Stanwix. Upon learning of the treaty, Ohio Indians were outraged at the cession. Not only Delawares but also Shawnees, Mahicans, Mesquakies, and Iroquoians in Ohio "complained much of the Conduct of the Six Nations giving up so much of the Country to the English without asking their Consent." The purchase included lands east of the Allegheny River between Kittanning and Fort Pitt and the area south and east of the Ohio River down to the Cherokee (or Tennessee) River. Besides lying near Ohio Delawares' eastern towns, the boundary line ran close to Iroquois settlements on the Ohio below Pittsburgh. Perhaps most importantly, the cession included hunting grounds south of the river in present-day Kentucky and West Virginia. Aggrieved "Ohio Senicas, Shawanese & Delawares" stated that "the most part of the Country which was Sold was their Hunting Ground down the Ohio."[28]

The Fort Stanwix treaty affected intergroup relationships in multiple ways. Not only did it further strain relations between the Iroquois and their Algonquian neighbors to the south and west, but it also caused divisions among the Iroquois themselves. A number of factors no doubt influenced Confederacy leaders' agreement to the boundary. Ending land disputes that threatened to erupt in renewed warfare was one consideration. The Six Nations probably also recognized the difficulty in wielding influence over the large area that they ceded. In addition, Confederacy leaders would have seen the benefit in focusing their attention on the preservation and control of lands closer to home threatened by Euro-American encroachment. It seems that various behind-the-scenes dealings, including insincere promises from Johnson, affected the final outcome of the treaty. In the end, the Six Nations appeared divided over the results, with some Senecas and Cayugas vocal in their discontent with the cession.[29]

The treaty also affected relations among Ohio Indians and worsened their relations with Euro-Americans. Some Ohioans cooperated in planning a response to the Euro-American settlers pouring into the areas south and east of the Ohio River. It was reported that Shawnees and Delawares had formed "a Confederacy" in May 1769 "occasioned by the Cessions Made by the Six Nations as it is positively said those Indians" opposed Euro-Americans "on the ceded Lands." In the fall, Senecas, Shawnees, and Delawares aired their complaints against the British in a meeting with Wyandots, Ojibwas, Ottawas, and Potawatomis on the Detroit River. In the year following the Fort Stanwix treaty, the Ohio Valley seemed once again on the verge of war. After Senecas killed a

"white man" and some livestock, Euro-Americans "around Pittsburg to Ligonier . . . abandoned their plantations," and Virginians on the Monongahela
"threaten[ed] to shoot the first Indian" who approached them.[30]

During the tense years after Pontiac's War, Delawares remained diverse.
Individuals were connected with various communities, with overlapping kin
groups formed through marriages or rooted in matrilineages, and with different ethnopolitical entities, particularly Munsee and Unami groupings.
Delaware leaders negotiated within this complex world in trying to define
their role and that of the people they represented. In doing so, they worked
to define the Delawares as a people. The situation became even more complex as Delawares formed ties or tried to reinvigorate existing alliances with
Shawnees, Wyandots, Ojibwas, and others sharing similar concerns about ensuring the safety of their homes and territories.

The Delaware Grandfathers

As war threatened to break out again, key Delaware leaders sought to place
themselves at the center of negotiations to prevent further hostilities and to
obtain security for their people. They continued to draw upon memories of
Delawares' friendship with Pennsylvania to underscore their nation's role as
alliance builders and mediators. When war did come in 1774, with the conflict known as "Dunmore's War," leading Delawares, including Netawatwees
and White Eyes, struggled to resolve differences between Indians and the
British. Although they did not have the support of all Delawares, they were
instrumental in constructing a vision that the Delawares were a people with
a particular peacemaking mission.

It was difficult, however, for Delawares to claim a central role in diplomacy if the Six Nations and Sir William Johnson held authority over
Delawares' affairs. Still unwilling to relinquish their affairs to negotiations
between Johnson and the Six Nations in Iroquoia, Delawares called now for
a "Council Fire at Fort Pitt." In a message that Killbuck carried to Philadelphia, they invoked tradition in justifying this meeting place in the west:
"There was formerly a Council Fire in these middle Provinces, kept by your
and our forefathers, but we perceive *that* fire is almost extinguished, and we
desire now that it may be renewed, that we may meet together as our forefathers used to do, and strengthen our Friendship." Delawares thus disputed
the need to go to Iroquoia with their concerns, and they later argued that

they could bypass Johnson. When Pennsylvania's governor tried to convince Netawatwees that the Delawares needed to deal with Johnson on a matter, the sachem replied, "I cannot agree to what you then recommended to me of going to Sir William Johnson to consult him upon that Business." Philadelphia, Netawatwees stated, was "where we . . . used to do all our Business with our Brethren the English."[31]

As they summoned memories of their "forefathers" and their connections with Pennsylvania, Delawares employed words similar to those heard at Fort Pitt in 1765, when Delawares had claimed a special role as "the first Nation that met the Quakers when first they came to Philadelphia." During the years after Pontiac's War, Delaware leaders planned to strengthen their position in the Ohio Country through an alliance with Pennsylvania. Furthermore, they seemed to believe that they could draw upon their historic connection with the Quakers to cement this alliance. Some Indians (probably Delawares) cited an affiliation with Quakers seemingly as part of religious revitalization efforts. Ohio Country Indians, it was reported in 1768, "were constructing a large meeting house," where Native preachers planned to hold forth with teachings that they linked to Quaker beliefs. Delaware leaders associated with Netawatwees's group around Gekelemukpechunk made overtures to the Friends. In spring 1771, Killbuck and his son Gelelemend traveled to Philadelphia, requesting a Quaker preacher and a schoolteacher. About a year later Delawares renewed this request with a message carried to Philadelphia by the Delaware Joseph Peepy.[32]

The claim to having a distinctive friendship with Pennsylvania and with the Quakers fit with Delawares' efforts to position themselves as alliance builders and peacemakers. Their actions were a continuation of a process seen in earlier references to Delawares as "women"; however, around the time of the Seven Years' War, another label, "grandfather," appeared increasingly important as a term for Delawares in relation to many neighboring Indians. "Grandfather" no doubt had various meanings, some of which are surely unrecoverable over two hundred years later. Like "women," the term seems to have highlighted the Delawares' reputation as constructors of alliances and peaceful relations. Unlike "women," it did not open the Delawares to the charge that they were subordinates of the Six Nations. In its maleness, the Delawares-as-grandfather language avoided certain negative connotations that some, especially Europeans, attached to the Delawares-as-women label. Significantly, it was the grandfathers, or elderly, who could attest to the early friendship with Penn and his people. In the Ohio Valley after Pontiac's War, there were still "some old people, who were in Philadelphia when the first houses were built there." These elderly Delawares nourished a vision of alliance through their stories about that time, recounting "how peaceably and agreeably the whites and Indians dwelt together, as if they had been one people, being ever ready each to serve the other." The elderly would have held authority as the witnesses of treaties with Pennsylvania and as the preservers of stories that Delawares could have used as evidence of their unique place in building connections with the English.[33]

Like the Delaware prophet's name "Neolin," the name "grandfather" suggested spiritual power and a link with the cardinal directions. According to one Delaware tradition, reported years later, three of the earth's four quarters were under the control of a grandfather spirit. *Muxumsa Wehènjiopàngw* was "Our Grandfather where the daylight begins," *Muxumsa Ehëliwsikakw* was "Our Grandfather where the sun goes down," and *Muxumsa Luwànàntu* was "Our Grandfather where it is winter." (A grandmother spirit oversaw the southern quarter.) "Grandfather" connoted the power of the winds and seasonal change. When applied to the Delawares, the term must have underscored their claims of influence.[34]

Grandfathers, and old people generally, deserved respect. Young people were told by their elders "above all things to revere old age and gray hairs and to be obedient to their words, because experience has given them wisdom." As Delawares urged their neighbors, particularly the Shawnees who were among their "grandchildren," to remain at peace with the English, they claimed deference. Although Shawnees from the Lower Town were more likely than Shawnees from the Upper Shawnee Town (Wakatomica) "to be obedient to their grandfather," Netawatwees and his associates repeatedly used their position to try to stop Shawnees from going to war. Furthermore, grandfathers gave something in return to their grandchildren. Delawares portrayed themselves to the Shawnees as "your grandfather," who "took you in my arms so that you should sit in peace and quiet"—apparently a reference to Delawares having provided Shawnees with "land for [their] residence." The title, "grandfather," then, also seemed to suggest that Delawares asserted special territorial authority, which would have competed with Iroquois claims.[35]

A flurry of references to Delawares as "grandfather" appeared during Dunmore's War in 1774, as Netawatwees, White Eyes, and their associates sought to stop the fighting. This brief war arose as a boundary dispute between Virginia and Pennsylvania added to the already tense situation in Ohio. The British army's withdrawal from Fort Pitt in 1772 had left unchecked the expansionist ambitions of both Virginians and Pennsylvanians as they sought to control the lands opened for Euro-American settlement at Fort Stanwix. As more and more colonists poured into the region, they came into increasing conflicts with already discontented Indians. By early 1774 intercolonial strife grew when Virginians occupied Fort Pitt, renaming it Fort Dunmore in honor of Virginia's royal governor, John Murray, fourth earl of Dunmore. Rival local governments vied for jurisdiction and popular support as Pennsylvanians opposed the claims to the Pittsburgh area made by Virginians. By mid-1774 the attempts of Dr. John Connolly, a hot-headed militia leader at Fort Dunmore, and others to solidify Virginia's hold on this region provoked a war between his colony and Ohio Indians.[36]

Dunmore's War began as a few incidents that were fanned into war by Connolly and other Virginians. There was a skirmish on April 27 at Pipe Creek below Wheeling, and a deadly encounter occurred three days later on the Ohio across from the mouth of Yellow Creek. In the latter case, Euro-Americans apparently took advantage of neighborliness that had developed—despite the tensions along the boundary line—between themselves and Indians from a "small" Yellow Creek community, consisting mainly, it seems, of Shawnees and Iroquois. One Indian woman "was in the habit of crossing" the Ohio "to get milk" from a "Mrs. Baker," who was reportedly "kind in giving her some for her 2 children." This Native woman had at least one child through her marriage to the Lancaster-born trader John Gibson. She and her fellow residents of Yellow Creek may have socialized frequently with Euro-Americans living across the Ohio River at a place called "Baker's Bottom." They apparently were unsuspecting when their neighbors invited them one spring day to come over and drink some rum. It seemed the Indians were still not suspicious when their hosts "chalenged" those who remained sober to a game of target shooting so that "the[y] emptied their Guns." With the Indians in this nearly defenseless state, the Euro-Americans easily overwhelmed them; by one account "nine Indians" were "Murthered and Scalped" at Baker's. Gibson's wife "lived long enough . . . to beg mercy for her babe, telling" her attackers "that it was a Kin to themselves."[37]

The violence aroused the ire of relatives of the deceased, who "took their Revenge by murdering a number of Virginians, settled to the Westward of the River Monongahela." These probably included attacks on an individual at Wheeling and on a family at Muddy Creek—a stream described as flowing "into the river Monongahela near Cheat river." A Shawnee captain explained that his people had limited war aims, saying that those "who live on their [the Indians'] land on the Ohio and who built a fort and killed seven Indians will be punished a little." John Logan, or Tachnedorus, a kinsman of the Yellow Creek Indians, also described his military goal as limited: after his raiding party obtained "Thirteen Scalps and one prisoner," he said he was now "sattisfied for the Loss of his Relations." Nevertheless, the violence did not stop, especially because Virginians were spoiling for a fight. When an account of Virginians "being killed" by Indians "proved false," some militiamen, "it was said," actually felt "sorry, exceedingly so," because they were "so desirous . . . for an Indian War." Peaceful Shawnees and Delawares, who had helped Euro-American traders reach safety in the Pittsburgh area, were "attacked, and one of them wounded by a Party of Virginians" under orders from Connolly. Virginia militia began to amass around Pittsburgh (or Fort Dunmore) and at the mouth of the Beaver River in preparation for continued warfare. By early August, Virginians had advanced on Wakatomica, now largely "abandoned," where they "burned" homes, "cut down the corn," "took three scalps," and captured "one prisoner."[38]

Dunmore's War placed Delawares such as Netawatwees and White Eyes in a position to test their influence as mediators. Following the massacre of the Yellow Creek Indians, Netawatwees headed a peace mission to Wakatomica, at which White Eyes served as his speaker. Although they failed to stop Shawnee retaliation against Euro-Americans, Delawares urgently continued their efforts as the conflict escalated. Not only did White Eyes continue to encourage moderation among Shawnees, but he also sought to calm Euro-Americans.[39]

As they worked to strengthen their influence as mediators, Delaware leaders centered around Gekelemukpechunk looked to Moravians and particularly the Moravian Indians as allies. Although not as strict as Quakers in their adherence to pacifism, Moravians advocated nonviolence and were apparently viewed as pacifists by Indians. Even those Delawares who did not adopt pacifism may have considered an association with Moravians as helpful in boosting their claim to be peacemakers in the region. As the missionary Heckewelder wrote, "an impression had for many years rested on the minds of" Indian mission leaders "that God having given the commandment to his people, 'Thou shalt not kill;' it must be a great sin . . . to murder men" and go to war. The notion that "believing Indians" did not fight was probably widespread; as one sachem said, "We see that the believing Indians are a peaceable people, [who] have nothing to do with war." The names of two Moravian towns, Friedenshütten ("huts of peace") and Langundo-Utenünk or Friedensstadt ("town of peace"), likely helped drive home the point. Moravian Christianity was depicted as different from other forms of Christianity, in part because of Moravians' pacifist leanings. Shawnees were told during a Moravian visit to one of their towns that "the Indians baptized by the French and English go to war," but in contrast, the Moravian Indians "do not kill people."[40]

Warriors associated Moravianism with nonviolence, recognizing that conversion would require them to reorient their lives. "I won't say that I won't convert sometime," one Indian captain explained, "but it is not yet time for me, because I still readily go to war." Some Shawnees related that "they could not live" like the Moravians, in part because they were unwilling to give up the sacred items that gave warriors power—their "Beson [i.e., medicine], which they received from God." If a warrior were to become a Moravian Christian, his battles were against sin, not against a physical enemy. Glikhikan, a Moravian convert who had once been an important war captain, said that after his conversion, he could "always be victorious. Sin can no longer overpower me as formerly."[41]

As Dunmore's War heated up, an association with the Moravians became important to Delawares who wanted to push a peace agenda. Netawatwees asked that two Gnadenhütten Indians—Joshua and John Martin—accompany him on his embassy to Wakatomica "as a sign that they also love peace." After this meeting failed to achieve the desired results, Netawatwees requested help from a larger number of Moravian Indians to press the Wakatomica Shawnees to stop fighting. In addition to pursuing help from an old and revered Christian convert Petrus Echpalawehund, Netawatwees sought assistance from "3 Mahicans" from Gnadenhütten and "3 Minisinks" from Schönbrunn. To Zeisberger, it seemed "the Chiefs in Gekelemukpechunk" were unwilling to act "without our Indian Brothers." The Moravian Indians were vital to Delaware leaders' plans. When White Eyes assured Pittsburgh residents of the Delawares' friendship, he claimed to speak not just for Gekelemukpechunk but also for Gnadenhütten and Schönbrunn. Although Moravian policy tried to limit Christian Indians' involvement in worldly "Chiefs' Affairs," Moravian Indians obviously believed that they had a role to play in peace efforts, in which they assisted Netawatwees.[42]

During Dunmore's War, Delawares also placed themselves in the position of mediators of intertribal alliances. In addition to maintaining older connections with Wyandots and struggling to hold onto fraying ties with Shawnees and Ohio Iroquois, Delaware leaders mounted an effort to ally with Cherokees, who had already made a peace agreement with the Six Nations several years earlier. Cherokees shared Delawares' concerns with Euro-

American encroachment. After the Fort Stanwix treaty, the boundary between Cherokee and Euro-American lands had remained in dispute, and
Cherokee holdings shrank through a number of land deals. The Cherokees,
like the Delawares, included some who took an accommodationist stance toward the colonists. In March 1774, these Cherokees said they sought "to enter
the same peace alliance" as the Delawares "had made with the English." The
next month, "over 100 Cherokees" were said to be on the way to the Muskingum Valley, and in June Cherokees arrived at Gekelemukpechunk where
they formed an alliance with Delawares, Wyandots, Mahicans, and Shawnees
from the Lower Town.[43]

Delawares described this intertribal alliance as an important aspect of
their work as mediators between Indians and English. The "Chiefs of the
Delawares" at Gekelemukpechunk assumed the English would approve of
their recent conference. "When the late unhappy disturbances happened,"
they said in a message to the English at Pittsburgh, "you desired us to be
strong and to speak to the other Tribes of Indians, to hold fast the Chain of
Friendship subsisting between the English and them." These Delawares could
now report that "we sent for our Uncles the Wiandots, and our Grand Children the Shawanese, and also the Cherokees, and we have desired them to be
strong and inform all other Nations, and hold fast the Chain which our
Grandfathers made." The conference at Gekelemukpechunk in June 1774 offered yet another way for the Delawares to convince others, as well as their
own people, that their nation was central to the work of peace keeping in the
region.[44]

Not all Delawares, however, rallied around Netawatwees and White
Eyes. The two leaders encountered opposition to their pro-English approach,
especially from Munsees at a place called Mochwesung (Moquesin or Bullet's
Town), about twenty miles below Gekelemukpechunk. It was said that
Netawatwees and his associates "had no leaders from the [Munsee] nation
upon whom they could depend," which was another reason he sought assistance from Moravian Indians, among whom were prominent Munsees. The
Mochwesung Munsees lived relatively close to Wakatomica and shared in the
militancy of that place. Within a month after the killings of the Yellow Creek
inhabitants, Mochwesung residents "held a war dance . . . because they believed that war had fully broken out." Critical of militant Shawnees, Zeisberger believed the "Munsees below in Mochwesüng" were "no better than
Shawnees"; however, the Mochwesung Indians probably thought missionaries were no better than other whites encroaching on Native lands. As fearful

reports of Virginian patrols circulated, Mochwesung Indians tried to convince Schönbrunn residents to leave the Moravians and move to the Lower Shawnee Town for safety.[45]

Intertribal alliances were also highly important to militants. Mochwesung Munsees claimed that the Wyandots, Miamis, Cherokees, and "other Nations had thrown in their lot with the Shawnees to help them against the whites." Zeisberger dismissed this claim as "untrue"; however, even if the Munsees exaggerated, their statement revealed a concern to gather intertribal aid. Some of the youthful warriors who died during Dunmore's War were Wyandots and Caughnawagas. Reports from the culminating battle of Dunmore's War, which occurred on October 10 at Point Pleasant at the mouth of the Kanhawa River in present-day West Virginia, suggest that Shawnees and Ohio Iroquois had found at least some intertribal support for their cause. One English lieutenant believed that the combatants at Point Pleasant included not only Shawnees and Ohio Iroquois but also Ottawas, Delawares, and peoples of "several Other Nations." Other English reports, although omitting identifying details about the Indians, remarked on the large size of the Native force. "We had 7 or 800 Warriors to deal with," wrote one colonel. An English captain stated that "there are many conjectures with regard to the number of Indians &c; some think eight hundred, some one thousand." Even if these accounts were exaggerated, it seems the militants had some success in expanding their range of support.[46]

It was said that "several of the Monsys who live close to [Wakatomica]" had "assisted the Shawnees" and had "paid for it by falling on the battlefield or by being badly wounded"; however, evidence does not suggest that large numbers of Delawares decided to fight in Dunmore's War. At the end of the war, White Eyes, Netawatwees, and other leaders had reason to believe that they could convince the English that Delawares were peacemakers and friends of the British. Through this friendship, however, Delawares risked damaging their image as mediators and alliance builders among Indians. White Eyes had passed along details of Shawnee warriors' movements to the British. The British believed that they had received a promise from White Eyes that he would "join the Virginia Militia, if they cross the River to attack the lower Shawanese." After the war Lord Dunmore promised White Eyes "some Satisfaction" for "serving with him on Campaign." A Shawnee, angry at Delaware support for the British, threatened "Mischief" against Gekelemukpechunk and said that the "Grand father's, the Delawares had thrown them [the Shawnees] away." Point Pleasant undoubtedly made Shawnees even more outraged at White Eyes and his associates. Described as "a hard fought Battle" that "lasted from half an hour after [sunrise], to the same time before Sunset," the encounter ended in defeat for the Indians. Outraged Shawnees who had survived the war accused Delawares of being "Virginians" or "Schwoneks" (also "Schwonnack").[47]

The tasks that Delaware leaders set out to accomplish in the years after Pontiac's War were formidable and significant. They worked to build connections among far-flung Delaware friends and relatives by gathering them into closer proximity in western locations. Sharing physical space had been a crucial component of alliance building since early times in homeland regions. They also forged wider connections that included Shawnees, Wyandots, Ohio Iroquois, and Cherokees. Increasingly, the language of a grandfather relating to his grandchildren supported the notion that Delawares had an especially powerful ability to influence events and convince Indians to work together under Delaware guidance. Through these complex processes of migration and mediation, Delawares formed themselves into a people that included both Munsees and Unamis, who lived in many different communities and were part of many different kin groups. Constructing and extending alliances, Delawares claimed authority in peacemaking. This claim and the special mission they envisioned helped them define the Delawares as a people distinct from other peoples.

Delawares also returned to the old idea of the "Chain of Friendship" linking Indians with the English. Netawatwees, White Eyes, Killbuck, and other Delawares invoked the "Chain of Friendship" in a message to Pittsburgh sent in the months after the attack near Yellow Creek. White Eyes added a reminder about the tradition behind this chain, which had "so long subsisted between" his people and the English: "Let us call to our remembrance the Amity made by our Forefathers and their Wise People, which is no doubt still impressed upon the hearts of our Great men." Attempting to put aside the years of conflict and warfare, Delawares who invoked the "Chain of Friendship" placed hope in strengthening their people through a process of building alliances upon alliances in a widening range of connections, even though plans to include Euro-Americans within this set of alliances were hotly contested.[48]

Chapter 6
Striving for Unity with Diversity, 1768–83

In the 1760s and 1770s, Delawares sought unity while recognizing the diverse groups involved in this process. The established pattern of living in small and dispersed, yet connected, communities had long revealed a tendency to unite with neighbors while retaining diverse localized attachments. The boundaries delineating the Delawares as a group were permeable; however, their leaders continued to try to create a more defined sense of the Delawares as a people. Peacemaker, alliance builder, "grandfather," and "the first nation" to negotiate with William Penn—all were aspects of this definition. Distinguishing themselves as a people also involved defining Delaware land rights. The effort to gather Delawares in the Ohio Country coincided with Delaware attempts to clarify and communicate their land claims in the west. The American Revolution sabotaged Delaware attempts to find consensus and come together as a people. In this time of turmoil, Delawares tried to steer a neutral course but ended up splitting into opposing factions. After the war, however, they did not abandon their hope in alliance building.

Mediation in a Complex World

Governing by persuasion rather than by coercion, Delaware leaders who emphasized their role as alliance builders would have been aware of the need to convince many different people about the importance of this work. Netawatwees and other Delaware leaders sought supporters from diverse groups and individuals. They also recognized the need to overcome disagreements among the Delawares themselves, and they utilized their experience with practices of mediation as they sought reconciliation.

An examination of the individuals living in the vicinity of the Delaware communities in the Muskingum Valley suggests the range of peoples that

Netawatwees and other Delaware leaders would have considered as they attempted to gain supporters. Besides the main Delaware ethnic groups—the Munsees and the Unamis—there was the small, infrequently mentioned Unalachtigo group. Some Mahicans resided in the environs of Gekelemukpechunk. Additional Mahicans arrived with the Moravian migration, and the main contingent of Moravian Mahicans lived at the mission town Gnadenhütten. Netawatwees referred to Gnadenhütten as the "place" of "my Grand Children the Mahicans," although they seem to have made up only a small proportion of the population. Other ethnic groups lived at least in small numbers in the area, including Moravian Wompanosch. Ohio Moravian Indians also included Nanticoke and Conoy individuals, a Cherokee man married to an Unami woman, and an Onondaga man with his son. An Iroquoian named Agnes was married to the Munsee Moravian Glikhikan.[1]

Here and there among the Delawares lived a few Euro-Americans, such as the trader named Thompson married to Isaac Nutimus's daughter, and various Moravian missionaries. In the early years of the Revolutionary War, missionaries in the Muskingum towns included David Zeisberger, John Heckewelder, Johanna and Johann Schmick, Anna and Johann Jungmann, and William Edwards. At least a couple of Euro-American women in the Delaware towns had been war captives. Margaret ("Peggy") Boyer Conner was released from captivity by the Shawnees at the end of Dunmore's War, and she and her husband Richard lived at Schönbrunn. A Philadelphia-born woman named Rachel, married to the Ohio Delaware sachem Welapachtschiechen, had been captured at age nineteen by White Eyes and Glikhikan during the Seven Years' War.[2]

African Americans also resided among the Delawares. Although their names are mostly unknown today, some information about them exists. White Eyes stated that there were "two Negro Women and two Children in our Towns." An African American woman lived with her Delaware husband Jonathan at Schönbrunn. Some African Americans in Indian country were runaway slaves or war captives unwilling to return to slave masters. Shawnees said that while they were still living in the east, "Severall negro Slaves used to Run away and Come amongst us." At Pittsburgh in 1761, an African American claimed by a storekeeper named Levy was said to have "run away with the Indians." White Eyes explained that some African Americans in the Delaware towns were actually "in the hands of the Shawanese"—in other words, they were Shawnee war captives. In 1775, the Shawnee Cornstalk told about "one Negro Man," apparently a former war captive, who had "runaway from the

Mouth of Hockhockan [Hocking River]," avoiding a forced removal to the English.[3]

Colonists appealed for the return of African American captives but faced resistance. At the end of Pontiac's and Dunmore's wars, English expected Indians to turn over African American prisoners; however, Indians seemed unwilling to go out of their way to accomplish returns. In the Johnson Hall meeting of 1765, the Delaware Squash Cutter offered to release African American captives, without actually promising that the Indians would effect the return themselves. "We are very glad to hear that the King will forgive what is past," he stated, and "we . . . are now resolved to deliver up" the captives; nevertheless, he told the English, "we wish you would stretch out your hand and fetch them." At the Pittsburgh treaty of 1775, the Shawnee Cornstalk explained that in order to obtain an "old" African American woman, the English should come for her themselves. "You may Get" her, Cornstalk said, "if you will bring her home upon your backs for she is not able to walk." Indians resisted returning children born to Indian and African American couples. Cornstalk stated, "It is true there are two Negro Children which were begotten by my People," whom "we are not Willing to give up." Zeisberger expounded on this attachment: "Indians and negroes intermarry and their mulatto children are as much loved as children of pure Indian blood."[4]

In order to attain the power that came when people united, Delawares needed to overcome suspicions and disagreements among themselves. Charges of witchcraft arose with the anguish that came in the wake of epidemics, and some of these charges were made by Delawares against other Delawares. Disease raged through Muskingum Valley communities in the late 1760s and the early 1770s. An old woman reported that "often 6 people were buried in a day" at Gekelemukpechunk during the winter of 1767–68. In 1770, Allegheny-area Indians learned of deaths from "a bad epidemic among the Indians" to the west. At Schönbrunn "a bad fever" struck and lingered. In 1777, "sudden death" carried off many there, and a number of survivors were "unable to shake the fever." Not unlike their seventeenth-century ancestors in the Delaware Valley, eighteenth-century Indians suspected that supernatural power, which had been turned to a bad purpose, was the source of epidemics. Ohio Delawares sought to root out the responsible parties.[5]

Delawares believed that certain individuals were employing secret knowledge of a supernaturally powerful medicine, called *Machtapassican*. They described the power to kill as closely related to the power to cure. Those who first possessed the knowledge of *Machtapassican* learned of "a Root which being Eaten by one of them poisoned him directly"; however, "upon Eating of another Root . . . was Cured directly." Unfortunately, no one seemed to remember anything about the healing root. All that remained apparently was the knowledge of the poisonous one. Delawares believed that *Machtapassican* knowledge originally came from the Nanticokes. According to one account, the Nanticokes received it through a spirit disguised as a baby. This infant "grew of a short & thick size" and "took to kill the others Children." People tried repeatedly to kill it, "but still it became alive again." Finally, the spirit worked out an agreement that "if they would obey it & serve it," which probably entailed the performance of certain rituals, "it would learn them how to do mighty things." Delawares said they "knew nothing" of this *Machtapassican* until they were in contact with Nanticokes in the Susquehanna Valley.[6]

In 1768, some at Gekelemukpechunk blamed the Munsee prophet Wangomen, then living on the Allegheny, for the onslaught of disease. The Moravian Indians also fell under suspicion as a faction of Delawares disagreed with those who thought an association with Moravians could help their people. A story started making the rounds that Moravians baptized Indians with a "powder" made from the "brain" and "heart" of "a certain pious minister." Perhaps this belief related to the notion that baptized Indians formed "one mind" and "one heart" with Moravian missionaries, extending the metaphor used in many early treaties with Euro-Americans. Although this potion was believed to impart positive attributes—wisdom and piety—the power associated with Moravians was also considered dangerous by some. At Friedenshütten, the Munsee leader Papunhank had faced allegations of using *Machtapassican* to sicken people. In Ohio, Moravians were said to have "accepted" and "protected" Native "sorcerers"—a charge leading to "harsh accusations" that *Machtapassican* was available in Moravian communities.[7]

Leaders faced a considerable task of reconciliation, particularly between Moravian Indians and their adversaries. On the Allegheny River, missionaries had faced firm opposition from those who saw the arrival of any Euro-Americans as an intrusion. A Seneca from Venango criticized Allemewi for inviting the Moravians, saying that other whites would shortly follow to "lay out a town on this river and take the land." Some Goschgoschunk residents disapproved of fellow Munsees who worshipped with the Moravians, warning that they would "become a slave of the white people." Zeisberger complained of Indian "women who go to great lengths to seduce the people so that they are not attending our service[s]." Wangomen's claim to healing powers—his ability "to cure when he blew upon the sick"—stood in contrast with the destructive power believed to be among the Moravians. His ill sister convinced Wangomen that "she must die if he went to . . . [Moravians'] meetings."[8]

Those considered witches, or practitioners of the *Machtapassican,* may have been blamed, not just for the deaths of individuals but also for undermining group solidarity. At a time when Delawares were trying to encourage a consolidation of their people in Ohio, divisions between Christian and anti-Christian factions threatened to destroy hopes for a strong Delaware coalition. Attempting to overcome these differences, Delawares turned to mediation techniques and worked to find common ground. Wangomen and his supporters appeared concerned that if they drove away the missionaries, "a great number of Indians would follow them." Furthermore, the Munsee Glikhikan threw his support behind the Moravians, which made their opponents more open to compromise. As one of Custaloga's councilors, Glikhikan was "a respected man among the Indians, a speaker for the chiefs," and, as we have seen, a well-known warrior. He was also a brother of Wangomen, which probably enhanced his influence over Wangomen's supporters. When Glikhikan visited the Allegheny mission Lawunakhannek in 1769, local Indians were said to have "waited for him this entire year" and were "eager to hear" his view of the Moravians. Munsees worked out an alliance with the Moravians and hence with their Indian friends. In so doing, they utilized the familiar technique of invoking a kin connection between allies, in this case with the Moravians. Munsees said that they "publicly and unanimously decided to receive the Brethren as . . . kin [*Freunde*] belonging to us." To preserve this relationship, they proposed using a "middleman," named Woathelapuenk. Wangomen explained, "what you hear from him [the middleman] shall be the truth and what we hear from him we will consider likewise." Negotiating through this middleman and building an alliance within the framework of kinship, Delawares sought to end disagreements and find unity.[9]

Still, accusations about *Machtapassican* followed the Moravian group to the Muskingum. Moravian Indians aroused suspicions that they would undermine attempts to unite Delawares. In 1770 Netawatwees had requested, with wampum, that Custaloga search for the source of the *Machtapassican.* This message included the warning that he "who . . . will not accept this belt shall be seen as an enemy and murderer of his Nation." Refusal to uncover knowledge of the *Machtapassican* was portrayed as a profoundly antisocial act, damaging to the Delawares as a whole. In 1773 Delawares tried again to root out sorcery. A message from Gekelemukpechunk urged the Christian Indians to hold "a council to see if they could discover something about the *Machtapassican*." Glikhikan, by now baptized and renamed Isaac, took offense at the request, perhaps especially because of its implication that witches were operating among the Christians. "It is not our business to hold a council about the Machtapassican and it does not pertain to us but rather to you," Glikhikan declared. Boldly, he "threw" the "string" of wampum accompanying the message "on the floor in the middle of the Council" at Gekelemukpechunk. Attenders of this meeting were disturbed by this response. It seemed to signal a lack of concern for the larger group by implying that the Delaware Council should "bear everything alone"—that is, bear all the responsibility for finding the source of the many deaths—without aid from the Moravian Indians.[10]

Yet Moravian Delawares seemed to regret their position, which appeared to undermine the plan to bring Delawares together. Netawatwees sought out the Christian group once again, approaching the Munsee Allemewi for aid in healing the breach. About two weeks after Glikhikan's outburst at Gekelemukpechunk, Allemewi (by now baptized Solomon) participated in a meeting of Netawatwees's council. It was said that Delaware leaders wanted to "discover from him because he is already an old chief, what he had heard in days of old about the Machtapassigan." In contrast to Glikhikan's noncooperation, Allemewi "passed on as much information as he knew, though he said that so much had he heard but never seen with his own eyes." On the Muskingum, as on the Allegheny, Delawares turned to compromise in order to try to build unity out of disparate groups.[11]

Like sachems in generations before them, Ohio Delaware leaders had to employ persuasive powers. Delawares depended on the cooperation of many different leaders, representing different groups. Netawatwees sought the support of individuals such as Echpalawehund, considered "the oldest in his *Freundschaft*." Echpalawehund was responsible for performing an annual ceremony for his *Freundschaft*, possibly a matrilineage, to ensure the health and well-being of its members. This important duty, along with his seniority, seem to have qualified him to serve as a major councilor for Netawatwees. In 1773 Echpalawehund stated that "up until now he had always" been "a councilor" to Netawatwees, who "had not done anything in the chiefs' affairs without" consulting him. Netawatwees also eagerly expected help from the

Munsee sachem Newollike en route from the Susquehanna. When Newollike finally reached the Muskingum in 1774, Netawatwees "had already waited a long time" for the Munsee, who he "hoped" would become "a faithful assistant." Drawing together Delawares from far-flung places thus had an added benefit—it could expand the circle of available councilors.[12]

Delaware governance attempted to balance unity with diversity. The continuing importance of fundamental units of association—kin groups and small communities—meant that there were indeed many different groups to be consulted. Council governance provided an opportunity for many voices to be heard in building connections among Delawares. Netawatwees was known "to lay all affairs of state before his council for consideration." At council meetings, affairs were "often very thoroughly and extendedly discussed," with the various "chiefs and counsellors in turn" offering "their opinions and suggestions." Dealings with non-Delawares also highlighted the approach of combining unity with diversity. Delawares worked together, attempting to unify, while recognizing that diverse groups needed to make their own contributions to the whole. Coordination among various individuals in Delaware communities occurred when wampum was gathered to construct alliances with neighboring peoples. Leaders needed to "be supported and maintained in their positions in order to settle necessary affairs among themselves as well as with other nations." In arranging for a treaty, Delaware heads requested contributions "in all the towns, usually wampum, sometimes also pelts." Gathering a sizable number of contributions was important. As Zeisberger wrote, "An alliance or league is hardly arranged by two peoples with less than twenty belts of wampum. Often thirty or more are required."[13]

The Delawares in Ohio recognized diversity within a larger unity in another way—by dividing into three main groups, called the Turtle, Turkey, and Wolf, while creating an interlocking leadership structure that encouraged coordination among these entities. Documentary evidence of the Turtle, Turkey, and Wolf groups is sparse, and the age of the tripartite division is unknown. These groups may have gained importance beginning around the time of Pontiac's War, when the three divisions were mentioned at a treaty with Bouquet in the Muskingum Valley. The Turtle, Turkey, and Wolf divisions apparently incorporated a number of different matriclans; accordingly, the three divisions have been termed "phratries." In the nineteenth century, Lewis Henry Morgan found twelve named subgroups under the Wolf division, ten under the Turtle, and twelve under the Turkey. For example, "Big

Feet," "Yellow Tree," "Pulling Corn," and "Dog standing by Fireside" were the names of some of the groups within the Wolf phratry.[14]

Phratries appear to have served both as markers of difference but also as a way to expand Delaware support networks. They apparently helped cut across the divide between Munsees and Unamis as these peoples came together in the Ohio Country. Despite cultural differences, a Munsee and an Unami might have shared the same phratry affiliation. Phratry membership may have acted as a link for people who had once been unrelated or only loosely connected with each other. For example, a Turtle member in one place might have had an affinity with Turtle members in other places, creating connections between Delaware communities.[15]

The selection of a phratry head also seems to have reinforced bonds among different groups of Delawares. When a phratry leader died, Turtle division members did not select his replacement, but rather Wolf and Turkey members performed this duty. "Similarly," Zeisberger explained, "if a chief of the Wolf or Turkey Tribe were to be elected, the tribe concerned would have no part in the election." The public ceremony for installing a new phratry sachem probably highlighted that phratry members held responsibility for the well-being of Delawares outside of their own phratry. "The two chiefs" involved in the selection moved at the "head" of a "procession toward the town where the election is to take place." They arrived "singing in a tone used on this and no other occasion," which would have underscored the special nature of the event. In the council house "one of the two chiefs, in a singing tone," began "the proceedings by explaining the object of the meeting, condoling with the chief elect." Then this individual pronounced the new phratry head "to be Chief in the Place of the Deceased." Showing his support for the selected leader, this sachem from outside of the new leader's phratry cautioned "the People present . . . to be obedient unto their Chief and to assist him wherever they can." Zeisberger believed that this ceremony ensured that "the new chief enters upon his office by consent of the tribe and the whole nation."[16]

Being Delaware meant being part of groups within groups that overlapped with and crosscut one another. The Ohio Delawares consisted of diverse peoples with differing community ties, affinal and matrilineal relations, linguistic/ethnic groups (especially Munsees and Unamis), and religious associations. Amidst this diversity, religious associations aroused some of the sharpest controversies, as fears of dangerous supernatural power became directed at Moravianism. Especially prior to the mid-1770s, however, Ohio Delawares found ways to mediate and compromise. As they sought to strengthen the Delawares' place in the region, leaders tried to promote Delaware solidarity by gaining support from many groups and leaders.

Land and Authority

Land was crucial to Delaware attempts to bolster their position in the region. Jurisdiction over land also helped the Delawares define themselves as a people with authority. Alliances were constructed in physical space. An Indian group with territory could strengthen its position by welcoming Native allies onto its lands, often those who had suffered from war, epidemics, and dispossession. The Iroquois, for example, had exhibited this authority when they had invited the Tuscaroras to settle among them earlier in the century. Should their territorial claims be recognized, the Delawares would have a powerful tool—land—to help them lead in the construction of alliances. Authority over land also promised to give Delawares a greater voice in dealing with Euro-Americans. Without land and the power to handle its disposition, Native peoples lost influence with Euro-Americans. One Onondaga man complained to a Pennsylvania negotiator, "you don't like to see us any more" ever since "you got all our lands that you wanted from us." Now, he said, "our fate is the same as our Cousins the delawares & Mohickans." Delawares were determined not to accept that fate. They did not consider themselves landless, and they developed approaches to demonstrate their land rights and to establish their authority in the Ohio Country.[17]

Between about 1772 and 1775 Delawares developed a two-pronged strategy to try to secure title to Ohio lands. They planned to send representatives directly to the king of England in order to gain acknowledgment of Delaware possession. Also, they set about firming up an agreement with the Wyandots, who, it was said, had granted a significant portion of the Ohio Valley to the Delawares. Netawatwees and White Eyes seem to have been major architects of this strategy; White Eyes, in particular, was an important figure in attempting to implement it.

Delawares made various appeals for assistance in accomplishing a trip to England. Their relationship with Pennsylvania and with the Quakers seemed possible sources of help—suggesting another reason why Delawares emphasized these alliances in this period. Netawatwees apparently made two requests to Pennsylvania in 1772. "I am ready to go over the Great Waters to see that Great King," Netawatwees informed Pennsylvania's governor, and "I desire you to prepare a Ship for me next Spring." Reminding the governor that this request came from an ally, described in kinship terms, Netawatwees added, "I am your Brother and I am your friend." When three Quakers paid a visit to Gekelemukpechunk in 1773, Delawares asked them for help in sending "some of their people to England in order to have a conference with the king."[18]

Delawares planned to seek the king's recognition of their land rights. By drawing parallels between their old ties with the Quakers and their present association with the Moravians, they apparently believed they could make a more convincing case. They designated a "belt to be shown to the king." This wampum belt, "which they had gotten from old Penn," had been a sign of "friendship." Penn also presented it, they said, so that the Delawares would "receive the Word of God, which he preached to them." Back in those early days of Pennsylvania, the Delawares said, "they did not understand" that Penn's preaching "should contribute to their everlasting good." "Now though," they added, they were ready "to receive" God's Word "because . . . they hear among the Brethren [Moravians] it is very necessary and healing." This approach resembled that of Captain John and Tatamy, who had backed up their request for land in the Forks during the 1740s with the declaration that they had "embraced the Christian Religion."[19]

None of these appeals achieved the desired result. Nevertheless, White Eyes believed he had another ally, Lord Dunmore, who he hoped would assist the Delawares in meeting the king. White Eyes expected gratitude from Lord Dunmore for the help the Delawares had provided Virginia in 1774. Because White Eyes had spent so much time negotiating with Shawnees during the war, he complained that he had become "a very poor Man and had Neglected to raise Corn . . . and . . . his wife and Childerin [*sic*] were now almost starving for Bread." In return for White Eyes's aid and sacrifice, "Lord Dunmore . . . had promised him his Interest in procuring a Grant from the King for the Lands claimed by the Delawares." It seems that White Eyes had received an assurance that Dunmore would draw up "a deed on the Delaware Indians' land" for White Eyes to carry to the king. Delawares wanted once and for all to stop Euro-Americans from pushing them off their land, "as has always occurred up until now," Zeisberger wrote.[20]

The second part of the Delawares' strategy—to establish that their land had been a gift from the Wyandots—was also meant to secure title, as the Delawares wanted a portion of the Ohio Valley to "remain for them and their descendants for hunting and dwelling." The Delawares planned to show the king of England a white wampum belt, indicating the agreement between the Wyandots and the Delawares, as evidence of the grant. It is unclear when Delawares first arranged matters with the Wyandots. Sometime prior to 1772, Netawatwees and the Wyandots met together and viewed a map, which depicted the grant's extent. It was claimed that "the Wyandots . . . gave the Delawares Land between the Beaver Creek [River], the Cayuga River, Lake Erie, the Sandusky River, from there to the heads of the Hocking River and so on the Ohio up to Shingas's Town [near the mouth of the Beaver]."[21]

This is not the only extant description of the boundaries of the Wyandots' gift. White Eyes portrayed it as "that Tract of Country Beginning at the Mouth of Big Beaver Creek and running up the same to where it interlocks with the Branches of the Guyahoga [Cuyahoga] Creek and down the said Creek to the Mouth thereof where it empties into the Lake along Side of the Lake to the Mouth of Sanduskey Creek and up the same to the head untill it interlocks with Muskingum down the same to the Mouth where it Empties into the Ohio and up the said River to the Place of Beginning." The main difference between the two descriptions lay in the western boundary—the Hocking in the first case and the Muskingum in the second. An account from 1776 differed from both of these descriptions in the location of the grant's northeastern boundary, which it placed at Presque Isle instead of Cuyahoga. There seemed little disagreement among the accounts, however, about the Muskingum Valley. All of the accounts included this important area of Delaware settlement within the Wyandots' grant.[22]

After seeing their England trip repeatedly postponed, Delawares decided to hold a council with the Wyandots in order to thank them properly for their land grant. They may have feared the agreement was on shaky ground "because the Delaware Nation has not yet rendered gratitude and thanks for the land presented to them." Besides recognizing the need to reciprocate, Delawares likely saw it would be wise to confirm their agreement with the Wyandots in order to strengthen their case for Delaware possession. By early 1775, leaders were soliciting donations from Delaware communities to send the Wyandots "thanksgiving for the land." The Moravian Indians sent along three wampum belts—one of these was from Schönbrunn and another from Gnadenhütten. That summer it was reported that Delawares had been at a "Great Council" in the "Wiandots['] Towns."[23]

Meanwhile, the Six Nations continued to claim Ohio Country lands. The Delawares' two-pronged strategy omitted soliciting Iroquois approval, although at one point White Eyes did "Acquaint" his "Uncles the Six Nations" about the Wyandot grant. By trying to base their possession on the Wyandot grant and on a direct meeting with the king of England, Delawares probably hoped that they could bypass conflicting Iroquois claims. Not surprisingly, the effort to firm up their land claim coincided with the Delaware attempt to get a "Council Fire at Fort Pitt."[24]

In 1776 White Eyes offered another justification for the Delawares' possession of the Ohio Country, and this time he directly disputed Iroquois ownership of the area. He told of an ancient war between Lenapes and a nation called "Dallagae," who had once occupied the Ohio Valley. "We conquered the Nation Dallagae," White Eyes said, "we took them Prisoners, and gave them as a Present to the Six Nations, but we did not give them the Lands we took from them when conquered." Heckewelder recorded a similar account of an ancient people known as "*Talligewi*" or "*Alligewi*," said to have had "many large towns built on the great rivers." As Lenapes, in some distant period, left a western country to arrive at what would become their eastern homelands, they were said to have encountered the Alligewi. In the war that ensued, the story went, the Iroquois and the Lenapes fought together, and as victorious allies "divided the country between themselves; the Mengwe [or Iroquois] made choice of the lands in the vicinity of the great lakes, and on their tributary streams, and the Lenape took possession of the country to the south."[25]

By the time White Eyes offered his remarks about the "Dallagae," the American Revolution was under way. James Wood, an envoy from Virginia, informed White Eyes in July 1775 about the "disputes subsisting between Lord Dunmore and the People of Virginia." In the circumstances, Delawares needed to rethink their strategy; the plan of approaching the king of England seemed moribund. Across the Ohio Country Indians observed the conflict and formulated responses. A few months after the clashes at Lexington and Concord, War Post, a Wyandot at Upper Sandusky, said that his people "had always Understood that the English had but one King who lived over the Great Water"; hence "they were Much Surprized to hear" about the war and "would be glad to know the Cause of the dispute." As the war escalated, Delawares worked at sorting out their relationships with the parties involved. Although they altered their strategies, they did not give up on trying to secure land.[26]

In the early phases of the war, the revolutionaries pressed Indians to remain neutral. At a treaty in Pittsburgh in 1775, John Walker, representing Virginia, told Ohio Iroquois, Wyandots, Shawnees, Ottawas, and Delawares, "we only ask of you to Stay at home, to take Care of your Women and Children, and follow other Usual Occupations." The Seneca Blacksnake remembered being told at Pittsburgh, "This is a family quarrel Between us and old England, you Indians are not Concerned in it." Like the revolutionaries, the British initially recommended the Indians remain neutral; indeed, the superintendent for the northern department had stated, "Indians should never be engaged in our differences." Nevertheless, Britain and the United States came to abandon this policy and tried to enlist Indian allies.[27]

Amid the turmoil Delawares continued to attempt to gain recognition of their land rights. Now, however, instead of planning an overture to the king, leaders shifted their strategy toward building a relationship with the new United States, while trying to steer a middle course to keep Delawares out of the fighting. Delawares treated with U.S. representatives at Pittsburgh in 1775 and 1776. Custaloga, Pipe, and White Eyes all attended the 1775 treaty, as did Moravian Delawares Billy Chelloway, Nathanael (formerly James Davis), and Glikhikan. Pipe, John Killbuck (Gelelemend), White Eyes, and Welapachtschiechen were among those at the 1776 meeting. Custaloga was dead by the time of this treaty; an ailing Netawatwees attended but died during a recess in the proceedings and was buried at Pittsburgh. Three Delawares—White Eyes, John Montour, and Wingenund—helped a U.S. messenger, William Wilson, meet with Wyandots in the summer of 1776. White Eyes traveled to Philadelphia and appealed to the Continental Congress to provide the Delawares with a schoolmaster, minister, "a mill, a miller," and "a couple of farmers"—an attempt to demonstrate Delaware interest in adopting Euro-American civilization as he continued to seek support for Delaware land claims. While there, he again utilized Delawares' connections with Quakers, suggesting that Delawares hoped they could build on old friendships. Delaware connections with the Moravians also probably reinforced their friendship with the United States, whose officers frequently received information about the state of the frontier from Zeisberger.[28]

The relationship that the Delawares had constructed with the United States culminated in the Pittsburgh Treaty of 1778. Article 6 of the treaty seemed to reflect the Delawares' concern to achieve recognition of their land rights. It stated, "the United States do engage to guarantee to the aforesaid nation of Delawares, and their heirs, all their territorial rights in the fullest and most ample manner." There were a couple of qualifications: the agreement was "bounded by former treaties," and it stipulated that the "guarantee" of Delaware lands lasted only "as long as they the said Delaware nation shall abide by, and hold fast the chain of friendship now entered into." Article 6 also seemed to speak to Delawares' long-standing interest in the construction of Indian-Indian alliances. "And it is further agreed on between the contracting parties," the article stated, "should it for the future be found conducive for the mutual interest of both parties to invite any other tribes who have been friends to the interest of the United States, to join the present confederation, and to form a state whereof the Delaware nation shall be the head, and have a representation in Congress." Although the treaty suggested major Delaware concerns—land rights and intertribal relations—it offered few certainties as the United States tried to maintain an alliance with the Delawares while avoiding unqualified commitments.[29]

Delawares approached their role in distinctive ways. They highlighted their place in the history of Pennsylvania, and they invoked their position as a grandfather for other Indians. Although Delawares did not achieve the security they sought, the struggle for land rights contributed to this process of defining who they were as a people. It is impossible for outsiders to know all the ways this struggle shaped the Delawares. Yet it was clearly a major effort, and it involved significant planning, strategizing, and cooperation. Through the process of trying to ensure land for themselves and subsequent generations, Delawares vocalized their own sense of their history and revealed how they saw themselves vis-à-vis their neighbors. In particular, Delawares tried to define their relations with the Six Nations, the Wyandots, and the new United States.

Division and Survival

More and more, Delawares found it difficult to resolve their differences and find consensus during the war. Delawares' attempts to build good relations with the United States angered other Indians, who were trending toward the British. Many of these pro-British Indians were ones with whom Delawares had built alliances and relationships in years past. Thus Delawares increasingly struggled with internal dissension as their former allies encouraged them to join the fight against the United States. The role of peacemaker was one that Delawares struggled to maintain for themselves, and they resisted providing outright military support for either side during the first few years of the war. With some exceptions, Delawares remained noncombatants for a longer period than many of their neighbors.

Delawares who chose this path would have built on past experiences, especially diplomatic ones. Dunmore's War likely influenced how some
Delawares responded to the renewed fighting. Unlike Shawnees, whose
Wakatomica settlements had been burned, Delawares had managed to avoid
an assault on their Muskingum towns in 1774. Although White Eyes had
made enemies because of his part in Dunmore's War, his opponents could
not claim success after the Battle of Point Pleasant. Furthermore, White Eyes
and other Delawares apparently hoped that, in attempting to secure their
lands, they could build on previously constructed relationships with
colonists, such as Quakers and Moravians who might support Delaware
claims in negotiations with the United States. The Pittsburgh Treaty of 1775,
at which Congress's commissioners promised not to encroach on Indian
lands, excluding the Fort Stanwix cession, may have left some Delawares at
least vaguely hopeful about their approach of building a relationship with the
United States while trying to remain militarily neutral.[30]

Holding to this approach was difficult, however. Frontier fighters from
the United States had a dismal record when it came to respecting Native
lands and lives. Indians' anxieties that they would continue encroachments
ran high. In the early months of the war, War Post said that he had "heard the
People of Virginia were now building a Fort on Kentucke and intended to
drive off all the Indians and take Possession of their Lands." Probably still discontented with the Fort Stanwix cession, the Shawnee Kishanosity "complained of the Encroachments of the Virginians" who "were now settling in
Great Numbers in the Midst of their Hunting Grounds on the Kentucke
River." These Virginians did not stop there, he said: "many . . . Crossed the
Ohio" and "killed and drove off their Game."[31]

Not only did settlers and hunters from the United States pose a threat to
Native subsistence, but also their frequent readiness to kill even friendly Indians made them unlikely allies. As one Indian proceeded to Pittsburgh to
negotiate with commissioners from the Continental Congress, he was "shot
at by two Men in long white hunting Shirts," leading him to fear that "all the
Indians near this place were Murdered." White Eyes was not exempt from
such threats, despite his helpfulness toward the United States. "If White Eyes
passes this way he will Be in danger of Being killed," wrote one officer, referring to danger from white Americans. Indeed, White Eyes evidently was later
murdered while assisting the United States. Gen. Edward Hand described the
problem of keeping his men from attacking friendly Indians: "the situation
of the Delawares embarraces me much. I wish to preserve their friendship,

how to do this & keep small parties in the Indian Country . . . & steer clear of the Delawares I cant tell."[32]

Indians' grievances against Euro-Americans were similar to ones in years past; the Revolutionary War did not change the fundamental complaint against encroachments. Native hostility was directed at newcomers pushing along the Ohio, the Allegheny, and the Monongahela. Indians targeted "the waters of Turtle Creek," a Monongahela tributary, "where the people are a living thick." A small raid occurred at Kittanning on the Allegheny River. On the Ohio, Indians struck around Wheeling, on Raccoon Creek in present Beaver County, and at "Muchmore's plantation, about forty-five miles" below Fort Pitt. In this last attack, "the widow Muchmore and her three children, were found almost burned to cinders, and her late husband killed and scalped near where the house stood, opposite the mouth of Yellow Creek." The location of this raid suggests that it was a response to the slaughter of Yellow Creek Indians during Dunmore's War.[33]

Native warriors included a mix of ethnicities. At about the time of the assault on Muchmore's, an Irish trader, James O'Hara, learned of a party of fifteen Shawnees, an Ohio Iroquois, and a couple of Wyandots who were "ready to go to war." Another group of warriors consisted of "24 Warriors," including Ohio Iroquois, and "some Wyondots & Mohickons." Wyandots, Ottawas, and Ohio Iroquois were blamed for an attack at the mouth of Wheeling Creek in fall 1776. The next year a war party gathering before an assault on Fort Henry (Wheeling) was said to include Ottawas, Ojibwas, Wyandots, Ohio Iroquois "of all sorts," Shawnees, "Woaponos," and Potawatomis. A variety of warriors gathered around Pluggy's Town (present-day Delaware, Ohio) on the Olentangy, a branch of the Scioto. Virginians complained that "Repeated hostilities" were "Commited" by these Indians. The son of the town's namesake, Pluggy, captained a party of "Wapanaws, Mohickons, and Munsies" ready to attack Turtle Creek in 1777.[34]

Like the warriors commanded by Pluggy's son, at least a few Delawares broke with the noncombatants and took part in fighting by 1777. The Delaware "Wiondoughwalind with his Men" participated in an attack on Wheeling. Wiondoughwalind was probably the "Windaughalah" who had once lived near the Shawnees at "a small Delaware Town of about twenty Families" on the southeast bank of the Scioto River, about ten miles above the mouth. In 1751 his settlement was referred to as the "last Town of the Delawares to the Westward." This Delaware leader may have lived as early as 1739 on the south side of the Ohio River (present-day West Virginia bordering Meigs County, Ohio) on the Great Bend. A long residence in the Ohio Country would have given Wiondoughwalind many opportunities to build connections with Shawnees, Ohio Iroquois, Wyandots, and other peoples who later attacked Fort Henry. Some of the earliest Revolutionary-era militants among the Delawares apparently came from the Walhonding and Cuyahoga areas. Previously constructed relationships between Munsees and Ohio Iroquois—some perhaps through intermarriage—probably played a role in influencing Munsees to join Ohio Iroquois war parties. In March at a town "on the Walhonding," an Ohio Iroquois "was discovered" making some inroads enlisting Munsees as warriors. A few months later a small party of warriors, consisting of six Ohio Iroquois and "1 Minisink," appeared at Gnadenhütten.[35]

Yet many—probably most—Delawares remained out of the fighting throughout 1777 and into the next year. George Morgan, Congress-appointed Indian agent for the Middle Department, learned from Pipe in April 1777 that the Munsees "intend to collect themselves at Shaningas" [probably Shenango, near present-day Sharon, Pennsylvania] "to be out of the way of the bad people—That they . . . will contribute all in their power to preserve Peace and Friendship with the United States." A little more than three months later, it was said that "the [Delaware] chiefs and captains . . . were altogether agreed not to receive the war belt," when the Wyandots tried to compel them to accept it. The next day the Delawares gathered their people at their town of Coshocton in the Muskingum Valley and "ordered that no one let himself be seduced and that they take no part in the war, which they also all promised to do."[36]

These promises would not have represented the views of all Delawares, some of whom joined war parties; however, leaders such as Pipe, White Eyes, Welapachtschiechen, Gelelemend, and Glikhikan, with the Delawares around Coshocton, continued to avoid a military response. They probably hoped that their previous work in building alliances would help them sway others to their position. Wyandots reportedly had concerns that "so many nations stood in alliance" with the Delawares. Respect for the Delawares as "grandfathers" was said to restrain pro-British Indians from attacking them. Zeisberger received a report in September 1777 that Miamis, Weas, and Kickapoos had "all agreed not to take the Tomhawk but to follow the Example of their Grandfather the Delawares." As late as 1780 Col. Daniel Brodhead of the Continental army believed that the Delawares had "influence . . . over near twenty different Nations."[37]

Just as they had done during Dunmore's War, Delawares tried to use their influence to stop Indian neighbors from going to war. Invoking memories of "ancient Friendship," delegates, apparently from Coshocton and/or the Moravian towns, "were sent to Pluggys Town & Sandusky" to urge peace. In November 1777, Pipe, who was apparently living at Cuyahoga, convinced "the greater part" of a war party including Delawares to halt their advance against Ligonier on the Loyalhanna Creek. White Eyes met with "the Head Chief of the Chipaways" and with Wyandots, pressing them to "take hold of our chain of Friendship." And he received assurances from the Shawnees that they would "join their Grandfather" in attending a treaty at Fort Pitt. This "chain of Friendship" was one linking Delawares with the United States. Although advocating peace, Delawares did not necessarily remain politically neutral.[38]

Yet the United States continued to prove itself a questionable ally, and Delawares friendly toward the U.S. had an increasingly difficult time finding supporters among their people. Their approach was severely tested in February 1778, when General Hand gathered four or five hundred Westmoreland County militia, who attacked Munsees in the Beaver River Valley. Hand's original plan was to strike a supply center at Cuyahoga; however, high waters blocked access to this region. Expecting to find a sizable warriors' camp up the Beaver, Hand made alternate plans to travel along the river and attack there. Upon reaching the forks of the Shenango River and the Neshannock Creek (present-day Newcastle, Pennsylvania), Hand discovered "only one Man with some Women & Children." The small Indian community, which lay along the east side of the Shenango, included family members of Pipe—his mother, his brother, and this brother's wife and children. The soldiers were "Impetuous" and primed to kill. While defending his family, Pipe's brother was shot and tomahawked in the head. An old man was wounded in the leg, then tomahawked, and finally shot dead. Hand's men next proceeded up the Mahoning to Salt Lick, where they killed three Indian women and "a small Indian boy out with a gun shooting birds."[39]

Surprisingly, Pipe asserted his readiness to remain a noncombatant after these events. Morgan was pleased "to hear that Capt. Pipe" was among the Delawares who had determined "to remain our Friends." Despite the violence in the Beaver River Valley, Delaware leaders at Coshocton retained some influence in preventing retaliation against the United States. When "twenty eight Munsy warriors," arrived there in June, "the Chiefs stopped . . . the greater part" from going "to war."[40]

Although it marked an alliance between the United States and the

Delawares, the Pittsburgh Treaty of 1778 ultimately struck a serious blow at that alliance. Gelelemend and Welapachtschiechen signed a complaint, stating that "some of their Chiefs" had been "induced" by Gen. Lachlan McIntosh and congressional commissioners "to sign certain Writings, which to them were perfectly unintelligible which they have since found were falsely interpreted to them & contain'd Declarations and Engagements they never intended to make or enter into." They objected to a treaty provision that indicated the Delawares agreed "to join the troops of the United States . . . with such a number of their best and most expert warriors as they can spare." "The Delaware Nation," they declared, "have ever been, dureing the present War betwen Brittain and the United States, & still are of opinion, that it is their Interest & the Interest of the United States that the said Nation should observe the strictest Neutrality." Delawares must have found it difficult to square this provision with the role they had been constructing for themselves as alliance builders and peacemakers. Several months after the treaty, "a rumor . . . that the Delawares would be obliged to fight aginst those Nations which with they were connected" led to "much disturbance." The "Tomahawk and Belt" given us by the United States, they said, "have created great confusion among Us." George Morgan, who believed that the U.S. negotiators had dealt unfairly with the Delawares, wrote, "There never was a Conference with the Indians so improperly or villainously conducted." Gelelemend stated, "I have now looked over the Articles of the Treaty again & find that they are wrote down false."[41]

Delawares became increasingly divided about how to respond to the shift in U.S. policy. Supporters of the United States could no longer argue, as White Eyes once had, that the United States "had never as yet, called on" the Delawares "to fight the English, knowing that wars were destructive to nations." Not only did the treaty provide for the Delawares' entry into the war, but it also called for U.S. intervention in Indian country and the establishment of a fort, later known as Fort Laurens. Word that the army was coming created turmoil. "The confusion among the Indians cannot be described," Zeisberger wrote. Past experience would have taught Delawares that they could not be certain Euro-Americans would distinguish between neutral and combatant Indians. The U.S. general Lachlan McIntosh showed no signs of compromise as worried Delawares faced the prospect of invasion. When Munsees, through Pipe's intervention, sought pardon and a peace agreement, they "received no favorable answer from the General." Soon thereafter, in fall 1778, Pipe and Wingenund "with most of the Indians" on the Walhonding were said to have "crossed over" to the British, although in 1780 there seemed to be a brief improvement in Pipe's relationship with the revolutionaries. Gelelemend, who continued to side with the United States, lost the support of many of his councilors, except Welapachtschiechen and several others.[42]

Even those Delawares still allied with the United States found the revolutionaries poor trading partners. The articles from the Treaty of 1778 had mentioned a "well-regulated trade"; however, such did not develop. Delawares complained that Congress had agreed "to supply" them with "Cloathing and other Goods" "in exchange for their Peltries" but instead had left them "poor & naked." Pennsylvania was unable "to furnish" even "a few Indian goods." "They are not to be procured," a state official explained, adding that "the People in the Back Counties" were unlikely to allow delivery of supplies anyway, "so violent are the Prejudices against the Indians." The small, badly provisioned Fort Laurens on the Tuscarawas offered little opportunity for trade. At a particularly low point, the fort's soldiers were themselves forced to subsist on "Herbs Salt & Cowhides." Finding better trading opportunities elsewhere, Pipe declared, "Was it not for the English, we would have to suffer, and perhaps many of us perish for want."[43]

Nevertheless, the fate of Gelelemend and his remaining supporters became increasingly intertwined with that of the United States. These Delawares "sent down three Children of their principal Chiefs to be placed at School by Congress." Two were relatives of Gelelemend—his son John Killbuck (age sixteen) and his half brother Thomas (age eighteen). George, just eight years old, son of the now deceased White Eyes, was also included. These boys lived in George Morgan's home in Princeton, New Jersey. Delawares portrayed sending their youth as a sign of alliance, of forming "one Peopl[e] with our Brethren of the United States." Eventually Delawares provided military support as well. "A young Delaware Chief named Nanowland (or George Wilson)" joined a party of revolutionaries to fight "some warriors led by a Muncy Capt., who was killed." Despite initial opposition to requests for military aid, Gelelemend "used strong expressions" in an August 1779 speech to other Delawares "to convince" them "to go with Col. Br[odhead] against the enemy Indians." In 1780 Welapachtschiechen sent several "Young Men" to assist the army and promised more would follow.[44]

Delawares' relationship with the United States deteriorated, however. A shortage of goods for Native allies continued to hurt relations. Trust between Delawares and U.S. military personnel waned. In late 1780, Brodhead complained that about "forty men from the neighbourhood" around

Hannastown (between Pittsburgh and Ligonier) had "attempted to destroy" Delawares who had agreed to assist the United States Army. Brodhead showed a lack of faith in his allies. "I conceive that much confidence ought never to be placed in any of the [Indians'] colour," he wrote. The United States could barely hold onto its remaining Indian supporters. In February 1781, Gelelemend, now increasingly isolated from other Delawares, wrote to Brodhead from one of the Moravian towns, "Every body here now knows, that the Coochockung [Coshocton] Men are getting ready to fight you." Three men from Coshocton, "near relations" to a Delaware named William Penn, and another man, "a Friend to White Eyes Cousin," had "already" gone "towards Wheeling." Believing the Coshocton Delawares, "very few excepte'd, have declare'd in favor of the British," Brodhead launched an expedition. On the evening of April 19, his forces destroyed Coshocton as well as Lichtenau, which was now inhabited by non-Moravian Indians. Brodhead reported that "about three hundred men, (nearly half the number Volunteers from the Country,) . . . killed fifteen warriors and took upwards of twenty old men, women & children." These warriors were not killed in battle; instead, the soldiers scalped and executed them after capture.[45]

By now, those Delawares who had decided to support the British probably saw the Moravian Indians and missionaries as one of the main reasons their nation remained divided. Pipe and Wingenund had moved to the Sandusky area, as had other Delawares. Pro-British Indians sought to convince the Christian Indians to join them in the west. The Delaware war leader Buckangehela ("Pachgantschihilas"), with eighty men, arrived at Gnadenhütten and urged the Moravian group to unite with them. "I myself come to bid you rise and go with me to a secure place!" he said. That place seems to have been on the Maumee River, "where," Buckangehela promised, "your fields shall yield you abundant crops; and where your cattle shall find sufficient pasture; where there is plenty of game; where your women and children, together with yourselves, will live in peace and safety." The Moravian Indians included those Delawares especially resisting war with the United States. Most declined Buckangehela's invitation, no doubt increasing British-allied Indians' resentment at the influence—or control as they saw it—of the missionaries ("teachers") over Christian converts. Buckangehela commented that "he had often heard it said that the believing Indians were slaves to their teachers, and what these commanded them to do, they *must* do, however disagreeable to them!" Wyandots who had failed to gain full Delaware support in the war effort "ascribed" this resistance "to the influence the missionaries had in the council of the nations."[46]

These frustrations came to a head in August 1781, when a large war party entered the mission town of Salem, which ironically had been constructed the previous year to be farther away from gatherings of militants. Soon there were "about 300 warriors" there and at nearby Gnadenhütten. They included Wyandots led by Pomoacan (called the Half King), Delawares under Pipe, Shawnees, Ojibwas, Ottawas, and the British captain Matthew Elliot. Like Buckangehela, Pomoacan pressed the Moravian Indians to relocate—in this case near the Wyandots who lived at Sandusky. Pomoacan warned that the "long knives (Virginians) would certainly one day fall upon and kill" them, if they were not first attacked by Ottawas and Ojibwas. Nor, he said, would "the Six Nations . . . suffer" them to remain. The Moravian "Indians were not of one mind" about what to do, but there was significant reluctance to move. In response, the war party forced the residents of the three Moravian towns on the Tuscarawas—Gnadenhütten, Salem, and New Schönbrunn—to leave their homes and travel to Upper Sandusky.[47]

Soon after the Moravian party arrived at Upper Sandusky, Maj. Arent Schuyler de Peyster, the British commandant at Detroit, called for the missionaries to come in for questioning. Not only were Zeisberger and his associates viewed as an obstacle to Christian Indians uniting with British-allied Indians, but they were also suspected of assisting the United States. At a council meeting where the missionaries appeared, Captain Pipe presented them to the commandant, who he said had "ordered" the warriors "to bring the believing Indians with their teachers from the Muskingum." De Peyster explained these orders: "he had heard complaints" about the missionaries, "especially that" they "had corresponded with the rebels and from time to time given them news when the warriors wished to make attacks on their settlements, whereby many warriors came to harm, that many lost their lives." Furthermore, "the warriors had always said they could have done more" if the missionaries had been out of the way.[48]

The loss of their homes just as their crops were ripening and winter was approaching left the Christian Indians in a terrible state. According to the Moravian John Schebosch, by mid-October "the most Part of our People had eat up all their Provision they took with them. . . . [I]n all the Parts ware we are there [is] nothing to be had." To sustain themselves, the Indians returned to their abandoned fields and towns to search for food. "We [have] nothing to eat but what [we] fetch from our old townds," Schebosch wrote. While the former residents of the Moravian towns sifted through the remains of their fields in search of sustenance for themselves and their families, Pennsylvania militia were on the move. In February 1782, the militia, numbering 160 men, left the Monongahela "in order to destroy the towns on the Muskingum because they imagined, and perhaps had not been instructed otherwise, that the Indian attacks on the settlements had primarily been executed from there." The expedition's organizers assumed that the Moravian Indians had "now all gone over to the English side."[49]

Reaching Gnadenhütten on March 7, the militia imprisoned the Indian men in one house and the women in another. Next the militia "gave them to understand that they must bring them as Prisoners to Fort Pitt. . . . They were ordered to prepare themselves for the Journey and to take all their Effects along with them. Accordingly they did so." But the plan to transport the prisoners to Fort Pitt was not yet settled: "In the Evening the Militia held a Council, when the Commander of the Militia told his men that he would leave it to their choice, either to carry the Indians as Prisoners to Fort Pitt, or to kill them; when they agreed they should be killed." The militia leader Col. David Williamson gave a chilling portrayal of how his men reached this decision. Questioned later about why the militia decided to kill the Moravian Indians, he stated "they died according to God's will." "After holding them as prisoners for three days," he explained, his men "drew lots three times" to decide "whether they should kill them." Two of the lots cast indicated that the prisoners be exterminated; hence "God's will" was discerned, he claimed. Williamson may have known that Moravians drew lots to obtain divine guidance; if so, then he applied this knowledge in a cruelly ironic way.[50]

Knowing they were about to die, the Indians requested time to pray, and "hereupon the women met together and sung Hymns & Psalms all Night, and so did likewise the Men and kept on singing as long as there were three alive." One soldier taunted an Indian by pretending to offer him his hatchet with the words, "Strike me dead!" When the man answered, "I strike no one dead!" the soldier swung at the Indian and "chopped his arm away." All the while, the Indian kept singing "until another blow split his head." According to another report, "The Militia chose Two houses, which they called the Slaughter Houses, and then fetch'd the Indians two or three at a time with Ropes about their Necks and dragged them into the Slaughter Houses where they knocked them down." A boy who escaped by crawling under the floor of one building said, "the blood flowed in the house like a river." The militia slaughtered Indians not only from Gnadenhütten but also from Salem. Some, though not all, Indians from New

Schönbrunn recognized the danger and escaped to Sandusky. Reported death tolls varied, but it is certain that the dead numbered at least ninety, including about thirty-five children as well as some older youths.[51]

A large number of the massacred were Delawares, including two major leaders, Welapachtschiechen and Glikhikan. Also among the dead were Netanewand (or Johannes) and his son Joseph, a grandson and great-grandson of Netawatwees. Some victims were individuals from the Harris-Evans family, formerly from the New Jersey-Lehigh Valley area. Related to this line were the three sisters Anna Benigna, Lucia, and Rebecca—probably daughters of Teedyuscung. A couple of the older converts, both baptized in 1749, had roots in the Connecticut Wompanosch population. Phillipus was born at Potatik, Connecticut, in 1739 to a Wompanosch father and Esopus mother. Christina was a widow, about age fifty-four, whose birthplace was near New Milford, Connecticut. Her father had been the sachem Mauweehu, an important figure in Moravian missions in western Connecticut.[52]

Before the massacre, there had been three to four hundred mission Indians at Upper Sandusky. With a large group of them now dead, the remaining ones struggled to survive. In doing so, they utilized the familiar practice of turning to Indian neighbors, who shared territories with them. About half of the Moravian Indians moved to the Shawnees, who were at that time gathered around the upper Great Miami and a tributary, the Mad River. Despite their past differences with Captain Pipe's group, some Moravian Indians went "into the neighborhood of Pipe's town" around Upper Sandusky. This move occurred at about the time that Pipe and his associates revenged the Gnadenhütten slaughter by capturing, torturing, and killing the U.S. colonel William Crawford. Some of the Moravian Indians planned a move to the Miamis, probably in the vicinity of the Maumee River. The Mahican Mark said that the Miamis "had given him a district to live on," and he hoped the "scattered Indian brethren would then move there." By 1784 Mark and his group, including a former Coshocton resident named Masktschilitis, were living in the future Fort Wayne area. Some Moravian Indians headed with the missionaries to a spot on the Clinton River above Detroit, where they received help from, and traded with, neighboring Ojibwas.[53]

The Clinton River group faced extreme food shortages in unfamiliar surroundings. At first they had trouble with their corn crop because of the short growing season. Yet they found ways to cope. They improved their chances at hunting by using snowshoes during the extremely snowy winter of 1783–84. At the end of that long hard season, they found wild potatoes along Lake St. Clair. In June they gathered wild cherries, and in August whortleberries. Ojibwas taught them where they should "block up the creek" so that "fish, which are very large, could not get back into the lake, and in this way, all summer long, they could have fish enough."[54] They hired themselves out to harvest crops for nearby Euro-Americans. In addition, they sold hand-made items—baskets, brooms, and canoes.[55] In short, Indians adapted in some ways that would have been familiar to their predecessors in the Delaware and Hudson valleys.

Delawares who had been gathering in the Ohio Country struggled to find unity. For a long time they had approached survival by forming alliances. Attempting to work together, Delawares associated alliances and unity with power. Unity did not mean the erasure of differences. It meant forming a complex coalition of groups. Tending to relations among various components of this Delaware coalition was an ongoing process, and mediation skills were vital to this work. The decade between Pontiac's War and the American Revolution were crucial years for the Delawares. During this time they constructed meanings about who they were as a people, and they sought to take the lead in forging alliances; however, their efforts received a serious blow after war broke out between Britain and the colonies.

The Revolutionary War ended, but the Delawares' struggles did not. In the postwar period survivors drew upon their long experience in dealing with hard times. Through the years, Delawares had gained a great deal of knowledge, out of necessity, about the process of moving to new places and relating to new neighbors. They brought along versatility in their approaches to land and its resources, as the Clinton River inhabitants demonstrated. They continued to adjust their economic practices to new circumstances. They organized communities and reorganized social relations. In addition, Delawares continued to consider how they might draw their people together and continued to approach alliances as a source of power.

Epilogue
"Sit down by us as a nation"

Colonial records are replete with language used to describe the process of forming alliances. Chains, linked arms, roads and paths between peoples, "one heart," "one mind," "one body," and people eating out of "one dish" with "one spoon" were all invocations of alliance. The sheer number of expressions indicates the importance of this process among a variety of Indians, not just Delawares. The phrase to "sit down" connoted alliance building as well as peacemaking in general. It also implied the act of sharing physical space, as in the place where meetings were held and peoples sat down together. Indian allies frequently moved onto each other's territories. Native peoples came to learn, however, that sitting down with Euro-Americans at a treaty was unlikely to result in any long-term option of sharing territories with them.[1]

The history of the peoples who came to be known as Delawares reveals the profound implications of land sharing among Indians. The mixing and merging of peoples were tools for surviving the rigors of life in the Hudson and Delaware valleys. Deeply rooted approaches toward land encouraged overlapping land usages that smoothed the way for Indians to move into neighboring Indians' home areas. Flexibility in forming alliances combined with a deep-seated commitment to small groups with localized orientations. Amid massive change, these approaches were used again and again in new places where Delawares reconstructed their lives from the seventeenth into the eighteenth century.

Even before the outbreak of the bloody Seven Years' War, relations between Delawares and Euro-Americans were far from easy. Pennsylvania was founded against the backdrop of a recent epidemic among Indians of the Delaware Valley. Evidence suggests that at least some Indians may have held Euro-Americans responsible for the illness, perhaps associating it with a supernatural power among the Christians turned against them. Although

Indians set up "one heart" connections with William Penn that promised amicable land arrangements between neighbors, in the following decades Native peoples complained of trade abuses and blamed Euro-Americans for the damage done by alcohol sales. During the volatile 1720s Delawares on the Schuylkill and the Brandywine protested dispossession, as did Delawares in the Forks during the 1730s and 1740s.

Nevertheless, here and there Delawares worked out friendships with Euro-American neighbors. Among these friendships, some Delawares placed special significance on those they formed with Quakers and Moravians. Delaware leaders around the middle of the eighteenth century were in the process of defining who they were as a people, and these friendships played a role in that formulation. After participating in the violence of the Seven Years' War, Delawares began to pull back from it and tried to place themselves at the head of mediation efforts to reestablish peace. As they did so, they drew upon long experience in shaping and being shaped by alliances. Relationships created with pacifist Quakers and Moravians helped Delawares highlight their peacemaking mission. Furthermore, the story of their dealings with William Penn became especially important in building a case for the Delawares' role as alliance leaders.

Delawares' definition of themselves as a people able to marshal the power of many nations developed vis-à-vis conflicting claims of the Six Nations to authority over lands where Delawares lived. This conflict and the problem of encroaching Euro-American settlement sharpened Delawares' definition of themselves, stimulating them to clarify, with the help of oral tradition, their claims to lands in Ohio. Delawares also sought to gather other Delawares in Ohio and to resolve disagreements among themselves as they tried to handle negotiations and secure the Ohio Country for its Indian residents. Delawares disagreed about whether accommodation with Euro-Americans was wise, with some rejecting the viewpoints of individuals such as Tamaqua and White Eyes. Nevertheless, attachment to the goal of leading in the formation of alliances with other Indians cut across these differences. By the time the Revolutionary War broke out, the Delawares had gone a long way toward defining themselves as authorities in forming alliances.

The dramatic changes did not stop after the war. Delawares faced multiple instances of Euro-American encroachment. They passed through epidemics and famine. Frontier fighting scarcely ceased with the war's official end—the Treaty of Paris in 1783. But there were certain continuities in Delawares' approaches to these problems. Delawares remained committed to alliance building and forging networks across communities, some of which were spread over great distances. Although widely dispersed after the American Revolution, Delawares also returned, at times, to the notion of consolidating their people in a particular region. Building and maintaining connections with non-Delaware Indians remained an important tool for survival, especially as different groups shared territories far from their earlier homelands.

After the war, the area around Gigeyunk (or Kekionga), where the Maumee River forms at the intersection of the St. Marys and St. Joseph rivers, was a focal point of Delaware settlement. Not only was this a site of Delawares coming together, but it also was a site of Delawares sharing space with other Indians. In 1785 Delawares were moving "in large numbers" up the Maumee. One Delaware town lay on the east side of the St. Joseph, and two others were established on the St. Marys. Among the leading Delawares on the Maumee were Buckangehela, who had urged the Moravian Indians to move there in 1781, and Welandawecken, who had become head of the Turkey phratry. Besides the Mahican Mark, who had been gathering former residents of the Moravian mission after the war, Shawnees were also relocating to this region. Delawares who arrived in this area would have relied on Miamis already settled there to share their territory with them. One report said that Miamis as well as Ottawas had "given the Delawares land from the Miami [Maumee] to the Wabash, so that now again they have their own land to live on."[2]

Delawares did not all head for the Maumee Valley after the war. Some continued to live close to Wyandots on the Sandusky. Among these were Captain Pipe and a Munsee captain named Titawachkam. Moravian Indians left the Clinton River in 1786 but did not join those who had earlier separated from the mission and gone to Gigeyunk. Considering the possibility of eventually returning to the Muskingum, Moravian Indians moved to the south side of Lake Erie, settling first on the Cuyahoga and a year later on the Pettquotting (or Huron) River near present Milan, Ohio.[3]

Disease and famine wracked the Delawares and their neighbors during this period. In fall 1786 Indians were struck by "a severe fever," and it was reported that "sicknesses" were "prevalent everywhere among the Indians," including an illness that caused "swollen necks." Over the next two years Indians at Sandusky suffered outbreaks of smallpox. The Wyandots at Lower Sandusky were hit especially hard, with only "fifteen men" left alive after the contagion spread in spring 1788. Later that year practically a "whole town" at

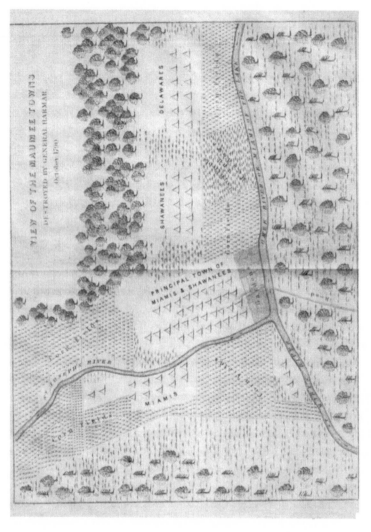

Figure 9. Gigeyunk (or Kekionga), in the Maumee Valley, where Delawares and other Indian peoples gathered after the Revolutionary War. *Military Journal of Major Ebenezer Denny, an Officer in the Revolutionary and Indian Wars* (Philadelphia: HSP, 1859). Courtesy of Archives and Special Collections, Dickinson College, Carlisle, Pennsylvania.

Sandusky was reported to have "died out," with "only two families" remaining. The survivors "burnt the old town" and "built on another site." Not only Wyandots but also Munsees contracted smallpox. On the Pettquotting in 1787, Zeisberger wrote of an outbreak of "yellow fever, which attacks the head," so that "they who have it lie for many days speechless." Indians in the region were probably more prone to disease because of nutritional deficits. Among residents of the Maumee Valley, there was a "very great famine" in spring 1787, with "no corn nor means of living to be had" so "that the children waste away from hunger." The same area saw famine the following year, as did Sandusky. Hopes for a successful harvest were dashed at Sandusky in 1789, when "hard night-frosts" in September left "the tender corn . . . injured." By October, "most people" there had "no harvest."[4]

These conditions undoubtedly aroused great anxiety. A further source of Indians' worries came from the United States' efforts to push its borders north of the Ohio River. At the Fort Stanwix Treaty of 1784, pressure was put on the Iroquois to relinquish their claims to lands west of Pennsylvania. The next year at the Treaty of Fort McIntosh, a substantial portion of what would later be the state of Ohio was declared within U.S. jurisdiction. Delawares, Wyandots, Ojibwas, and Ottawas signed this agreement. Verbalized by U.S. commissioners but left out of the treaty document itself was a version of the familiar promise to reserve Native hunting rights within the cession, at least temporarily. Under duress, Shawnees the following year signed a treaty that enlarged the U.S. claim to land south and west of the Fort McIntosh boundary. There was widespread Native opposition to the outcomes of these treaties. Indians generally preferred retaining the 1768 Fort Stanwix boundary line along the Ohio River. When land surveyors appeared in the aftermath of the Fort McIntosh Treaty, it was said that their actions "had the effect to unite the Indians, and induce them to make a common cause" against U.S. encroachment.[5]

Native warriors launched numerous small-scale raids. "The murders that have been committed lately upon the inhabitants passing up and down the Ohio," a U.S. military officer stated, "indicate great dissatisfaction prevailing amongst the Indians." What these Indians saw with disgust was a flood of Euro-Americans entering the region. Already by 1785, one report stated there were "upwards of three hundred [Euro-American] families" settled at the Hocking River's falls, and "at the Muskingum a number equal." "More than fifteen hundred" had come to live in the Scioto and the Miami river valleys. Killings of Euro-Americans on the Hocking were blamed on a party of

Delawares and Wyandots. Shawnees captured and tortured to death Charles Builder, who had captained militia involved in the 1782 massacre of Moravian Indians. Violence also erupted between Kentuckians and Indians living on the Wabash and Mad rivers.[6]

Indian opponents of the United States formed a confederacy, though their task was difficult given the many communities, ethnicities, and political loyalties among them. Indians under the Miami Little Turtle and the Shawnee Blue Jacket gained a range of allies, including Delawares, to defeat U.S. forces led by Gen. Josiah Harmar in 1790 and Gen. Arthur St. Clair in 1791. Nevertheless, Harmar's army succeeded in burning down many of the Indians' homes at Gigeyunk and destroying a huge amount of harvested corn there. Seeking a safer location, Indians began to congregate by 1792 in another area—farther down the Maumee at its intersection with the Auglaize River (present-day Defiance, Ohio).[7]

The Delaware Big Cat, called a "Wenaumie" [Unami] sachem, and Buckangehela resided at this place, called the Glaize, as did the Mahican sachem Pohquonnoppeet. Also living there were Shawnees, Miamis, Conoys, Nanticokes, Ohio Iroquois, Cherokees, Creeks, and Euro-American traders and captives. The sheer complexity of the population gathered at the Glaize hints at the continuation of the approach to survival among Delawares and their neighbors of seeking alliances and sharing territory with various groups.[8] Life at the Glaize was soon disrupted, however. A failure to gain British support seriously undermined the Indian confederacy, which had become increasingly divided. In summer 1794 Maj. Gen. Anthony Wayne, with a force of 3,500, established Fort Defiance at the Glaize. On August 20 at a spot between the Glaize and the mouth of the Maumee, Wayne's army defeated the Indian confederacy in the Battle of Fallen Timbers. At the Greenville Treaty the following year, Wyandots, Delawares, Shawnees, Ottawas, Ojibwas, Potawatomis, Miamis, and Indians from several Wabash-area groups signed a document that declared approximately the southern two-thirds of Ohio within U.S. possession, as well as certain tracts beyond this line, including Fort Miamis near the mouth of the Maumee, Fort Defiance, Fort Wayne, and Detroit. Following the wartime destruction on the Maumee, many Delawares relocated to the White River, a tributary of the Wabash.[9]

Delaware communities were strung out along the White River (including its West Fork) in the area of the present-day Indiana counties of Delaware, Madison, Hamilton, and northern Marion. Among the Delaware leaders on the White River were Tetepachsit, Buckangehela, Kikthawenund (or William Anderson), and Hockingpomska. The first three of these had signed the Greenville Treaty, with Tetepachsit (or Tetabokshke) labeled the "Grand Glaize King" at the time. In 1799, Hockingpomska (or Hakinkpomsga) was referred to as "the successor of Pipe." A small Moravian mission was located near Kikthawenund's town (vicinity of present-day Anderson) between 1801 and 1806. Echoing an earlier policy in Ohio, Delawares encouraged relocations to the White River, saying that the Miamis had "given us this entire river . . . on both sides of which we have enough land to keep us here together."[10]

Some Delawares moved back to Ohio after the Greenville Treaty as the violence subsided. In 1798, Moravian Indians, including the former Coshocton leader Gelelemend (now baptized and renamed William Henry), returned to the vicinity of their former towns on the Tuscarawas, establishing a new community called Goshen (in the area of New Philadelphia, Ohio). In 1807, the United States reserved two other places in Ohio for Delawares, one near the Jerome Fork of the Mohican River and another at Greentown, approximately a dozen miles from Mansfield. Greentown was described as "a village consisting of some 60 cabins, with a council-house about 60 feet long, 25 wide, one story in height, and built of posts and clapboarded." Its population numbered "several hundred" before the War of 1812. After the Greenville Treaty some Delawares continued to live near Wyandots in the Sandusky area. Having passed through epidemics, famine, and war, Delawares and Wyandots had come to depend on each other. In 1799 it was reported that these two groups at Sandusky "had agreed to consider themselves henceforward as one nation, and that their chiefs should accordingly sit together in council."[11]

Various land cessions had diminished the holdings of Delawares and other Indians in the Midwest by the early nineteenth century. The Shawnee Tecumseh gathered an intertribal alliance to try to stop cessions and to end Euro-American encroachment. As fighting between the United States and Indians merged with the British-American War of 1812, Delawares in Ohio faced increasing hostility from whites, who imprisoned the Jerometown Indians and took the Greentown Indians under guard into Mansfield. One Indian was shot while trying to escape, and Greentown Indians later returned to kill Euro-Americans on the Mohican River. The dwindling Goshen population also faced intimidation from whites, who called for the destruction of the mission. New Philadelphia residents—"above 20 men, all armed with rifles, swords or pistols"—threatened Goshen. Euro-Americans "declared that if they saw a strange Indian" at the mission, "they would shoot him, & shoot any Indian who would take their part." In 1813, when Col. John B. Campbell led a force against the Miamis, Munsees living near them on the Mississinewa River moved to Piqua, Ohio, where Delawares had been congregating and receiving supplies from U.S. Indian agent John Johnston. William Henry Harrison's invasion of Canada that same year threatened Moravian Indians, who had left Pettquotting in 1791, briefly settling on the Detroit River and then moving the following year to the Thames River in Canada. On October 5, 1813, the Battle of the Thames occurred west of the Moravian mission town of Fairfield, at which time the British were defeated, Tecumseh was killed, and Fairfield was plundered and burned by the U.S. forces under Harrison.[12]

After the war the U.S. government turned to a plan of removing Delawares across the Mississippi, a policy increasingly applied to other eastern Indians as well. In the 1818 Treaty of St. Marys, Delawares ceded "all their claim to land in the state of Indiana." In return, the United States promised "to provide for the Delawares a country to reside in, upon the west side of the Mississippi, and to guaranty to them the peaceable possession of the same." Delawares from the White River of Indiana relocated to the James Fork of the White River in southeastern Missouri. They were joined by fifty-eight Delawares from Sandusky. Some Delawares were already living west of the Mississippi by this time, having moved there while the region was under Spanish governance. In 1793 the Spanish had offered Delawares land in the Cape Girardeau area along the Mississippi. Because of increasing Euro-American settlement around Cape Girardeau, Delawares in this region relocated to present-day Pope County, Arkansas, and to Texas in 1807–15.[13]

Meanwhile, developments in the east indicated how Delawares, though widely dispersed, maintained connections across long distances and forged alliances with new neighbors. At the turn of the nineteenth century some Delawares were still living at the Brotherton reservation in New Jersey under difficult economic conditions. By 1801 a majority of the Brothertons had decided to sell their land and relocate. Their move and resettlement involved relationships with multiple groups outside of New Jersey. One group consisted of Indians who had relocated from the Christian mission town of Stockbridge, Massachusetts, in the mid-1780s and who invited the Brothertons to join them in their new home southwest of Oneida Lake in Iroquoia. These former Massachusetts residents had a town called New Stockbridge. Another group was the Oneidas themselves, who shared their territory with the immigrants. Yet another group, called Brothertowns, after the name they gave their community near New Stockbridge, was composed of Algonquians from Long Island and southern New England, who had earlier gained permission from the Oneidas to settle in the area. Delawares from New Jersey became neighbors of peoples from all three of these groups.[14]

Indians in Oneida territory had connections with Delawares living on the White River in Indiana as well. The relationship between Mahicans and Delawares had long been close, and Stockbridge Indians included not only Mahicans but also Munsees. As Euro-American settlement impinged on them, some Stockbridge-Munsees supported moving to the White River. For their part, Delawares in the west encouraged the migration. "When we rise in the morning," White River residents wrote to their friends in Oneida country, "we have our eyes fixed toward the way you are to come, in expectation of seeing you coming to sit down by us as a nation." By the time a party from New Stockbridge arrived in Indiana, however, the 1818 Treaty of St. Marys had already been held, and "the lands had all been sold." Nevertheless, some of the New Stockbridge group remained in the Midwest, and in spring 1819 they were in the area of Piqua, Ohio.[15]

Finding a long-term place in Ohio and Indiana was unlikely, and residents of New Stockbridge and Brothertown soon redirected their attention to lands near Green Bay in Michigan Territory (future Wisconsin). At the same time, land speculators were pressing for the removal of New York's Indian neighbors and seeking help from the federal government for this purpose. There was strong opposition to removal among the Six Nations, but Indians at New Stockbridge and Brothertown decided to relocate to lands on the Fox River in the early 1820s, and a portion of the Oneidas also moved to Michigan Territory. In addition, Stockbridge-Munsees who had been in Ohio and Indiana relocated to the Fox River in 1822 or 1823. These migrations involved working out relations with Menominees and Winnebagos, who sold land to the newcomers. They also involved formalizing an alliance between Stockbridge-Munsees and Delawares formerly from New Jersey. Articles of agreement signed at Vernon, New York, in 1823 indicated that the Brothertons from New Jersey were "to be considered as a component part of the Muhheconnuck or Stockbridge nation" with "an equal right title interest claim" to lands obtained from the Menominees and Winnebagos. Furthermore, these articles indicated that there were still some "scattered brethren in the state of New Jersey," who were also entitled to these rights.[16]

Menominee and Winnebago criticism of treaties with the Indians from Oneida territory as well as Euro-American pressures in the Fox River area led to another removal of the Stockbridge-Brothertown group, this time to the east side of Lake Winnebago around 1834. After the War of 1812, the Moravian Indian community (New Fairfield or Moraviantown) had been reestablished on the Thames, about forty miles from a Munsee community (Muncey Town). In 1837, some Delawares from the Thames relocated to the Stockbridge-Munsee community. Stockbridge-Munsees were divided into different factions by the 1840s, with one party urging the acceptance of U.S. citizenship and individual land holding and another party supporting the continuation of communal lands and government annuity payments. The federal government obtained a cession of the Stockbridge-Munsee lands east of Lake Winnebago and moved toward allotment, issuing patents to some Indians. For those who did not accept allotments, communal land holding continued at a reservation in Shawano County, Wisconsin, established in 1856.[17]

While Stockbridge-Munsees had lived along the Fox, they had received additional Munsee immigrants, possibly some who had lived at Cattaraugus in Seneca country. Certain Cattaraugus Delawares had earlier moved to Canada close to the mouth of the Grand River at present-day Dunnville. Eventually they relocated upriver to a portion of the Six Nations Reserve (Hagersville area), where they lived in close association with Cayugas. Delawares in this region claimed descent from Teedyuscung as well as from the Montour family. Their population also included Mahicans and apparently Munsees from Esopus.[18]

When the contingent from the Thames arrived in Wisconsin in 1837, a portion of the group moved on to Kansas, where Delawares who had left Missouri were already living. The Thames immigrants became part of a Moravian mission at Westfield (near Munsie, Kansas). Following a treaty in 1829, Delawares along the James Fork had moved to a reservation at the intersection of the Kansas and Missouri rivers, "extending up the Kansas River, to the Kansas Line, and up the Missouri River to Camp Leavenworth." The treaty stated that this land was set aside "for the permanent residence of the whole Delaware Nation." This area of Kansas seems to have been more suitable than the James Fork, where the hunting had been poor and Delawares had fought with local Osages over limited resources. Some Stockbridge-Munsees also moved to "lands of the Delaware Indians, five miles below Ft. Leavenworth," in other words, to the Kansas reservation. The U.S. commissioner of Indian Affairs reported that "sixty-nine souls of the Stockbridges and one hundred and five of the Munsees and Delawares, under the chief

Thomas T. Hendrick, of the former" had left for lands on the Missouri River, probably near the end of 1839.[19]

In Kansas, Delawares maintained their long-standing connections with the Wyandots. Wyandots had resisted leaving the Sandusky area, where they had reserved lands well into the nineteenth century. The federal government tried unsuccessfully for years to convince the Wyandots to leave these Ohio lands and move west of the Mississippi. At a treaty in 1842 Wyandots finally ceded all of their Ohio holdings, which amounted to about 109,144 acres. In the summer of 1843, approximately seven hundred Wyandots, including some from the Huron River in Michigan, were on their way to Kansas. The new lands Wyandots obtained came from their old allies the Delawares, with whom they had shared territory in years past. Wyandots bought from the Delawares thirty-six sections of land at the junction of the Missouri and Kansas rivers (the future site of Kansas City) and received a gift of three more sections from the Delawares.[20]

Delawares' history also remained intertwined with that of the Shawnees, who had a reservation in Kansas just south of the Kansas River, adjoining the Delaware reservation. Those Delawares who had moved to Texas also lived near Shawnees. After Texas became independent from Mexico in 1836, Delawares and Shawnees experienced relatively good relations with the Republic of Texas under the presidency of Sam Houston; however, in 1838, the next president, Mirabeau B. Lamar, tried to eradicate Indians. Once Houston returned to the executive office in 1841, he sought to repair the damage done to Indian-white associations. Delawares were among those Houston depended on to promote peace. At a treaty in 1844 on Tehuacana Creek, Delawares under their leader St. Louis assumed the role of grandfather and urged Texas Indians to "make a strong peace" with their Euro-American neighbors.[21]

Important connections developed between Delawares and another Indian group, the Caddos, who had also supported peace with the Republic of Texas. "Look at my people, and the Delaware," the Caddo leader Bintah said at the Tehuacana Creek Treaty, "we are like brothers; we listen to the whites and we do well." This expectation of success through friendship with Euro-Americans was overly optimistic. After the United States annexed Texas in 1845, Euro-American and Indian relations in the state deteriorated. Delawares, Caddos, and other Texas tribes faced Euro-American encroachment, causing relocations and outbreaks of violence. In 1854, Texas set up an Indian reservation on the Brazos River, where Delawares lived close to

Caddos. Continuing threats from Euro-Americans led Delawares, Caddos, Wichitas, and other Indians to leave Texas in 1859 and move to the western portion of Indian Territory (later Oklahoma). In this area, known as the Wichita and Affiliated Tribes Reservation, Delawares lived with Caddos on the Washita River. During the disruptions of the Civil War, Delawares and Caddos relocated from there to the mouth of the Little Arkansas River in Kansas but, after the war, returned to western Indian Territory. Between 1874 and 1879, Delawares and Caddos were so closely allied that they shared the same council and were led by the same chief.[22]

Delaware-Cherokee relations, which had a long history, became especially significant in the period immediately after the Civil War. Once Kansas became a territory in 1854, mounting pressure from white squatters, land speculators, and railroad interests led to cessions of Delaware lands through four treaties. The last of these treaties, held in 1866, resulted in removal to Indian Territory, except for those Delawares who agreed to accept an allotment in Kansas. Planning to cut administrative costs, the U.S. government pressured the Delawares into leaving Kansas and merging with the Cherokee Nation. In order to purchase lands in Indian Territory, Delawares entered into articles of agreement with the Cherokees, who held the property. Delawares preparing to leave Kansas signed a document that stated they would "become members of the Cherokee Nation, with the same rights and immunities, and the same participation (and no other) in the national funds, as native Cherokees. . . . And the children hereafter born of such Delawares so incorporated into the Cherokee Nation shall in all respects be regarded as native Cherokees." Kansas Delawares began to relocate to the Little Verdigris (or Caney River) in the northeastern part of the Territory in late 1867, leaving behind the lands they had once been promised would be their "permanent residence." Despite the geographical separation between Delawares in western Indian Territory and in the Cherokee Nation, there was a "continuum of contacts" that linked Delawares in the two areas. In Oklahoma, as well as in Canada, groups of Delawares drew inspiration from practicing a traditionalist Delaware Big House Religion (or Gamwing). Certain Delawares continued to be influenced by Christianity, including that of Baptist and Methodist missionaries in Oklahoma.[23]

By the middle of the nineteenth century, Delawares were in locations that would represent Delawares' present-day areas of settlement, including northeastern Oklahoma (Bartlesville, Dewey, Copan areas); western Oklahoma (Anadarko area); Ontario (Moraviantown, Munceytown, and the Six

Nations Reserve); Kansas; and the Stockbridge-Munsee Mohicans' Reservation (Bowler, Wisconsin, area). Some with Munsee ancestry continued at the Cattaraugus (Seneca) Reservation in New York. In addition, some modern-day Lenapes live in or near their eastern homelands. Whether Delawares remained farther east or moved to Oklahoma, Canada, or elsewhere, their actions from the end of the American Revolution to the mid-nineteenth century revealed their continuing dedication to forming alliances and sharing territories with other Indian peoples. Furthermore, Delawares worked on strengthening connections with other Delawares—connections that sometimes spanned substantial distances. Through their actions, Delawares exhibited a deep-seated commitment to the notion that gathering peoples and constructing alliances were sources of power. Not all intergroup relations were smooth. For example, Delawares sometimes fought Comanches and Osages. The incorporation of the Delawares into the Cherokee Nation also caused conflicts. Nevertheless, responding to stresses and disruptions, Delawares continued to take shape as a people out of long-term processes of building alliances and sitting down with others in many different times and places.[24]

Abbreviations

AGL	Helen Hornbeck Tanner, ed., *Atlas of Great Lakes Indian History* (Norman: University of Oklahoma Press, 1987)
APS	American Philosophical Society, Philadelphia
BD, 1	Kenneth G. Hamilton, trans. and ed., *The Bethlehem Diary*, vol. 1, *1742–1744* (Bethlehem, Pa.: Archives of the Moravian Church, 1971)
BD, 2	Kenneth G. Hamilton and Lothar Madeheim, trans., and Vernon H. Nelson, Otto Dreydoppel Jr., and Doris Rohland Yob, eds., *The Bethlehem Diary*, vol. 2, *January 1, 1744–May 31, 1745* (Bethlehem, Pa.: Moravian Archives, 2001)
BDZ	Eugene F. Bliss, trans., *Diary of David Zeisberger, a Moravian Missionary among the Indians of Ohio*, 2 vols. (Cincinnati, Ohio: Robert Clarke, 1885)
BP	S. K. Stevens et al., eds., *The Papers of Colonel Henry Bouquet*, 6 vols. (Harrisburg: Pennsylvania Historical and Museum Commission, 1972–94)
DS	William A. Hunter, "Documented Subdivisions of the Delaware Indians," *Bulletin of the Archaeological Society of New Jersey* 35 (1978): 20–40.
DW	Reuben Gold Thwaites and Louise Phelps Kellogg, eds., *Documentary History of Dunmore's War, 1774* (Madison: Wisconsin Historical Society, 1905)
EAID	Alden T. Vaughan, ed., *Early American Indian Documents: Treaties and Laws, 1607–1789*: Vol. 1, *Pennsylvania and Delaware Treaties, 1629–1737*, ed. Donald H. Kent (Washington, D.C.: University Publications of America, 1979) Vol. 2, *Pennsylvania Treaties, 1737–1756*, ed. Donald H. Kent (Frederick, Md.: University Publications of America, 1984)

Vol. 10, *New York and New Jersey Treaties, 1754–1775*, ed. Barbara Graymont (Bethesda, Md.: University Publications of America, 2001)

Vol. 18, *Revolution and Confederation*, ed. Colin G. Calloway (Bethesda, Md.: University Publications of America, 1994)

FAUO   Louise Phelps Kellogg, ed., *Frontier Advance on the Upper Ohio, 1778–79* (Madison: State Historical Society of Wisconsin, 1916)

FDUO   Reuben Gold Thwaites and Louise Phelps Kellogg, eds., *Frontier Defense on the Upper Ohio, 1777–1778* (Madison: Wisconsin Historical Society, 1912)

FEPW   *Friends and Enemies in Penn's Woods: Indians, Colonists, and the Racial Construction of Pennsylvania*, ed. William A. Pencak and Daniel K. Richter (University Park: Pennsylvania State University Press, 2004)

FL   Carl. John Fliegel, comp., *Index to the Records of the Moravian Mission among the Indians of North America*, 3 vols. (New Haven, Conn.: Research Publications, 1970)

Friedenshütten   (Schmick and Zeisberger), Moravian diary from Friedenshütten, *RMM*

FRUO   Louise Phelps Kellogg, ed., *Frontier Retreat on the Upper Ohio, 1779–81* (Madison: State Historical Society of Wisconsin, 1917)

GA   Peter Lindeström, *Geographia Americae with an Account of the Delaware Indians Based on Surveys and Notes Made in 1654–1656*, trans. Amandus Johnson (Philadelphia: Swedish Colonial Society, 1925)

GMP   Lois Mulkearn, ed., *George Mercer Papers Relating to the Ohio Company of Virginia* ([Pittsburgh]: University of Pittsburgh Press, 1954)

Gnadenhütten, Ohio   (Schmick et al.), Moravian diary from Gnadenhütten, Ohio, *RMM*

Gnadenhütten, Pa.   (multiple writers), Moravian diary from Gnadenhütten, Pa., *RMM*

Goschgoschunk   (Zeisberger), Moravian diary from Goschgoschunk, *RMM*

Goshen	(Mortimer), Moravian (English) diary from Goshen, *RMM*
HCID	Francis Jennings et al., eds., *The History and Culture of Iroquois Diplomacy: An Interdisciplinary Guide to the Treaties of the Six Nations and Their League* (Syracuse, N.Y.: Syracuse University Press, 1985)
HF	Timothy Horsfield Papers, APS
HNAI	William C. Sturtevant, ed., *Handbook of North American Indians* (Washington, D.C.: Smithsonian Institution, 1978)
HSP	The Historical Society of Pennsylvania, Philadelphia
ICDB	Indian Commissioners Papers, Simon Gratz Collection, Collection 250B, HSP
IVPN	George P. Donehoo, *A History of the Indian Villages and Place Names in Pennsylvania* (1928; Lewisburg, Pa.: Wennawoods, 1998)
JD	Bartlett Burleigh James and J. Franklin Jameson, eds., *Journal of Jasper Danckaerts, 1679–1680* (New York: Charles Scribner's Sons, 1913)
JEP	John Ettwein Papers (microfilm), Moravian Archives, Bethlehem, Pa.
JO	Amandus Johnson, *The Swedish Settlements on the Delaware: Their History and Relation to the Indians, Dutch, and English, 1638–1664. . . .* , 2 vols. (New York: University of Pennsylvania and D. Appleton & Company, 1911)
KJ	"James Kenny's 'Journal to Y^e Westward,' 1758–59," ed. John W. Jordon, *PMHB* (1913): 395–449; John W. Jordan, ed., "Journal of James Kenny, 1761–1763," *PMHB* 37 (January 1913): 1–47, (April 1913) 152–201
Langundo-Utenünk	(Zeisberger), Moravian diary from Langundo-Utenünk, *RMM*
LAP	*Letters and Papers Relating Chiefly to the Provincial History of Pennsylvania with Some Notices of the Writers* (Philadelphia: Crissy and Markley, 1855)
Lawunakhannek	(Zeisberger), Moravian diary from Lawunakhannek, *RMM*
LCA	James Logan Collection, APS

Lichtenau	(Zeisberger), Moravian diary from Lichtenau, *RMM*
LPIA	Logan Family Papers, Indian Affairs, Collection no. 37, HSP
MB	Jonathan Edwards and Sereno Dwight, eds., *Memoirs of Rev. David Brainerd: Missionary to the Indians on the Borders of New-York, New-Jersey, and Pennsylvania . . .* (New Haven, Conn.: S. Converse, 1821)
MCT	Fliegel catalog of Indians, box 3191, *RMM*
MJNY	William M. Beauchamp, ed., *Moravian Journals Relating to Central New York, 1745–66* (Syracuse, N.Y.: Dehler Press, 1916)
MPC	*Minutes of the Provincial Council of Pennsylvania, from the Organization to the Termination of the Proprietary Government,* 10 vols. (Harrisburg and Philadelphia, 1851–52)
NASP	*The New American State Papers: Indian Affairs: General,* vols. 1 and 2 (Wilmington, Del.: Scholarly Resources, 1972)
NEP	Albert Cook Myers, ed., *Narratives of Early Pennsylvania, West New Jersey, and Delaware, 1630–1707* (New York: Charles Scribner's Sons, 1912)
NNN	J. Franklin Jameson, ed., *Narratives of New Netherland, 1609–1664* (New York: Charles Scribner's Sons, 1909)
NYCD	E. B. O'Callaghan and B. Fernow, eds., *Documents Relative to the Colonial History of the State of New York,* 15 vols. (Albany: Weed, Parsons and Company, 1853–87)
NYHM 1974	Arnold J. F. Van Laer, trans., and Kenneth Scott and Kenn Stryker-Rodda, eds., *NYHM: Dutch,* vol. 5, *Council Minutes, 1638–1649* (Baltimore: Genealogical Publishing, 1974)
NYHM 1977	Charles T. Gehring, ed., *New York Historical Manuscripts: Dutch, Vols. XX–XXI, Delaware Papers (English Period): A Collection of Documents Pertaining to the Regulation of Affairs on the Delaware, 1664–1682* (Baltimore: Genealogical Publishing, 1977)
NYHM 1980	Charles T. Gehring, trans. and ed., *NYHM: Dutch, Volumes GG, HH & II, Land Papers* (Baltimore: Genealogical Publishing, 1980)

NYHM 1981	Charles T. Gehring, trans. and ed., *New York Historical Manuscripts: Dutch, Vols. XVIII–XIX, Delaware Papers (Dutch Period): A Collection of Documents Pertaining to the Regulation of Affairs on the South River of New Netherland, 1648–1664* (Baltimore: Genealogical Publishing, 1981)
OIEAHC	Omohundro Institute of Early American History and Culture
OVGLEA	Ohio Valley-Great Lakes Ethnohistory Archive, Glenn Black Laboratory of Archaeology, Bloomington, Indiana
PA	Samuel Hazard et al., eds., *Pennsylvania Archives* (multiple series and volumes; Philadelphia and Harrisburg)
PG	*Pennsylvania Gazette*, Accessible Archives website
PJ	Frederick Post journal in *Early Western Travels, 1748–1846*, ed. Reuben Gold Thwaites (Cleveland, Ohio: Arthur H. Clark, 1904)
PM	Penn Manuscripts, Indian Affairs, Penn Family Papers, Collection no. 485A, HSP
PMHB	*Pennsylvania Magazine of History and Biography*
PP	Richard S. Dunn et al., eds., *The Papers of William Penn*, 5 vols. (Philadelphia: University of Pennsylvania Press, 1981–86)
PSA	Pennsylvania State Archives, Harrisburg
PSL	Pennsylvania State Library, Harrisburg
RMM	*Records of the Moravian Mission among the Indians of North America*, photographed from original materials at the Archives of the Moravian Church, Bethlehem, Pa., microfilm, 40 reels (New Haven, Conn.: Research Publications, 1970), cited by item, folder, box, and reel number (e.g., 1/4/135/8). These records are in German unless otherwise noted, and I have translated brief German quotations into English.
RUO	Reuben Gold Thwaites and Louise Phelps Kellogg, eds., *The Revolution on the Upper Ohio, 1775–1777* (Madison: Wisconsin Historical Society, 1908)
Schönbrunn	(Zeisberger and copyist), Moravian diary from Schönbrunn, *RMM*
SCP	William Henry Smith, ed., *The St. Clair Papers: The*

	Life and Public Services of Arthur St. Clair . . . , 2 vols. (Cincinnati, Ohio: Robert Clarke & Co., 1882; repr., New York: De Capo Press, 1971)
SWJP	James Sullivan et al., eds., *The Papers of Sir William Johnson*, 14 vols. (Albany: University of the State of New York, 1921–65)
THDC	Tribal History Documents Collection, OVGLEA
WP	Conrad Weiser Papers, Collection no. 700, HSP
Z.	David Zeisberger

Notes

Prologue

1. C. A. Weslager, *Dutch Explorers, Traders, and Settlers in the Delaware Valley, 1609–1664* (Philadelphia: University of Pennsylvania Press, 1961), 121–26; *NEP*, 18–19 (quotations on 19).

2. *NEP*, 18 ("stock-fish"), 19, 20 ("Armewanninge"); Weslager, *Dutch*, 125–26.

3. *NEP*, 20–21.

4. Ibid., 21 ("Indian corn," "kettles"); Archer Butler Hulbert and William Nathaniel Schwarze, ed., *David Zeisberger's History of the North American Indians* (Columbus: Ohio State Archaeological and Historical Society, 1910), 100 ("to sit down . . . signifies declaring a truce").

5. *NEP*, 20. With my focus on "Indian-Indian relations" and "internal processes" of Native societies, my work reflects recommendations made decades ago as part of the movement for a "new" Indian history. Robert F. Berkhofer, Jr., "The Political Context of a New Indian History," *Pacific Historical Review* 40 (August 1971): 357–58, 368. On these and other aspects of the "new" Indian history, see Nancy Shoemaker, ed., *Clearing a Path: Theorizing the Past in Native American Studies* (New York: Routledge, 2002), viii–ix. No longer "new," of course, this scholarly trend, however, fits well with a more recent trend to move away from the dichotomous view of "the frontier" and instead to recognize multiple frontiers of "kinetic interactions among many peoples." This approach to frontiers highlights the "mosaic of diverse Indian groups" involved in these interactions, something that I emphasize as well. Furthermore, fluidity, dynamism, and complexity characterize this notion of frontiers—all appropriate terms for the history of the Delawares. Andrew R. L. Cayton and Fredrika J. Teute, eds., *Contact Points: American Frontiers from the Mohawk Valley to the Mississippi, 1750–1830* (Chapel Hill: University of North Carolina Press for the OIEAHC, 1998), 1–8 (quotations on 2, 8). See Fredrik Barth, ed., *Ethnic Groups and Boundaries: The Social Organization of Culture Difference* (1969; Long Grove, Ill.: Waveland Press, 1998), for examinations of "the persistence of cultural boundaries" along with the "flow of personnel across" these boundaries, a view that highlights ethnic groups as the product of social interactions and dynamism (pp. 23–24).

6. Ives Goddard, "Delaware," in *HNAI*, vol. 15: *Northeast*, ed. Bruce G. Trigger (Washington, D.C.: Smithsonian Institution, 1978), 213, 235–36. Some spellings within quotations in my book have been modernized, particularly by writing the thorn as "th" and "ff" as "F" as well as removing superscripts in abbreviations.

7. Mary A. Druke, "Linking Arms: The Structure of Iroquois Intertribal Diplomacy,"

in *Beyond the Covenant Chain: The Iroquois and Their Neighbors in Indian North America, 1600–1800*, ed. Daniel K. Richter and James H. Merrell (Syracuse, N.Y.: Syracuse University Press, 1987), 29–33; Gregory Evans Dowd, *A Spirited Resistance: The North American Struggle for Unity, 1745–1815* (Baltimore: Johns Hopkins University Press, 1992), 3 ("successful interaction," "ability"); Richard White, *The Middle Ground: Indians, Empires, and Republics in the Great Lakes Region, 1650–1815* (Cambridge: Cambridge University Press, 1991), 35 ("source of influence").

8. See Robert Grumet's discussion of the problems in the approaches of both "lumpers" and "splitters," who describe the early Delawares. Neither did the Delawares seem to live in isolated autonomous villages nor did they gather in sizable unified tribes. Robert Steven Grumet, "'We Are Not So Great Fools': Changes in Upper Delawaran Socio-Political Life, 1630–1758" (Ph.D. diss., Rutgers, The State University of New Jersey, 1979), 23–28. On the Delawares coming together in the West in the eighteenth century, see Michael N. McConnell, *A Country Between: The Upper Ohio Valley and Its Peoples, 1724–1774* (Lincoln: University of Nebraska Press, 1992), 225–29; *DS*, 35; Goddard, "Delaware," 223.

9. Rachel Wheeler portrays the Mahicans as viewing themselves as "peacekeepers and mediators." "Living upon Hope: Mahicans and Missionaries, 1730–1760" (Ph.D. diss., Yale University, 1999), 18. Given the close connections between Mahicans and Delawares and their overlapping histories, this similarity is not surprising. James H. Merrell, *Into the American Woods: Negotiators on the Pennsylvania Frontier* (New York: W. W. Norton, 1999), 34–38 ("looks less peaceful" on 37). Also, on the state of Euro-American and Native American relations in early Pennsylvania, see Daniel K. Richter and William A. Pencak, Introduction, in *FEPW*, ix–xxi; James O'Neil Spady, "Colonialism and the Discursive Antecedents of *Penn's Treaty with the Indians*," in ibid., 18–40. For examples of coexistence and adjustment between Native Americans and Euro-Americans, but ultimate divisions along racial lines in Pennsylvania, see Jane T. Merritt, *At the Crossroads: Indians and Empires on a Mid-Atlantic Frontier, 1700–1763* (Chapel Hill: University of North Carolina Press for the OIEAHC, 2003).

10. *MPC*, 8:307 ("sit down and smoak"); 7:320 ("I clear the Ground"); 4:647 ("to sit down and not to revenge themselves"); *PA*, 1st ser., 4:509 ("to sit down and Listen"). The first two statements are by Delawares, the third is from the Iroquois (or Six Nations), and the fourth seems to have been made by Ohio Iroquois and delivered by Delawares. This source uses the word "Mingo" (from the Algonquian *mengwe*, meaning "stealthy"). Because of the negative connotation of this term, I avoid its use in this study. The term "Mingo" was typically applied to Iroquois in Ohio. Paul A. W. Wallace, ed., *Thirty Thousand Miles with John Heckewelder* (Pittsburgh: University of Pittsburgh Press, 1958), 425. See the discussion of "Mingo" and of Wallace's contribution in Barbara Alice Mann, *Iroquoian Women: The Gantowisas* (New York: Peter Lang, 2000), 17–18.

Chapter 1

1. Tantaqué was also called Jasper. *JD*, 76–78, 175 (quotations on 77–78).
2. John Heckewelder, *History, Manners, and Customs of the Indian Nations* . . .

(Philadelphia: HSP, 1876), 250 (quotations); M. R. Harrington, "A Preliminary Sketch of Lenápe Culture," *American Anthropologist* 15 (April–June 1913): 232–33. For a summary of traditional stories: John Bierhorst, *Mythology of the Lenape: Guide and Texts* (Tucson: University of Arizona Press, 1995). Although different in other respects, Iroquois cosmology also included an origin story about the creation of the world on the back of a turtle. Daniel K. Richter, *The Ordeal of the Longhouse: The Peoples of the Iroquois League in the Era of European Colonization* (Chapel Hill: University of North Carolina Press for the Institute of Early American History and Culture, 1992), ch. 1.

3. Allen W. Trelease, *Indian Affairs in Colonial New York: The Seventeenth Century* (Ithaca, N.Y.: Cornell University Press, 1960; repr., Lincoln: University of Nebraska Press, 1997), 25–26; *NNN*, 53 (Dutch report), 31–34. For application of the term "River Indians" to Delaware Valley Indians (1656): *NYCD*, 1:597. For its application to Hudson River Indians (1687): ibid., 3:444. For its application (1698) to New England Indians who migrated into New York: ibid., 4:381. On the importance of rivers to the Delawares, see Lynette Perry and Manny Skolnick, *Keeper of the Delaware Dolls* (Lincoln: University of Nebraska Press, 1999), 21–39.

4. Carol E. Hoffecker et al., eds., *New Sweden in America* (Newark: University of Delaware Press, 1995), 11; *NEP*, 70 (New Sweden historian); *GA*, 170 (Swedish observer); *NNN*, 45–47, 53.

5. Richter, *Ordeal*, 1, 16–17, 29; Neal Salisbury, "The Indians' Old World: Native Americans and the Coming of Europeans," *William and Mary Quarterly*, 3rd ser., 53 (July 1996): 436–37; Jonathan D. Hill, ed., *History, Power, and Identity: Ethnogenesis in the Americas, 1492–1992* (Iowa City: University of Iowa Press, 1996), 7; Herbert C. Kraft, "Indian Prehistory of New Jersey," in *A Delaware Indian Symposium*, ed. Herbert C. Kraft (Harrisburg: Pennsylvania Historical and Museum Commission, 1974), 33–34; Ted J. Brasser, *Riding on the Frontier's Crest: Mahican Indian Culture and Culture Change* (Ottawa: National Museums of Canada, 1974), 3; Kathleen J. Bragdon, *Native People of Southern New England, 1500–1650* (Norman: University of Oklahoma Press, 1996), 72. On the Susquehannock-Lenape relationship, see Chapter 2 below. On the Wendats, see Chapter 4 below.

6. *GA*, 241 ("somewhat cleverer"), 205 ("of one nation"), xix and n. 17 ("art of fortification," editor quoting from a Swedish document, "*Mijne K. förälldrar . . . ,*" Lindeström, March 19, 1657); Herbert C. Kraft, "The Minisink Indians," in *The People of Minisink: Papers from the 1989 Delaware Water Gap Symposium*, ed. David G. Orr and Douglas V. Campana (Philadelphia: National Park Service, 1991), 33–35; Barry C. Kent, *Susquehanna's Indians* (Harrisburg: Pennsylvania Historical and Museum Commission, 1989), 93–95; *NYCD*, 1:282 ("the next of kin"); *NEP*, 4–5, 15, 17 ("the friends"). The references to retaliation over the death of kin suggest that Hudson and Delaware Valley Indians used a variation of the "mourning war" practiced by the Iroquois, but there is no reference here to taking captives to replace dead kin, a function of the mourning war among the Iroquois. See Daniel K. Richter, "War and Culture: The Iroquois Experience," *William and Mary Quarterly*, 3rd ser., 40 (October 1983): 528–59.

7. Lynn Ceci, *The Effect of European Contact and Trade on the Settlement Pattern of Indians in Coastal New York, 1524–1665* (New York: Garland, 1990), 12–26, 191–208; Adriaen van der Donck, "A Description of the New Netherlands," in *Collections of the*

New York Historical Society, 2nd ser. (New York, 1841), 1:206; *NNN*, 288. For corrected translations of parts of Van der Donck's "Description," see Ada van Gastel, "Van der Donck's Description of the Indians: Additions and Corrections," *William and Mary Quarterly*, 3rd ser., 47 (July 1990): 411–21. *NNN*, 288; *PA*, 2nd ser., 5:191; Richter, *Ordeal*, 29, 84: Neal Salisbury, "Toward the Covenant Chain: Iroquois and Southern New England Algonquians, 1637–1684," in *Beyond the Covenant Chain*, ed. Richter and Merrell, 61–62.

8. Van der Donck, "Description," 194; *NNN*, 106; *GA*, 195; *NYCD*, 1:281 ("They twine").

9. *HCID*, 138–39; Mary A. Druke, "Iroquois Treaties: Common Forms, Varying Interpretations," in ibid., 88–89.

10. Karen Ordahl Kupperman, "Scandinavian Colonists Confront the New World," in *New Sweden*, ed. Hoffecker et al., 102–4; *NEP*, 105 (quotation).

11. *NNN*, 13, 18 (officer quoted), 49 (Hudson quoted); Richter, *Ordeal*, 16, 29; Herbert C. Kraft, *The Lenape: Archaeology, History, and Ethnography* (Newark: New Jersey Historical Society, 1986), 274 n. 3; Mary Ann Levine, "Native Copper in the Northeast: An Overview of Potential Sources Available to Indigenous Peoples," in *The Archaeological Northeast*, ed. Mary Ann Levine, Kenneth E. Sassaman, and Michael S. Nassaney (Westport, Conn.: Bergin & Garvey, 1999), 196 (N.J. examples), 183–99.

12. *NEP*, 226–27 (Penn); C. A. Weslager, *The Delaware Indians: A History* (1972; New Brunswick, N.J.: Rutgers University Press, 1989), 40; Anthony F. C. Wallace, "Woman, Land, and Society: Three Aspects of Aboriginal Delaware Life," *Pennsylvania Archaeologist* 17 (1947): 16; Brasser, *Riding*, 2. For a contemporary's description of the Hudson area's landscape: *NNN*, 205–8. On climate and growing seasons in the New Jersey portions of the Delaware Valley: Peter O. Wacker, *Land and People, a Cultural Geography of Preindustrial New Jersey: Origins and Settlement Patterns* (New Brunswick, N.J.: Rutgers University Press, 1975), 8–10. On subsistence practices: William W. Newcomb, *The Culture and Acculturation of the Delaware Indians* (Ann Arbor: University of Michigan, 1956), 13–20.

13. Ceci, *Effect*, 52, 93–134; Robert S. Grumet, " 'Strangely Decreast by the Hand of God': A Documentary Appearance-Disappearance Model for Munsee Demography, 1630–1801," *Journal of Middle Atlantic Archaeology* 5 (1989): 135. Marshall Becker argues that the Delaware Valley Indians practiced only very limited gardening. Marshall Joseph Becker, "A Summary of Lenape Socio-Political Organization and Settlement Pattern at the Time of European Contact: The Evidence for Collecting Bands," *Journal of Middle Atlantic Archaeology* 4 (1988): 79–83. The documentary evidence I offer suggests that corn and other crops, while varying in importance according to location, were, or had become, a notable part of the diet of Algonquians in the Hudson and Delaware watersheds by the seventeenth century. *NNN*, 261 (Jogues quotation).

14. Van der Donck, "Description," 186–87; *NEP*, 48 ("covered"); *NNN*, 21 ("eares"), 49 ("enough"), 208 ("little capable"); *GA*, 154 (on the "Sironesack" group). Ceci, *Effect*, 116–17.

15. *NEP*, 355–56, 385 ("They plant"); *NNN*, 221–22 (about blackbirds); *GA*, 170 ("their dwellings"); Brasser, *Riding*, 4.

16. *GA*, 179; *NNN*, 107 (De Rasieres), 100, 219 (De Vries).

17. *NNN*, 107–8 (De Rasieres), 218–19 (De Vries); *NEP*, 334.

18. *NNN*, 107–8; Van der Donck, "Description," 193 ("We seldom"); *NEP*, 232; *NYCD*, 1:283 ("mix this").

19. *NEP*, 232 ("Roasted"); *NNN*, 219–20 ("They gather"); Van der Donck, "Description," 193–94 ("When they intend").

20. Kraft, "Indian Prehistory," 43–44 ("single opening," "room partitions"); Kraft, "Minisink Indians," 34–35; Newcomb, *Culture*, 24–25; *GA*, 211; Richter, *Ordeal*, 18. Anthony F. C. Wallace offers the view that the longhouse was possibly a summertime residence. Wallace, "Woman," 17. Lindeström reported that longhouses were constructed in the fall and served as dwellings throughout the winter. His suggestion, however, that the longhouses were not important during the growing season is open to question, for his statement that "during the summer they [the Indians] have no certain dwellings, but move about here and there around the country" makes little sense given his own references to Native agriculture. It seems that here Lindeström was focusing on male hunting activities and ignoring women's tending of corn and other crops that would have continued in villages throughout the summer; thus his statement about a lack of "certain dwellings" does not disprove the use of longhouses in planting settlements. *GA*, 211.

21. Goddard, "Delaware," 217.

22. *GA*, 213–14 ("Now at that time"; brackets added in volume); *NEP*, 18, 22 ("great fires").

23. Van der Donck, "Description," 150 (quotations); *NEP*, 18, 22. On Indians' burning of forests in New England: William Cronon, *Changes in the Land: Indians, Colonists, and the Ecology of New England* (New York: Hill and Wang, 1983), 48–51.

24. *NNN*, 220 (quotations).

25. *NNN*, 108 ("baskets woven"), 70 ("dwellings . . . commonly circular"); *NEP*, 232 ("In Travel"); *NYCD*, 1: 282 ("Their dwellings are constructed"); Brasser, *Riding*, 5; Wallace, "Woman," 16–17. Wallace suggests that the dome-shaped lodge might have served as a wintertime dwelling (17), as does Newcomb (*Culture*, 25). Stephen Aron, "Pigs and Hunters: 'Rights in the Woods' on the Trans-Appalachian Frontier," in *Contact Points*, ed. Cayton and Teute, 194. For the Iroquois, Richter notes that among various "locales, the seasonal camps and hunting grounds may have been the most permanent, for migrating fishes, birds, and animals returned predictably to the same venues each year, but towns and hamlets came and went." Richter, *Ordeal*, 24.

26. *GA*, 223; Daniel Denton, *A Brief Description of New-York* (1670; New York: Columbia University Press, 1937), 7; *NNN*, 57; Van der Donck, "Description," 193 ("Dry beans").

27. *NNN*, 18 ("some in Mantles"), 106 ("In the winter time"), 217 ("their clothing"); *NEP*, 434 ("instead of shoes"); *GA*,199 ("On their feet").

28. Kraft, "Indian Prehistory," 23–25; Kraft, "Minisink Indians," 31, 37; *NNN*, 105 (De Rasieres quotation, brackets in source), 222 ("seines"); *GA*, 219–20 ("when the river").

29. *NEP*, 25 (De Vries), 48 (English contemporary), 21 (Juet), 17, 24; Van der Donck, "Description," 198.

30. Van der Donck, "Description," 197 ("villages"). *NNN*, 71, 207; *NEP*, 434 (Pastorius); *JD*, 176–77 ("a hut" and subsequent quotations), 176n, xiii; n. 25 above.

31. Kraft did not find archaeological evidence of stockaded towns in the upper Delaware Valley within New Jersey. Kraft, "Indian Prehistory," 32, 34, 43. Shirley W. Dunn, *The Mohicans and Their Land, 1609–1730* (Fleischmanns, N.Y.: Purple Mountain Press, 1994), 103–5; *NNN*, 280–81; Trelease, *Indian Affairs*, 78–79; my Chapter 2 below (on warfare); Van der Donck, "Description," 197. Another less well-documented location of community life and subsistence was a group's collecting area, which could be rich in wild foods. De Vries reported, "There also grow here hazelnuts, large nuts in great quantities, chestnuts, which they dry to eat, and wild grapes in great abundance, which they also use." *NNN*, 219. In the Delaware Valley, once the corn crop was planted, Indians "gathered wild pease, which grew along the river, and dried them." *NEP*, 73.

32. Lewis H. Morgan, *Ancient Society or Researches in the Lines of Human Progress from Savagery through Barbarism to Civilization* (Chicago: Charles H. Kerr, [1877]), 176n, 176–78. Morgan refers to these as "sub-gentes." See discussion of terminology in Newcomb, *Culture*, as well as another listing of Morgan's "sub-gentes" (48–49). Delawares seem to have followed a form of segmentary lineage system. On this system: E. E. Evans-Pritchard, *The Nuer: A Description of the Modes of Livelihood and Political Institutions of a Nilotic People* (Oxford: Clarendon Press, Oxford University Press, 1940), 192–211; Marshall D. Sahlins, "The Segmentary Lineage: An Organization of Predatory Expansion," *American Anthropologist* 63 (February 1961): 322–45; *NEP*, 335.

33. Wallace, "Woman," 6–14; "Some Remarks and Annotations concerning the Traditions, Customs, Languages &c. of the Indians in North America, from the Memoirs of the Reverend David Zeisberger, and other Missionaries of the United Brethren," copied from John Ettwein by Jared Sparks, [1788?], no. 100, JEP. A quotation from Zeisberger with further discussion of his statement appears in Chapter 5 below. Frank G. Speck, *The Celestial Bear Comes Down to Earth: The Bear Sacrifice Ceremony of the Munsee-Mahican in Canada as Related to Nekatcit* (Reading, Pa.: Reading Public Museum and Art Gallery, 1945), 3–4 (quotations on 4); Richter, *Ordeal*, 39.

34. Wallace, "Woman," 6 ("mixture of affinal and consanguine relatives"); Van der Donck, "Description," 199.

35. *NNN*, 106–7; Van der Donck, "Description," 198–99.

36. *NNN*, 107 ("That being done," editor's brackets); Van der Donck, "Description," 198–99; *NEP*, 231 ("Girls stay"); Richter, *Ordeal*, 20 ("the ideal").

37. *JD*, 156–59 (quotations on 158–59).

38. Ibid., 158–59.

39. Ibid., 159 (Danckaerts quotations), 160; *NEP*, 234–35 ("Their Government").

40. *PA*, 2nd ser., 5:99.

41. Van der Donck, "Description," 196–97 (emphasis mine); Goddard, "Delaware," 216. See later in this chapter for discussion of harvest rituals.

42. *NNN*, 57–58 ("They have"); *NEP*, 234–35; Newcomb, *Culture*, 51; Brasser, *Riding*, 9; Goddard, "Delaware," 216; Wallace, "Woman," 7–8, 14; Grumet, " 'We Are Not So Great Fools,' " 102–3; Van der Donck, "Description," 210.

43. *NNN*, 109 (De Rasieres), 302 ("Ordinarily"); *GA*, 255 ("She is the housekeeper"); Van der Donck, "Description," 198, 201. Helpful to my understanding of the sachem's role has been Bragdon, *Native People*, 153–54.

44. *NEP*, 233; Peter A. Thomas, *In the Maelstrom of Change: The Indian Trade and Cultural Process in the Middle Connecticut River Valley, 1635–1665* (New York: Garland, 1990), 39.

45. *NNN*, 50 ("Every thing"), 57; *NYCD*, 1:282; Kraft, *Lenape*, 163–65; *JD*, 172, 174; Neal Salisbury, *Manitou and Providence: Indians, Europeans, and the Making of New England, 1500–1643* (New York: Oxford University Press, 1982), 37–39.

46. *NNN*, 302; David Zeisberger (manuscript), "History of the Indians," 1/1/2291/33, *RMM*. The published English translation of this fails to translate "Freundschaft" in a consistent fashion. Hulbert and Schwarze, eds., *Zeisberger's History*, 136. One piece of evidence suggests that the Moravians used *Freundschaft* to refer to relatives within the same matrilineage: when mentioning members of the *Freundschaft* of Gehntachquishigunt (or Gottlieb), a missionary included only individuals who would have been from Gehntachquishigunt's matrilineage—that is, his mother, his mother's sister, and his own sister. Gnadenhütten, Pa., November 14, 1748, 1/4/116/4; Register of Adult Baptisms, Catalogs, Generalia, April 26, 1745, 3/1/313/33, *RMM*. For other examples of the use of *Freundschaft*: Gnadenhütten, Pa., January 18/29, 1748, September 7, December 17, 1749, 1/3 and 6/116/4. For a similar conclusion about *Freundschaft*: Hermann Wellenreuther and Carola Wessel, eds., *The Moravian Mission Diaries of David Zeisberger, 1772–1781*, trans. Julie Tomberlin Weber (University Park: Pennsylvania State University Press, 2005), 18. M. R. Harrington, *Religion and Ceremonies of the Lenape*, Indian Notes and Monographs, Museum of the American Indian, Heye Foundation, no. 19 ([New York?]: n.d.), 176–79 (quotation on 179), 172, 162–63.

47. *NEP*, 233–34 (Penn); *NNN*, 223 (De Vries); Kraft, "Minisink Indians," 39; Charles Wolley, *A Two Years' Journal in New York and Part of Its Territories in America* (Cleveland, Ohio: Burrows Brothers, 1902 [a reprint of original 1701 edition]; repr., Harrison, N.Y.: Harbor Hill Books, 1973), 60 ("a certain Tree"). For further evidence of the significance of the proximity of burials to home communities and the stress on grave tending: *NEP*, 340.

48. *NEP*, 234 (Penn); *GA*, 214–15 ("*Hägginj, hä,*" "They sing," "thus repeating").

49. *NEP*, 234 (Penn); Bragdon, *Native People*, 219 (on the Narragansetts). Bragdon's discussion of "Ritual and the Creation of Sacred Space" and of ritual's role in creating *communitas* (following Victor Turner's approach) has been useful in my own presentation of ritual (esp. 218–23); Goddard, "Delaware," 217; Heckewelder, *History*, 185–86; *NYCD*, 13:84 (sitting down to meet "under a tree").

50. *NNN*, 217–18 (De Vries); *GA*, 257 ("pour water").

51. *GA*, 257–58 (quotation on 258); Bragdon, *Native People*, 218–20.

Chapter 2

1. See, for example, *NEP*, 87; *NNN*, 67–68, 270–71.

2. Wallace, "Woman," 2 ("an element," "irrevocable," "exclusive"); Francis Jennings, *The Ambiguous Iroquois Empire: The Covenant Chain Confederation of Indian Tribes with English Colonies from Its Beginnings to the Lancaster Treaty of 1744* (New York: W. W. Norton, 1984), 325–28; Cronon, *Changes*, 62–65; Daniel K. Richter, *Facing East from*

Indian Country: A Native History of Early America (Cambridge, Mass.: Harvard University Press, 2001), 54–55. After I had written my ideas about shared lands, I discovered the following essay, which is also relevant here: Patricia Albers and Jeanne Kay, "Sharing the Land: A Study in American Indian Territoriality," in *A Cultural Geography of North American Indians*, ed. Thomas E. Ross and Tyrel G. Moore (Boulder, Colo.: Westview Press, 1987), 47–91. Thomas J. Sugrue, "The Peopling and Depeopling of Early Pennsylvania: Indians and Colonists, 1680–1720," *PMHB* 116 (January 1992): 21–22.

3. Clayton Colman Hall, ed., *Narratives of Early Maryland, 1633–1684* (New York: Charles Scribner's Sons), 440 ("Some of these Territories"); *PA*, 2nd ser., 5:266–67 ("hunting and fishing" on 266); *NYHM* 1980, 9 ("under the express"); Leon de Valinger Jr., "Indian Land Sales in Delaware," *Bulletin of the Archaeological Society of Delaware* 3 (February 1941): 25–26, 32; Cronon, *Changes*, 62–65; Grumet, "'We Are Not So Great Fools,'" 266–67. Weslager, *Delaware*, 126, also discusses the meaning of "selling land," from the Indians' perspective, as being essentially about "use rights" in the seventeenth century.

4. *EAID*, 1:43 ("Liberty") and n. 11; Edwin B. Bronner, "Indian Deed for Petty's Island, 1678," *PMHB* 89 (1965): 111–14; *NYCD*, 13:441–42; 12:290; *MPC*, 2:554; Richter, *Ordeal*, 23; Brasser, *Riding*, 4; Newcomb, *Culture*, 14.

5. *NYCD*, 14:474 (first quotation), 460 (second quotation); Minutes of the Commissioners on the Brandywine Indians Complaint, 1725 or 1726, p. 49, vol. 4, LCA ("tho' they sold"). For other examples of Native reserved usage rights: Robert S. Grumet, "The Indians of Fort Massapeag," *Long Island Historical Journal* 8 (Fall 1995): 35–36.

6. The quote "different groups . . ." is from Cronon (*Changes*, 63), whose conclusions about New England Algonquians' focus on usufruct rights and "flexible definitions of land tenure" are useful in trying to understand attitudes of Delaware Valley Algonquians toward land. Wallace, "Woman," 6; *PA*, 1st ser., 1:62–64 (quotations from deeds). These deeds appear in *PA* with inconsistent spellings. In describing Penn's early purchases, Donald H. Kent notes that most had "vague limits, and overlapping areas." Kent, *Iroquois Indians I: History of Pennsylvania Purchases from the Indians* (New York: Garland, 1974), 11. See also De Valinger, "Indian Sales," 27, 28, 32.

7. Wallace, "Woman," 6 ("communal territories"); *NYHM* 1980, 2 (second and third quotations).

8. *NNN*, 18–19, 21, 22, 23 (quotations). Gift giving was meant to cement treaty relationships, as a large number of documents show. See the "Peace made between the Dutch and Indians on the Lower Hudson" in April 1643 (*NYCD*, 13:14), stating, "For the confirmation and ratification of this treaty presents were mutually given." On the idea of land sales as forms of alliance gifts: Grumet, "'We Are Not So Great Fools,'" 269–71.

9. For variations on the oral tradition: Heckewelder, *History*, 71–74; *Turtle Tales: Oral Traditions of the Delaware Tribe of Western Oklahoma* (Anadarko: Delaware Tribe of Western Oklahoma Press, 1984), 9; *The White Deer and Other Stories Told by the Lenape* (New York: William Morrow and Company, 1995), 104–6; Weslager, *Delaware*, app. 3, 475–76; *PA*, 2nd ser., 5:265 ("We will rather sell"), 261 ("willing to present");

J[ames]. L[ogan]. to Sassoonan or Allumapies, August 13, 1731, p. 35, vol. 1, PM ("When Wm. Penn"); *NEP*, 233 ("sold," "others presented"). For Hudson Valley agreements that seem to have involved gifts of land: *NYCD*, 13:533–34 and 571.

10. *NEP*, 72 (quotation). For some examples of Indian witnesses: various deeds in *PA*, 1st ser., 1:62–68; *NYCD*, 13:399, 402–3.

11. For payment goods: *PP*, 2:262; various deeds in *PA*, 1:62–68; *NYHM* 1980, 62–63. *NEP*, 233 (Penn quotations); Declaration of Moses Tetamy, Papers Relating to the Friendly Association for Regaining and Preserving Peace with the Indians by Pacific Measures, 1:407, Philadelphia Yearly Meeting Indian Committee Records, ca. 1745–1983, Special Collections, Haverford College Library, Haverford, Pa. (Nutimus quotation).

12. *PA*, 2nd ser., 5:265 (quotation); *EAID*, 1:43 and n. 11; *PP*, 3:611, 612 n. 1, 613 n. 7; *PP*, 2:243 n. 4; Marcel Mauss, *The Gift: Forms and Functions of Exchange in Archaic Societies*, trans. Ian Cunnison (New York: W. W. Norton, 1967), 1–11; Grumet, "Massapeag," 36 (example of an annual present included in land sale). Matchcoats appeared in various forms; see Marshall Joseph Becker, "Matchcoats: Cultural Conservatism and Change in One Aspect of Native American Clothing," *Ethnohistory* 52 (Fall 2005): 727–87.

13. On the standard use of "for Ever" in deeds, see, for example: *PA*, 1st ser., 1: 62–63, 65; *EAID*, 1:34, 43. *PP*, 3:32 (quotation), 41, 88–89. Jennings discusses the "Delaware expectation of perpetually renewed presents for use of the land" in *Ambiguous*, 328. See also Sugrue, "Peopling," 22–23.

14. *PP*, 3:131 ("long & chargeable"), 58 n. 15, 190 (Markham). On Penn's financial situation and Indian payments: ibid., 27 and 158.

15. Ibid., 2:569, 573 (quotations). Spady, "Colonialism," 36, draws a similar conclusion about the Indians' likely view of Penn's approach.

16. *NYHM* 1980, 2 (quotation). Baron van der Capellen and Cornelius van Werckhoven both claimed to have bought the Raritan country from the Indians at about the same time; no doubt conflicting land claims such as this were yet another factor contributing to a sense of fluidity in land ownership. *NYCD*, 13:31–32. On regulations requiring the seating of purchased lands with European colonists: *NNN*, 90; *PA*, 2nd ser., 5:737; *PP*, 2:120; *PA*, 2nd ser., 7:11. Dunn suggests that some Hudson Valley Algonquians may have seen the sales "in the nature of a loan of their land." Dunn, *Mohicans*, 100–101.

17. *GA*, 164 ("safely navigable"); *NEP*, 344n; Weslager, *Dutch*, 49–81 (esp. 64 and for *Schoon Eylandt*, 80); *JD*, 98.

18. *NYCD*, 12:48–49; *JD*, 97–98; *NYHM* 1977, 4–5, 305, 229–31; *PA*, 2nd ser., 5:603–4; Lucy L. Aiello, "Burlington Island," *New Jersey History* 91 (1973): 24–34; *PP*, 2:262, 267 n. 22.

19. *GA*, 128 ("whole tribes"), 127 ("sickness had formerly"). There was a bad spell in 1643, a year in which "many people died" among the Swedish colonists. This illness perhaps spread to the Swedes' Native neighbors, although New Sweden's governor, Johan Printz, spoke only of the vulnerability of the Swedes, because in that year "they had then to begin to work, and [had] but little to eat." *NEP*, 121. *NYHM* 1981, 126, 132, 174, 317 ("small-pox is drifting"); *PA*, 2nd ser., 5:339–40 ("fully more," "perished," and

"continual"); Van der Donck, "Description," 183 ("Indians . . . affirm"); *NYCD*, 13:191 ("mortality"); Denton, *Brief Description*, 7; Charles T. Gehring, "*Hodie Mihi, Cras Tibi*: Swedish-Dutch Relations in the Delaware Valley," in *New Sweden*, ed. Hoffecker et al., 69–85; Francis Jennings, "Dutch and Swedish Indian Policies," in *HNAI*, vol. 4, *History of Indian-White Relations*, ed. Wilcomb E. Washburn (Washington, D.C.: Smithsonian Institution, 1988), 17–18; Richter, *Ordeal*, 57–60; Salisbury, *Manitou*, 7–8; Grumet, "'Strangely Decreast,'" 129–45; Charles T. Gehring and Robert S. Grumet, "Observations of the Indians from Jasper Danckaert's Journal, 1679–1680," *William and Mary Quarterly*, 3d ser., 44 (January 1987): 107.

    20. *GA*, 127; Samuel Smith, *The History of the Colony of Nova-Caesaria, or New-Jersey* . . . (Burlington, N.J.: James Parker, 1765; repr., Spartenburg, S.C.: The Reprint Company, 1966 [reprint of reprint, Trenton, N.J.: William S. Sharp, 1890]), 101–2 (sachem quoted); *PA*, 2nd ser., 5:629, 630 (Tashiowycam quotation). Tashiowycam was probably associated with the Mantes Indians, who may have moved north and west from Mantua Creek. Referring to the two men, Alrichs stated that "the whole Nation of the Indians of whom these Murderers are, consists of about 50, or 60 persons." He added, "All the Mischeifs committed in Delaware [i.e., on the Delaware River] these 7 Years by Murder and otherwise, are said to be done by them." *PA*, 2nd ser., 5:630. Because Mantes Indians had been explicitly blamed three years earlier for killing some of Alrichs's servants, it is reasonable to think that the nation mentioned by Alrichs was indeed the Mantes or a portion of that group. Ibid., 602. In about 1647, a Mantes sachem, Siscohoka, bargained with the Swedes over an area that apparently included a portion of present Philadelphia to the falls. Siscohoka sold land west of the Delaware from Wychquahoyngh to Mechechason. *PA*, 2nd ser., 5:264. Wychquahoyngh was probably a variant of Wigquachkoing (also probably Wiccaco). Weslager, *Dutch*, 307–8 and n. 2; *NYHM* 1981, 16–18. Wiccaco was the site of a Swedish settlement on the north side of Hollander Creek near the Delaware River. *IVPN*, 252–53. Mechechason was probably in the falls area. *PA*, 2nd ser., 5:149. By the mid-1650s, Lindeström found Mantes Indians living in the falls region. *GA*, 165 and n. 36.

    21. John E. Pomfret, *The Province of West New Jersey, 1609–1702: A History of the Origins of an American Colony* (Princeton, N.J.: Princeton University Press, 1956), 106–7 (population), 88–89; Mahlon Stacy to George Hutcheson, August 12, 1680, in Edwin Robert Walker and Clayton L. Traver, *A History of Trenton, 1679–1929: Two Hundred and Fifty Years of a Notable Town with Links in Four Centuries* (Princeton, N.J.: Princeton University Press, 1929), 1:42; and Mary Murfin Smith narrative in ibid., 56; Thomas Budd pamphlet, quoted in Smith, *Nova-Caesaria*,100n; Samuel Hazard, *Annals of Pennsylvania, from the Discovery of the Delaware, 1609–1682* (Philadelphia: Hazard and Mitchell, 1850), 461–62. According to the remembrances of Richard Townsend, who traveled with Penn to North America in 1682, many passengers on their ship *Welcome* had smallpox, "out of which company about thirty died." It is possible that these immigrants helped transmit this disease in America, although many of the vulnerable Native individuals may have already been sickened by earlier contact with colonists. John Warner Barber, *The History and Antiquities of New England, New York, New Jersey, and Pennsylvania* . . . (Hartford, Conn.: Allen S. Stillman & Co., 1844), 545.

22. William Christie MacLeod, "The Family Hunting Territory and Lenape Political Organization," *American Anthropologist*, n.s., 24 (October–December 1922), 457–58; Goddard, "Delaware," 216. On territory sharing and adaptation among Native peoples in another context, see Albers and Kay, "Sharing the Land," 56–74.

23. *NNN*, 31–33, 45–47, 53 (quotation on 46). For other group labels: *PA*, 2nd ser., 5: map opposite 289.

24. William A. Starna and José António Brandão, "From the Mohawk-Mahican War to the Beaver Wars: Questioning the Pattern," *Ethnohistory* 51 (Fall 2004): 725–50; Brasser, *Riding*, 12–13; Bruce Trigger, "The Mohawk-Mahican War (1624–28): The Establishment of a Pattern," *Canadian Historical Review* 52 (September 1978): 277–82; Hendrick Aupaumut, "Extract from an Indian History," *Collections of the Massachusetts Historical Society* 9 (Boston, 1804): 100; *NNN*, 47, 43 n. 3, 89, 131, 157; Gordon M. Day, "The Ouragie War: A Case History in Iroquois-New England Indian Relations," in *Extending the Rafters: Interdisciplinary Approaches to Iroquoian Studies*, ed. Michael K. Foster, Jack Campisi, and Marianne Mithun (Albany: State University of New York Press, 1984), 39; *NYCD*, 13:161, 162, 308, 381, 302, 345, 420, 439–40, 491, 496, 508; 2:371. On Wattawyt: *NYCD*, 13:515, 517–18.

25. Day, "Ouragie War," 39. On Andros's activities: *NYCD*, 3:265; and Richter, *Ordeal*, 135–36. Michael Kammen, *Colonial New York: A History* (White Plains, N.Y.: KTO Press, 1987), 71–72, 88–89; Francis Jennings, *The Invasion of America: Indians, Colonialism, and the Cant of Conquest* (Chapel Hill: Institute of Early American History and Culture and the University of North Carolina Press, 1975), 313, 315, 317. For additional evidence suggesting Mahican involvement in Metacom's War: *NYCD*, 13:496. Lawrence H. Leder, ed., *The Livingston Indian Records, 1666–1723* (Gettysburg, Pa.: Pennsylvania Historical Association, 1956), 39; Brasser, *Riding*, 23; Jennings, *Invasion*, 322–23; Trelease, *Indian Affairs*, 235; Richter, *Ordeal*, 136.

26. Leder, *Livingston*, 37 (quotations). In a letter to the Massachusetts governor, New York's governor, Francis Lovelace, explained that the Highland Indians were "Wappingoes & Wickersheck" Indians. *NYCD*, 13:440, 345. On Wnahktukook: Brasser, *Riding*, 66; Samuel Hopkins, "Historical Memoirs Relating to the Housatonic Indians," *Magazine of History with Notes and Queries* 5, no. 17 (1911): 15. The fact that the Wecquaesgeeks and Wappingers had both become known as Highland Indians suggests the blending of populations. On the Wappinger-Stockbridge connection: Robert S. Grumet, "The Nimhams of the Colonial Hudson Valley, 1667–1783," *Hudson Valley Regional Review* 9 (September 1992): 80–99.

27. *NNN*, 205n–206n.

28. Ibid., 225 (quotations); Richter, *Ordeal*, 93–95; for another suggestion on the causes of the Mahicans' attack, see Paul Andrew Otto, "New Netherland Frontier: Europeans and Native Americans along the Lower Hudson River, 1524–1664" (Ph.D. diss., Indiana University, 1995), 204n, including comments on the possible role of the wampum trade.

29. *NNN*, 209 ("must be"), 213 and n. 1 and 2, 215, 273 ("cattle," "revenge"), 274–75, 276–77 ("vengeance" on 276); *NYHM* 1974, 187.

30. Brasser, *Riding*, 18 ; *NNN*, 172 ("yearly contribution"); Richter, *Ordeal*, 94; *NNN*, 274, 225 ("gun on his shoulder" and on numerical disparity).

31. Trelease, *Indian Affairs*, 76–77; *NNN*, 279, 282 ("about one hundred"), 282 n. 5, 283–84 (other quotations on 283).

32. *NNN*, 283–84 ("collected" on 284); Van der Donck, "Description," 202–3.

33. *NNN*, 230 and n. 1.

34. Ibid., 230 ("how they came," "they were out"), 208 (quotations about Raritans).

35. Ibid., 68 ("two," "Esopes"); *NYCD*, 13:84 ("how many of their people"), 290 ("some of his friends"); Trelease, *Indian Affairs*, 6–7.

36. Marc B. Fried, *The Early History of Kingston and Ulster County, N.Y.* (Marbletown, Kingston, N.Y.: Ulster County Historical Society, 1975), 14–15 (on Chambers); *NYCD*, 13:77 (quotation), 79, 81–83.

37. *NYCD*, 13:80, 84 ("*cacheus*"), 96–97 ("a certain"), 93–94, 99 ("to murmur"), 104 ("that their corn-pits," "had badly beaten"), 375. On the word "cacheus," see Ives Goddard, "The Delaware Jargon," in *New Sweden*, ed. Hoffecker et al., 140.

38. Grumet, "'We Are Not So Great Fools,'" 49–52; *NYHM* 1981, 195 ("eleven Menissing"), 337 ("Christians," "near the Menissingh"); *NYCD*, 13:169, 178, 173, 171, 179–81, 245–47, 328, 341, 342, 343, 372, 386–87, 376, 280 ("tried to involve"), 361, 290, 325 ("40 *Manissing*," "40 more"), 324.

39. *NYCD*, 13:172–73, 364, 386–87.

40. Ibid., 13:275 ("some *Esopus*"), 572 ("an old Esopus"), 279, 284, 287 ("one of the *Esopus* Sachems"), 288, 292 ("the *Wappinghs* and *Esopus* keep together"), 291 ("mostly hidden"). Brasser considers Catskill a Mahican area by 1650. Brasser, *Riding*, 66. Dunn argues that the Catskills were a subgroup of Mahicans. Dunn, *Mohicans*, 54. One of Wannachquatin's partners in the sale was "Mamanauchqua and her son Cunpaewn," apparently kin of Shabash, who would become a future Moravian leader at the Shekomeko mission (present Pine Plains, New York). Evidence for this identification appears in Shabash's family narrative, in which he mentioned his grandmother and uncle (mother's mother and mother's brother) "Mannanochquá" and her "minor" son. The 1683 sale may have been one of Mannanochquá's last official acts on behalf of her family, because Shabash's story mentions that she and her son died in an epidemic that would have occurred in the 1680s. Büttner, Historic Statement, 3/5/113/3, *RMM*.

41. *NYCD*, 13:325–26, 339, 338–39. Grumet has drawn attention to the importance of a flexible approach to settlement as a tool for survival. Grumet, "'We Are Not So Great Fools,'" 60, 91–92.

42. *NYCD*, 13:279 ("disperse"), 324, 325, 339, 329, 344, 273 ("all the prisoners," "guarded together"), 327 ("here and there"); Fried, *Early History of Kingston*, 66–84, 87–102.

43. Francis Jennings, "Susquehannock," in *HNAI*, 15:367; *NEP*, 103–4 n. 2, 70 and n. 5; Weslager, *Dutch*, 117–18, 120; Francis Jennings, "Glory, Death, and Transfiguration: The Susquehannock Indians in the Seventeenth Century," *Proceedings of the APS* 112 (February 1968): 17.

44. *NEP*, 22–24 (quotations from Dutch encounter), 38–40 (quotations from English encounter); *PA*, 2nd ser., 5: opposite 289. Sankiekans appears as "Sanhicans" on this map, and Armewamen as "Ermomex." In his work dated 1765, Smith placed Arwaumus "in and about where the town of Gloucester [N.J.] now is." Smith, *Nova-Caesaria*, 98. On Fort Nassau, see Prologue in this volume. Jennings notes evidence of

Susquehannock-Lenape warfare as early as 1626, but it is unclear whether competition over the fur trade was the cause of this fighting. Jennings, "Glory," 17.

45. Amandus Johnson, *The Swedish Settlements on the Delaware: Their History and Relation to the Indians, Dutch and English, 1638–1664* (New York: D. Appleton and University of Pennsylvania, 1911), 1:434–45; *PA*, 2nd ser., 5:262–63 (quotation from 1651), 266–67. Evidence that Matthehooren (or Mattehooren) and Sinquees were Armewanninges comes from the statement, in ibid., 257, that along with Alibakinne, they were "Sachems over the district of country called Armenveruis." This document is possibly the basis for Myers's editorial note that "Mattahoorn" may have been "Ermewarmoki": *NEP*, 87 n. 2. For the 1638 meeting with the Swedes: ibid., 86–89. Jennings makes the strong case that the Delaware Valley Algonquians did not become tributaries or "subject" peoples of the Susquehannocks at the end of the war period, in contrast to the assertion of the Swedish writer Thomas Campanius Holm. Jennings, "Glory," 17, 19–20, 50–53.

46. *NEP*, 38 ("had wholly"), 24 ("compelled").

47. Ibid., 40 ("who lived," "40 or 60"), 42 ("a lesser River"), 43 ("came aboard our shippes"), 44 (subsequent quotations in paragraph).

48. Ibid., 40 (quotation), 41–44.

49. *NYHM* 1981, 5.

50. *NEP*, 47–48 (Yong), 103 (Printz); *GA*, 170 (Lindeström); *PA*, 2nd ser., 5:250 (Dutch report).

51. *NEP*, 41 (Yong), 156–57 (Rising); Jennings, "Glory," 25.

52. *NEP*, 103 (Printz), 139 n. 2; *NYHM* 1981, 131 (Alrichs); Marshall Joseph Becker, "Lenape Maize Sales to the Swedish Colonists: Cultural Stability during the Early Colonial Period," in *New Sweden*, ed. Hoffecker et al., 121–36.

53. *NNN*, 19–26; Hazard, *Annals*, 443; Budd pamphlet quoted in Smith, *Nova-Caesaria*, 101n ("The Indians have been very serviceable to us"), 102n; Smith narrative in Walker, *History of Trenton*, 55. Mahlon Stacy also indicated that local Indians helped with provisioning at West Jersey. As he stated, "We have brought home to our houses by the Indians, seven or eight fat bucks of a day; and some times put by as many." Abstract of Mahlon Stacy letter to his brother Revell, June 26, 1680, in Smith, *Nova-Caesaria*, 112.

54. Goddard, "Delaware Jargon," 137–43; A. J. F. van Laer, trans. and ed., *Van Rensselaer Bowier Manuscripts . . .* (Albany: University of the State of New York, 1908), 306 (on Mahican); Ives Goddard, "Eastern Algonquian Languages," in *HNAI*, 15:72–73.

55. Fort Altena was formerly the Swedish Fort Christina. C. A. Weslager, *The English on the Delaware, 1610–1682* (New Brunswick, N.J.: Rutgers University Press, 1967), 155; Becker, "Maize Sales," 124; *NYCD*, 12:340 ("at the tavern"); *NYHM* 1981, 72, 76 ("five Indian men," "pail," "drunk and insolent"), 80 ("they had not received"), 184 ("brawling"), 185 ("canoe," "six Indians"), 266; *PA*, 2nd ser., 5:299; Peter C. Mancall, *Deadly Medicine: Indians and Alcohol in Early America* (Ithaca, N.Y.: Cornell University Press, 1995), 39–61. For similar findings in a later period: Merritt, *Crossroads*, 65.

56. *NYHM* 1981, 185 ("almost empty," "threatened," "saying that he had poisoned"); Budd pamphlet, in Smith, *Nova-Caesaria*, 101n–102n (quotation from sachems); *NYHM* 1977, 340 (quotations about Wheeler), 341, 311.

57. Jegou said he was attacked in 1670: "The Record of the Court at Upland, in

Pennsylvania, 1676 to 1681," in *Memoirs of the HSP* (Philadelphia: J. B. Lippincott, 1860), 7:140 ("lying and being"), 141 ("plundered"); *PA*, 2nd ser., 5:629–32; *NYHM* 1981, 235 ("the English have killed," "River chiefs do not trust"), 232–34; *NYHM* 1977, 18 ("to remain brothers"), 49–50; *NYCD*, 12:486–88.

58. *NYHM* 1981, 203.

"He knew the best how to order them"

1. *An Account of the Life of that Ancient Servant of Jesus Christ, John Richardson, Giving a Relation of many of his Trials and Exercises in his Youth, and his Services in the Work of the Ministry, in England, Ireland, America, &c.* (Philadelphia: Joseph Crukshank, 1783), 134; Thomas Campanius Holm, *Description of the Province of New Sweden . . .* (Philadelphia, McCarty and Davis, 1834; reprt., Millwood, N.Y.: Krause Reprint, 1975), 77 ("stroked"); *EAID*, 1:285 ("the Great Being").

2. *PP*, 2:243 n. 4; *An Account of Richardson*, 134–35.

3. *An Account of Richardson*, 137–38.

4. *MPC*, 2:14–18; *EAID*, 1:101–4; *MPC*, 2:469 ("Passakassy").

Chapter 3

1. *NEP*, 15–17, 87–89, 53; *EAID*, 1:2; *NNN*, 82–83, 86, 83 n. 3; Sten Carlsson, "The New Sweden Colonists, 1638–1656: Their Geographical and Social Background," in *New Sweden*, ed. Hoffecker et al., 176–78; Per Martin Tvengsberg, "Finns in Seventeenth-Century Sweden and Their Contributions to the New Sweden Colony," in Hoffecker et al., 284; Evan Haefeli, "The Pennsylvania Difference: Religious Diversity on the Delaware before 1683," *Early American Studies* 1 (Spring 2003): 41; *NYCD*, 12:176ff; *NYHM* 1981, 137–38; Weslager, *Dutch*, 252, 61n; *PA*, 2nd ser., 5:307.

2. Pomfret, *West New Jersey*, 106–7; *EAID*, 1:52–53; *PP*, 2:261–62; see various deeds in *PA*, 1st ser., 1:62–68, 91–96. *DS*, 22; Peter C. Mancall, *Valley of Opportunity: Economic Culture along the Upper Susquehanna, 1700–1800* (Ithaca, N.Y.: Cornell University Press, 1991), 73; *PA*, 1st ser., 1:69 ("80 houses," "300 farmers"); William Penn, "Some Proposals for a Second Settlement in the Province of Pennsylvania," 1690, vol. 1, Penn Letters and Ancient Documents, p. 66, APS ("good forwardness").

3. *PP*, 3:107 (first and second quotations), 112 n. 72, 113 n. 76; 2:261–62; Jennings, *Ambiguous*, 231; *PA*, 1st ser., 1:62, 64, 92–93; *MPC*, 1:435; J[ames]. L[ogan]. to Sassoonan or Allumapies, August 13, 1731, p. 35, vol. 1, PM ("Little Lad"). Sassoonan mentioned seeing Hithquoquean, Menanzes, and Tamanen at Perkasie. For lands associated with these individuals, see *PP*, 2:262, 266n, map on 491. *EAID*, 1:180; *MPC*, 3:316, 404.

4. *PP*, 3:452 ("Quanestaqua"). The Conestoga residents had "removed From Schoolkill," according to Markham. *IVPN*, 36, 146, 38; *NEP*, 69–70 n. 10; *MPC*, 2:389 (quotations on Evans's visit), 469 ("Chiefs of the Delaware Indians"); *EAID* 1:136 ("great Falls"); Merrell, *Into the American Woods*, 110–15.

5. Isaac Norris, Sam Preston, and James Logan to John, Thomas, and Richard Penn, November 13, 1731, p. 36, vol. 1, PM; *GA*, 128, 170, 168 n. 48; *EAID*, 1:180; *MPC*, 2:469, 545, 546 (also spelled "Scollitchy"), 557, 599–600 (Skalitchi); ibid., 3:316, 404.

6. *MPC*, 2:469, 26; 1:448; *EAID*, 1:135. Owechela may have been the same person as Machaloha who had sold land between the Delaware River and Chesapeake Bay to Penn. De Valinger, "Indian Sales," 30.

7. *MPC*, 2:469; *PA*, 1st ser., 1:63–64, 67; *PP*, 3:41.

8. *MPC*, 2:15; Charles Callender, "Shawnee," in *HNAI*, 15:622, 630; *EAID*, 1:478 n. 8; *IVPN*, 148–49, 152–53, 36–37; *MPC*, 3:97; Robert S. Grumet, "The Minisink Settlements: Native American Identity and Society in the Munsee Heartland, 1650–1778," in *People of Minisink*, ed. Orr and Campana, 177–79, 187; Kent, *Susquehanna's Indians*, 83–84, 93; White, *Middle Ground*, 29–31; Jennings, *Ambiguous*, 173–75; Charles A. Hanna, The *Wilderness Trail* . . . (New York: G. P. Putnam's Sons, 1911), 1:138, 142.

9. Christian F. Feest, "Nanticoke and Neighboring Tribes," in *HNAI*, 15:240–46, 249–50; William Hand Browne et al., eds., *Archives of Maryland* (Baltimore: Maryland Historical Society, 1883–1972), 24:101; 25:102–3; 26:42; *MPC*, 2:246 ("the Virginians"), 15 ("head of Potomac"), 656–57, 191, 246 ("settled some miles").

10. Feest, "Nanticoke," 240–41; Marian E. White, William E. Engelbrecht, and Elisabeth Tooker, "Cayuga," in *HNAI*, 15:501; Douglas W. Boyce, "Iroquoian Tribes of the Virginia-North Carolina Coastal Plain," in *HNAI*, 15:287–88; David Landy, "Tuscarora among the Iroquois," in *HNAI*, 15:518–20; Richter, *Ordeal*, 238.

11. *PA*, 1st ser., 1:67; Kekelappan came from Opasiskunk. *IVPN*, 137, suggests that Opasiskunk might have been around Conestoga Creek; however, Hunter (*DS*, 22) places it on White Clay as does Kent in *EAID*, 1:52. The documents bearing Kekelappan's name, quoted above, suggest that White Clay is a more likely location for Opasiskunk than is Conestoga. *PA*, 1st ser., 1:67 (first quotation); *PP*, 2:492 ("between Delaware River"); Jennings, "Glory," 46–47. Along with Kekelappan and other lower–Delaware Valley Indians, Machaloha later signed over to Penn a deed to lands between Duck and Chester creeks. Indenture at New Castle, October 2, 1685, p. 44, vol. 1, PM. In his article, *DS*, 22, Hunter suggests that Kekelappan and Machaloha were Lenapes. Also see Jennings, "Glory," 46–47 n. 128. See *PP*, 2:492 n. 1 for a suggestion that Machaloha might have been a Susquehannock. Although not objecting to the Indians' retaining access to certain hunting territories, Maryland claimed that Delawares had no guaranteed right "to hunt any where westward of Elk river" along Chesapeake Bay—hence disputing the Delawares' original claim to these lower-Susquehanna lands. The Marylander Talbot seemed to consider Machaloha a Delaware. Clayton Colman Hall, ed., *Narratives of Early Maryland, 1633–1684* (New York: Charles Scribner's Sons, 1910), 440–41 ("to hunt any where"), 439 ("declared," "should not be molested," "in Delaware").

12. On Iroquois claims to the Susquehanna Valley by right of conquest, see *EAID*, 1:227 and *MPC*, 4:708. Richter, *Ordeal*, 136–37; *PP*, 2:260; 3:671; *PA*, 1st ser., 1:80 ("people," "Jealous," "much opposed"); *PP*, 3:132, 159, 179; *PA*, 1st ser., 1:76–77 ("all of them"). Jennings argues, "The Iroquois, far from conquering the Susquehannocks, provided sanctuary and support for them." Jennings, "Glory," 16–17.

13. Jennings, *Ambiguous*, 228 ("neither a cession"), 229, 235; *MPC*, 4:708 (second and

third quotations); *PA*, 1st ser., 1:76, 81, 122–23; Gary B. Nash, "The Quest for the Susquehanna Valley: New York, Pennsylvania, and the Seventeenth-Century Fur Trade," *New York History* 48 (January 1967): 13–14, 22–24.

14. *PP*, 2:423 ("Claime," "the remainder"); *PA*, 1st ser., 1:133; *MPC*, 2:14–18.

15. *EAID*, 1:136 ("That the Land belonged"); *MPC*, 3:97 ("the Five Nations," "seemed to claim"); Jennings, *Ambiguous*, 303–4; *MPC*, 4:93 (third quotation). For variants of this Susquehannock leader's name, see *MPC*, 2:553 and *EAID*, 1:285.

16. Taquatarensaly's speech is in *EAID*, 1:227–29 ("When the Conestogoes," "Upon which Wm. Penn" on 227); *MPC*, 2:16 ("live Near"); *EAID*, 1:107 ("be good and kind," "confidence" [emphasis mine]), 85–86.

17. *MPC*, 1:448, 396–97 ("Kyentarrah"), 435 ("strange Indians"); *PA*, 1st ser., 1: 144. For suggested identifications of these Indians, see *EAID*, 1:476–77 nn. 2, 3. Callender, "Shawnee," 634. For evidence of a Delaware presence at the Articles of Agreement signing, see discussion about "Passauquessay" in the interlude between Chapter 2 and Chapter 3. *MPC*, 2:469.

18. *MPC*, 1:435 ("hee neither"); 3:97 ("People differed"); 2:601 ("lived," "entertained").

19. Ibid., 2:191.

20. Ibid., 2:141; 3:47 (Taquatarensaly and Sheeckokonichan quotations); Mancall, *Deadly*, 85–100.

21. *MPC*, 2:511 ("several persons"), 247 ("certain Orders"), 248 ("to take Care"), 554 ("since Lycenses"), 248; Mancall, *Deadly*, 101–10.

22. *MPC*, 2:553–54 (quotations on 554); *EAID*, 1:480 n. 32.

23. *MPC*, 2:601 (quotation), 556. For a discussion of Native and non-Native perspectives on the economics of trade, see Merrell, *Into the American Woods*, 123.

24. *MPC*, 3:45, 19–20 (quotations); *PA*, 1st ser., 1:144. For other joint actions involving Susquehannocks, Delawares, Shawnees, and Conoys, see *MPC*, 3:78–81; *EAID*, 1:187–90.

25. Register of Adult Baptisms, Catalogs, Generalia, November 15/26, 1748, 3/1/313/33, *RMM*. An English translation of the entire item about Depaakhossi, with the quotation, appears in Merritt, *Crossroads*, 316, app. A. *PA*, 1st ser., 1:213, 238; *EAID*, 1:188 ("A Dispute"); Richter, *Ordeal*, 237–38.

26. *MPC*, 2:546–47 (quotations from 1712 meeting on 547); Paul A. W. Wallace: Folder entitled "Wallace, Paul A. W. The Delawares-as-Women Problem," Paper read at the Iroquois Conference, Red House, October 1952, pp. 6, 14–15, Paul Wallace Papers, Series I: Correspondence, Wallace Family Papers, APS. Jennings points out that James Logan skewed the record of this conference to make it seem that the Delawares were "subjects" of the Iroquois. See also his view of the diversity among the Delawares. Jennings, *Ambiguous*, 263.

27. Manatawny appeared in various spellings: *MPC*, 2:390 and 3:304.

28. I. Daniel Rupp, *History of the Counties of Berks and Lebanon . . .* (1844; repr., Spartanburg, S.C.: Reprint Co., 1984), 82, 125, 87, 231; William C. Reichel, ed., *Memorials of the Moravian Church* (Philadelphia: J. B. Lippincott, 1870), 75n; J. Smith Futhey and Gilbert Cope, *History of Chester County, Pennsylvania, with Genealogical and Biographical Sketches* (Philadelphia: Louis H. Everts, 1881), 343–44; John W. Kleiner and Helmut T.

Lehmann, eds. and trans., *The Correspondence of Heinrich Melchior Mühlenberg* (1986; Camden, Maine: Picton Press, 1997), 2:20 n. 6; *IVPN*, 136; P. C. Croll, *Annals of the Oley Valley in Berks County, Pa.: Over Two Hundred Years of Local History of an American Canaan* (Reading, Pa.: Reading Eagle Press, 1926), 14, 17, 18 ("sin any more").

29. *EAID*, 1:485 n. 37; *IVPN*, 136; *MPC*, 3:319, 320–21 (quotations).

30. Francis Jennings, "Incident at Tulpehocken," *Pennsylvania History* 35 (October 1968): 337; *MPC*, 3:92, 321; *NEP*, 69 n. 10; Robert Proud, *The History of Pennsylvania . . .* (Philadelphia: Zachariah Poulson Jr., 1798; repr., Spartanburg, S.C.: Reprint Co., 1967), 2:245 (quotations on South Mountain). I. Daniel Rupp, *History of Northampton, Lehigh, Monroe, Carbon, and Schuylkill Counties: Containing a Brief History of the First Settlers, Topography of Townships, . . .* (Harrisburg: Hickok and Cantine, 1845), 110 (uses "*Lecha Hill*" and "South mountain" interchangeably); *IVPN*, 136; Reichel, *Memorials*, 75n (on Oley Hills); Isaac Norris, Sam Preston and James Logan, November 13, 1731, to John, Thomas, and Richard Penn, p. 36, vol. 1, PM ("Lechay Hills").

31. Isaac Norris, Sam Preston, and James Logan, to John, Thomas, and Richard Penn, November 13, 1731, p. 36, vol. 1, PM ("Lechay Hills"); *MPC*, 3:321–24 ("reached" on 322 and "had never" on 321–22); Jennings, "Incident," 338–39, 342–43.

32. Logan to Allummapis and Opekasset, March 13, 1730, and Logan to Allummapis, June 12, 1731, p. 50, vol. 4, LCA; Jennings, *Ambiguous*, 302–3 n. 38.

33. *MPC*, 3:303–5, 309 (the Shawnee message referred to the southern Indians as "Flatheads"), 295 ("upper parts of the River Susquehannah"), 213, 221 ("long hard Winter"), 210 (on Manawkyhickon as "Delaware"), 222 ("strange"), 223 ("foreign"), 209–10 (quotation about Philadelphia County); John H. Long, ed., *Pennsylvania: Atlas of Historical County Boundaries* (New York: Simon and Schuster, 1996), 170, 31; Helen Hornbeck Tanner, "Cherokees in the Ohio Country," *Journal of Cherokee Studies* 3 (Spring 1978): 95.

34. Rupp, *Berks and Lebanon*, 138, 111. On Chester County boundaries prior to 1729: Long, *Pennsylvania*, 45.

35. *PA*, 1st ser., 1:216, 218–20, 213–14 (quotations on 218, 219); *MPC*, 3:304, indicates that the killings took place at Cucussea; however, there is some confusion about this location. Samuel Whitaker Pennypacker indicates that John Roberts lived on the Skippack to the southeast of Tulpehocken rather than near the Winters at Cucussea. Merrell, *Into the American Woods*, 379 n. 11, cites him ("Bebber's Township and the Dutch Patroons of Pennsylvania," *PMHB* (1907): 1–18), and places the killings on the Skippack (161), though he mentions the alternative site of Cucussea as well. The colonial records I have cited, nevertheless, locate most of the trouble in this period on the Manatawny, the Cucussea, and at Tulpehocken, and I have relied on these sources for my discussion, although I have not resolved the disagreement over the location of Roberts's home.

36. *MPC*, 3:306 ("persons . . . all related," "we cannot expect"), 315 ("some of the Relations"); Rupp, *Berks and Lebanon*, 125 (on Molatton); *PA*, 1st ser., 1:227 (for Sassoonan at Shamokin); Patrick Gordon, *By the Honourable Patrick Gordon . . . A Proclamation . . . Now for prevention of all further and other breaches of the established peace and friendship . . . [May 16, 1728]* (Philadelphia: Andrew Bradford, [1728]) in

Early American Imprints, ser. 1, Evans no. 3087, Readex Digital Collections, Archive of Americana, American Antiquarian Society and NewsBank, 2002; Merrell, *Into the American Woods*, 158–67.

37. *PA*, 1st ser., 1:344–45. On Sassoonan's dissatisfaction with the payment for these lands, see Jennings, *Ambiguous*, 313–14.

38. *PP*, 2:448 ("secatareus"); *EAID*, 1:72; *PP*, 3:41.

39. *PA*, 8th ser., 2:1701 (first quotation), 1757–58. In 1725, Alphonsus Kirk and Samuel Hollingsworth, two area residents, suggested that indeed there had been some land set aside for the Brandywine Indians. Kirk remembered that "above thirty years Since he saw two Papers which Saccatarius or some other of the Chiefs of the Indians on Brandywine had in their possession." "The first," Kirk said, was "sign'd by Governor Penn recommending the Indians to the Regards and Friendship of the English." The second document indicated that the Indians were to retain their "Town on Brandywine . . . and one or two Miles round it." Although Kirk was unsure of the details in this second agreement, he had a "Notion . . . that there was more Land reserved to the Indians by the same Instrument besides the Town." Hollingsworth offered information that dated back to his childhood. Although he would have been only about ten years old at the time of the events he was describing, Hollingsworth could recall that "about one or two & forty Years Since [i.e., about 1684] Saccatarius the Indian Chief of Brandywine Shew'd to his father Valentine Hollingsworth and others[,] of whom the Said Samuel was one[,] a Paper Signed by Governor Penn declaring what Land the said Saccatarius had sold." Hollingsworth added that "he thinks there was Some reservation in it, which is all he knows further than that the Indians many years after claimed the Lands on Brandywine on which George Harland & himself & others lived." Statements of Alphonsus Kirk and Samuel Hollingsworth, [September 1, 1725, and no date], vol. 11, LPIA.

40. Futhey and Cope, *Chester County*, 189–92; Statement of Thomas Chandler, August 16, 1725, vol., 11, LPIA; Samuel Hazard, ed., *The Register of Pennsylvania Devoted to the Preservation of Facts and Documents, and Every Other Kind of Useful Information Respecting the State of Pennsylvania* (Philadelphia: W. F. Geddes, January–July 1828), 1:114; *PA*, 8th ser., 2:1701.

41. Edward Armstrong, ed., *Correspondence between William Penn and James Logan, Secretary of the Province of Pennsylvania, and Others, 1700–1750 . . .* (Philadelphia: J. B. Lippincott & Co., 1870 [also volume 10 of the *Memoirs of the HSP*]), 2:167 (first [emphasis mine], third, and fourth quotations); *PA*, 8th ser., 2:1758 (second quotation); Futhey and Cope, *Chester County*, 190 (map showing location of Abraham Marshall's land in 1730); Minutes of the Commissioners on the Brandywine Indians' Complaint, 1725 or 1726, p. 49, vol. 4, LCA.

42. Minutes of the Commissioners on the Brandywine Indians' Complaint (second and fourth quotations); *PA*, 8th ser., 2:1701 (first and third quotations).

43. Statements by Nathaniel Newlin and the Commissioners, [March ?] 1726, vol. 11, LPIA ("that he will not"); Futhey and Cope, *Chester County*, 191–92. *KJ*, 45 ("Sold by Old Newlin"), 176 (other quotations from Neemakcollen, or "E. McCollon"). A "Mr. Langdale" was a storekeeper at Pittsburgh in 1760. James Young to Richard Peters, August 14, 1760, vol. 11, LPIA.

44. *MPC*, 3:334 ("Brandywine Indians"); *EAID*, 1:285–88 ("Delaware Indians on Brandywine" on 285); *MPC*, 3:45 ("a chief"), 47; Wiggoneeheenah deed to Edmund Cartlidge, April 8, 1725, vol. 11, LPIA (quotations from Wiggoneeheenah). I assume that Wikimikyona may have been the individual named in Cartlidge's deed as "Wiggoneeheenah," who claimed to act "In behalf of all the Dellaware Indians." Wiggoneeheenah deed.

45. Marshall J. Becker, "Hannah Freeman: An Eighteenth-Century Lenape Living and Working among Colonial Farmers," *PMHB* 114 (April 1990): 249–69. Quotations from the beginning of the paragraph through "Aunts Betty & Nanny" are from the document "The Examination of Indian Hannah, alias Hannah Freeman (July 28, 1797), quoted in ibid., 251–52; subsequent quotations in this paragraph are from Henry Graham Ashmead, *History of Delaware County, Pennsylvania* (Philadelphia: L. H. Everts and Co., 1884), 314.

46. *IVPN*, 56–57.

47. Lenore Santone, "Resiliency as Resistance: Eastern Woodland Munsee Groups on the Early Colonial Frontier," *North American Archaeologist* 19, no. 2 (1998): 121–22; Grumet, "'We Are Not So Great Fools,'" 70–71; Weslager, *Dutch*, 64; *JD*, 96 (first quotation); *NEP*, 47 (the sailor was Yong's lieutenant). Also on the shortage of documentation about the early history of the Forks: Marshall J. Becker, "The Boundary between the Lenape and Munsee: The Forks of Delaware as a Buffer Zone," *Man in the Northeast*, no. 26 (1983), 5–6.

48. *NYHM* 1981, 195 ("from above"); *MPC*, 2:26 (quotes on "Oppemenyhook at Lechay"), 21–22; "James Letort's Petetion with his Accounts," 1704, vol. 11, LPIA. In this petition Le Tort also names debtors from his trade at Conestoga; however, given the proximity of the Forks to Pechoquealing, it seems likely that Oppemenyhook and other Indians from Lechay would trade at Pechoquealing rather than at Conestoga. *IVPN*, 148–49.

49. Alan Tully, *William Penn's Legacy: Politics and Social Structure in Provincial Pennsylvania, 1726–1755* (Baltimore: Johns Hopkins University Press, 1977), 3–6; Donna Bingham Munger, *Pennsylvania Land Records: A History and Guide for Research* (Wilmington, Del.: Scholarly Resources, in cooperation with the Pennsylvania Historical and Museum Commission, 1991), 5–6, 58–59; *The Scotch-Irish of Northampton County, Pennsylvania*, vol. 1 of Northampton County Historical and Genealogical Society (Easton, Pa.: John S. Correll, 1926), 430–31, 6, 18; A. D. Chidsey Jr., "The Penn Patents in the Forks of the Delaware" in *Publications of the Northampton County Historical Society*, vol. 2 (Easton, Pa., 1937; microfiche, PSL), 23, and map no. 9; A. D. Chidsey Jr., comp., *The Forks of the Delaware in Pennsylvania* . . . (Easton, Pa.: Northampton County Historical and Genealogical Society, 1938), in MG-11, Map Collection Items, PSA; Sherman Day, *Historical Collections of the State of Pennsylvania* . . . (Philadelphia: George W. Gorton, 1843), 510 ("dry lands").

50. Jennings, *Ambiguous*, 316–19 and 319n; Tully, *Penn's Legacy*, 11–12; Munger, *Land Records*, 5–6, 33–34, 66–67; John Penn to Thomas Penn, February 2, 1735, in "The Thomas Penn Papers, 1729–1832, at the Historical Society of Pennsylvania," ed. John D. Kilbourne (HSP, 1968), Special Collections Microfilm #1578, PSA; *Scotch-Irish of Northampton County*, 13, 35.

51. *EAID*, 1:441 ("endeavouring to raise War"); Jennings, *Ambiguous*, 334–35, 309, 331, 320–21; Anthony F. C. Wallace, *King of the Delawares: Teedyuscung, 1700–1763* (1949; Syracuse, N.Y.: Syracuse University Press, 1990), 24; *MPC*, 3:295–96, 315, 330; *PA*, 1st ser., 1:230, 215 ("that if he Did"); Grumet, "'We Are Not So Great Fools,'" 184–85, 187–88.

52. Nicholas Scull to Benjamin Eastbourn, September 9, 1734, box 36, reel LO 24.27, Records of the Bureau of Land Records, RG-17, PSA; Jennings, *Ambiguous*, 320–21, 334, 391; *SWJP*, 3:841; *PA*, 1st ser., 1:539; *EAID*, 1:457–59; "James Letort's Petetion with his Accounts," 1704, folder 4, vol. 11, LPIA; *IVPN*, 69; Wallace, *King*, 20–24; *EAID*, 2:24 ("begging & plagueing"—Jennings believes this statement was made at the Durham treaty [*Ambiguous*, 320–21]); John Penn to Thomas Penn, July 20, 1736, in "Thomas Penn Papers," microfilm roll 1 ("There is a very Large Quantity"). Delaware Indians' meeting with Proprietor, June 1733, p. 37, vol. 1, PM.

53. "A Connected Draft of 45 Tracts of Land, Situated in Lehigh and Northampton Counties . . . ," folio 1, sheet 9, Worksheets—Folder Pertaining to Northampton County, map no. 3312, Location 30–3312, RG-17, PSA; Chidsey, "Penn Patents," 25 and map no. 1; Indian Tract Survey, Book D-80, p. 237, copied surveys microfilm, RG-17, PSA; William J. Heller, *History of Northampton County [Pennsylvania] and the Grand Valley of the Lehigh* (Boston: American Historical Society, 1920), 2:490. Survey map of the land of Henry Tantlinger, Book A-64, p. 106, copied surveys microfilm, RG-17, PSA ("Survey'd").

54. *EAID*, 1:441; Jennings, *Ambiguous*, 322–23; "The Answer of the Chiefs of the Delaware Indians to the Governor's Message of March 27, 1741," May 12, 1741, p. 74, vol. 4, LCA.

55. *EAID*, 1:435–36, 441–43, 445, 446 ("no Land remaining"); *PA*, 1st ser., 1: 494, 498 ("the Land lying"); Statement of the Six Nations, October 1736, folder 25, vol. 11, LPIA; Jennings, *Ambiguous*, 321–23.

56. Jennings, *Ambiguous*, 329–33, 336–39; Wallace, *King*, 21–22, 25–26; Declaration of Moses Tetamy (see Chapter 2, note 11 in this volume); *EAID*, 1:80 (document used by proprietors as part of their claim to a purchase measured with a day-and-a-half walk).

57. *EAID*, 1:457–59; Jennings, *Ambiguous*, 330–40; Wallace, *King*, 25–28; William A. Starna, "The Diplomatic Career of Canasatego," in *FEPW*, 149–50; Gnadenhütten, Pa., February 19, 1749, 1/5/116/4.

58. Delaware Indians' meeting with Proprietor, June 1733, p. 37, vol. 1, PM (first quotation); *EAID*, 2:24 ("100 families," "We think," "We Desire"), 25 ("We are Very much Wronged"), 41.

59. *EAID*, 2:24 (quotation) and 473 n. 30.

60. Ibid., 2:33–35, 38, 42 (first quotation), 44, 45–46 (subsequent quotations).

61. Starna, "Canasatego," 152, 148 (quotation). On Iroquois troubles during this era: William N. Fenton, *The Great Law and the Longhouse: A Political History of the Iroquois Confederacy* (Norman: University of Oklahoma Press, 1998), 408. For Ohio Indians' resistance to Iroquois authority in the 1730s, see Jennings, *Ambiguous*, 314–15 and 315n, and on ambiguity in Delaware-Iroquois relations, 263–64.

62. Merritt, *Crossroads*, 220 (scholar quoted); Merritt also makes the point about Native women's ownership of property (220); *PA*, 2nd ser., 7:156 (Anameackhiska-

man). Dunn lists a number of deeds that include Algonquian women selling land in the Hudson Valley. See the sale of July 19, 1682, which included an Esopus woman and her son, as well as various sales involving Mahican women. Dunn, *Mohicans*, 293–94, 295, 298, 299. Wallace, "Woman," 25–26; *EAID*, 2:46 ("medling in Land-Affairs"), 212–15, 219 (final quotation).

63. "Wallace, Paul A. W. The Delawares-as-Women Problem," 14–15 ("might very well"). Wallace, "Woman," on ambiguity of this language, 23–24; Langundo-Utenünk, May 5, 1770, 1/1/137/8; Robert S. Grumet, ed., *Journey on the Forbidden Path: Chronicles of a Diplomatic Mission to the Allegheny Country, March-September, 1760*, Transactions of the APS, vol. 89, pt. 2 (Philadelphia: APS, 1999), 68 ("My Sister"); *SWJP*, 11:657 (last quotation). It is possible that Squash Cutter also used "Sister" to distinguish himself as a warrior apart from the peacemakers. See also the comment by the Delaware Tamaqua in 1758 that the Six Nations have "made me like a queen, that I always should mind what is good and right." Reuben Gold Thwaites, ed., *Early Western Travels, 1748–1846* (Cleveland, Ohio: Arthur H. Clark, 1904), 1:273 (Post Journal). McConnell, *Country*, 278. Frank G. Speck, "The Delaware Indians as Women: Were the Original Pennsylvanians Politically Emasculated?" *PMHB* 70 (October 1946): 377–89; Wallace, "Woman," 1–35; Wallace, *King*, 195–96; Jay Miller, "The Delaware as Women: A Symbolic Solution," *American Ethnologist* 1 (August 1974): 507–14; C. A. Weslager, "The Delaware Indians as Women," *Journal of the Washington Academy of Sciences* 34 (December 15, 1944): 381–88; and Weslager, "Further Light on the Delaware Indians as Women," *Journal of the Washington Academy of Sciences* 37 (September 15, 1947): 298–304. Nancy Shoemaker also discusses the importance of understanding this terminology in context in *A Strange Likeness: Becoming Red and White in Eighteenth-Century North America* (Oxford: Oxford University Press, 2004), 107–14. At the Pittsburgh treaty of 1775, Delawares attributed women's guidance to keeping the Delawares out of war. *RUO*, 88–89.

64. Reichel, *Memorials*, 72 (quotation, statement reported by Moravian leader); Jennings, *Ambiguous*, 263–64.

Chapter 4

1. *MB*, 205 ("not more"), 175 ("dispersed," "several"); *IVPN*, 158 (Pohopoco or Pochapuchkug); Gnadenhütten, Pa., May 2, October 16, 1748, 1/3 and 4/116/4 (Chestnut Hill or Kastanienberg). The Chestnut Hill site may have been at a gap in the mountains where Peter Doll later built a blockhouse "about a mile and a half northnorthwest of present Klecknersville, Northampton County." William A. Hunter, *Forts of the Pennsylvania Frontier, 1753–1758* (Harrisburg: Pennsylvania Historical and Museum Commission, 1960), 283. Also on Pohopoco (or Buchkabuchka), see Gnadenhütten, Pa., January 26, 1747, 1/1/116/4; *FL*, 3:935; Wallace, *King*, 20. On Meniolagomeka, see Reichel, *Memorials*, 35–36. *BD*, 2:74 ("little Indian towns").

2. *MPC*, 8:197, 199 (quotations on 199), 176. For another land complaint couched in the language of usage rights, see *MPC*, 7:325. Hulbert and Schwarze, *Zeisberger's History*, 17, 61, 104, 52.

3. On indebtedness, see *MB*, 274. Examination of David Zeisberger, November 22, 1755, pp. 61–62, vol. 1, HF ("pulling turnips"). *BD*, 2:99, 101 ("Indian family"). On handcrafted items, see Gnadenhütten, Pa., February 13, 14, 1747, 1/1/116/4; ibid., July 11/22, 1750, 1/1/117/5; Merritt, *Crossroads*, 152–53. For another example of this form of subsistence, see the example of the New Jersey Indian woman called Ann Roberts, who lived until 1894. Weslager, *Delaware*, 277.

4. *MPC*, 2:15 ("one Head," "one Heart," and "one People" in Articles of Agreement); ibid., 2:553 ("one body," "one heart," and "one mind"); ibid., 3:93 ("one Body, one Blood, one Heart, and one Head"), 363; ibid., 4:345 ("from one Woman"), 308 (A Delaware leader stated, "it was formerly said that the English and Indians should be as one Body or one People, half the one and half the other; but they were now to be all as one heart, not divided into halves, but entirely the same without any Distinction"); *EAID*, 1:228 ("same Flesh and Blood"); Jane T. Merritt, "Metaphor, Meaning, and Misunderstanding: Language and Power on the Pennsylvania Frontier," in *Contact Points*, ed. Cayton and Teute, 75. See also Shoemaker, *Strange Likeness*, 127–28.

5. Mancall, *Valley*, 72–74; *MPC*, 2:533; *PA*, 2nd ser., 19:572, 624, 625–26; *MPC*, 3:48; Draft (2 pieces) Conestogoe Manor 16,000 Acres Surveyed for Wm. Penn and His Heirs, Lancaster County, February 1718, map no. 3698, Location 119–2698, RG-17, Records of the Office of Land Records, Land Office Map Collection, PSA; Merritt, *Crossroads*, 28; *EAID*, 1:481 n. 4, 243; Jennings, *Ambiguous*, 268–69; Sugrue, "Peopling," 28. Memories of the Articles of Agreement were strong among these Indians, and in fact, Pennsylvania officials referred to the Articles years later in order to promote friendly relations with Indian peoples. *MPC*, 4:346, 337–41, 657 (Old Sack quotation); Merritt, *Crossroads*, 283.

6. *EAID*, 2:6–7; "Tat Tamany" Survey, Book A-24, p. 109, copied surveys microfilm, RG-17, PSA; *MB*, 210; William A. Hunter, "Moses (Tunda) Tatamy, Delaware Diplomat," in *Northeastern Indian Lives, 1632–1816*, ed. Robert S. Grumet (Amherst: University of Massachusetts Press, 1996), 259–61; *EAID*, 2:50–51 (quotations on 50); Stephen C. Harper, "Delawares and Pennsylvanians after the Walking Purchase," in *FEPW*, 171–72.

7. William N. Schwarze and Samuel H. Gapp, trans., *A History of the Beginnings of Moravian Work in America being a Translation of Georg Neisser's Manuscripts* (Bethlehem, Pa.: Archives of the Moravian Church, 1955), 18–19, 31–32; Calvin G. Beitel, *The Penn Titles to Northampton County Lands* (microfiche at PSL, n.p., 1900), 31, 33; Chidsey, *Forks of the Delaware*; Joseph Mortimer Levering, *A History of Bethlehem, Pennsylvania, 1741–1892* . . . (Bethlehem, Pa.: Times Publishing, 1903), 50, 45–46; Vernon H. Nelson, "Peter Boehler's Reminiscences of the Beginnings of Nazareth and Bethlehem," *Moravian Historical Society Transactions* (Nazareth, Pa.: Moravian Historical Society, 1992), 27:6–7, 18.

8. *BD*, 1:31 ("that he enjoy"); 2:209 ("to build"), 222 ("seventeen Indians"). "Captain John . . . decided, in return for a certain amount of compensation for his improvements to the land, to leave it and move away" (ibid., 1:129); Harper, "Delawares and Pennsylvanians," 171–72; *PP*, 2:128 ("Neighbours"). The Moravians had been in regular contact with the Indians living over the mountains (*BD*, 1:74, 169, 184, 188; 2:44, 97–98). Many of these visits were to Pohopoco.

9. *BD*, 2:225 ("great need"), 224 ("We visited"), 222 ("a large loaf"), and on obtaining timber, 2:20, 37.

10. Wheeler, "Living upon Hope"; Karl-Wilhelm Westmeier, *The Evacuation of Shekomeko and the Early Moravian Missions to Native North Americans* (Lewiston, N.Y.: Edwin Mellen Press, 1994); Frazier, *Mohicans of Stockbridge*; Corinna Dally-Starna and William A. Starna, "Picturing Pachgatgoch: An Eighteenth-Century American Indian Community in Western Connecticut," *Northeast Anthropology* 67 (Spring 2004): 1–22; Franz Laurens Wojciechowski, *Ethnohistory of the Paugussett Tribes: An Exercise in Research Methodology* (Amsterdam: De Kiva, 1992), 15, 45–47, 85–88, 90–91, 250–52; Bragdon, *Native People*, 21; Trudie Lamb Richmond, "A Native Perspective of History: The Schaghticoke Nation, Resistance and Survival," in *Enduring Traditions: The Native Peoples of New England*, ed. Laurie Weinstein (Westport, Conn.: Bergin and Garvey, 1994), 103–12; Carl Masthay, ed., *Schmick's Mahican Dictionary* (Philadelphia: American Philosophical Society, 1991), 60. Wojciechowski comments that "Wampano" meant "Easterner" (p. 15) as does Bert Salwen in "Indians of Southern New England and Long Island: Early Period," in *HNAI*, 15:175; Catalog of Baptized Indians, Generalia, 1742–1765, 1/5/313/33, *RMM*. William A. Hunter, "A Note on the Unalachtigo," in *Delaware Symposium*, ed. Kraft, 147–52; *MPC*, 7:506; 8:133; Goschgoschunk and Lawunakhannek, June 22, 23, 1769, 1/3/135/8.

11. *BD*, 2:247 ("until late"); 1:161 ("commenced"); 2:225 ("into their house"), 239 ("all the visiting"); Catalog of Baptized Indians, 1/5/313/33, *RMM*.

12. *BD*, 2:100 (comments of man from Tunkhannock or "Denkhannek"), 209 ("nice fence"); Merritt, *Crossroads*, 89–166. On care of graves, see *NEP*, 234.

13. Translation in Merritt, *Crossroads*, app. A, 311–12.

14. Ibid., app. A, 311, 313. According to Merritt, a portion of the Moravian document about Awialschashuak and her family includes a crossed-out statement, saying that the ill Englishwoman "wanted to get rid of her pregnancy" (ibid., 313).

15. Register of Baptized Indians, 3/1/313/33, *RMM*; "Catalogus aller Einwohner in Meniwolagomekah nach ihren Wohnungen," December 19, 1753, 1/4/122/6, *RMM*; Reichel, *Memorials*, 217; Wallace, *King*, 2, 20.

16. Register of Baptized Indians (German, quotation). An English translation of the entire item about Depaakhossi appears in Merritt, *Crossroads*, app. A, 316.

17. Lebenslauf of Anna Charitas, pp. 57–59, Bethlehem Diary, vol. 16—1756 (microfilm), Moravian Archives, Bethlehem, Pa.

18. All of these accounts appear in Hanna, *Wilderness*, 1:249 (Frankstown Path, 1766), 275 (Raystown Path, 1754), 282 (on Forbes Road, 1758), and 214 (Shamokin Path, 1772). Map insert at end of ibid.; Thwaites, *Early Western Travels*, 241–42; Michael N. McConnell, *Army and Empire: British Soldiers on the American Frontier, 1758–1775* (Lincoln: University of Nebraska Press, 2004), 7–12.

19. McConnell, *Country*, 1 (quotation), 5–7; *GMP*, 495 n. 111.

20. *PA*, 1st ser., 1:299, 301

21. *MPC*, 5:354–55, 519. At the Logstown meeting, Shannopin's name appears as "Shawanosson"; this appears to be the same person as "Shawanapon," mentioned in Gov. Hamilton's instructions from 1751. "Shawanapon" was reported here as one of the leaders who had said earlier, presumably at Logstown, that he would come to

Philadelphia to discuss a replacement for Sassoonan. Shannopin died before he could make the trip. *DS*, 32, equates Shawanosson and Shawanapon with Shannopin, and this correlation seems reasonable. On the Delaware brothers, see *DS*, 32–33; *MPC*, 3:404; *EAID*, 2:299; "The Examination of John Baker Servant Man of George Croghan aged about nineteen," March 31, 1756, p. 78, vol. 2, PM; *MJNY*, 8; *MPC*, 8:187–89; *DS*, 29; *MPC*, 3:321 ("Nedawaway or Oliver"); the notion that Netawatwees might have witnessed the Walking Purchase comes from *DS*, 25; *EAID*, 1:458 ("Nectotaylemet"); Untitled [communication from Croghan], n.d., p. 6, vol. 3, PM (Custalogo, "Chief" of "Delawares" at Venango ["an old Indian Town on Ohio"]); *DS*, 30; *BP*, 2:304 ("heads"); *KJ*, 157; Z. to Seidel, November 4, 1770, 19/3/229/32, *RMM*; Paul A. W. Wallace, *Indians in Pennsylvania*, 2nd ed. (Harrisburg: Commonwealth of Pennsylvania, Pennsylvania Historical and Museum Commission, 1986), 174. "Nectotaylemet" bears a resemblance to a version of Newcomer's name, "Natatwallamen," noted in 1773: *PA*, 1st ser., 4:469.

22. William A. Hunter, "History of the Ohio Valley," in *HNAI*, 15:588–90; Richter, *Ordeal*, 50–65; Marian E. White, "Erie," in *HNAI*, 15:412, 415–16; Callender, "Shawnee," 630; McConnell, *Country*, 5, 9; *MPC*, 4:234. While living on the Beaver River in 1771, Zeisberger heard a story of how the Iroquois had nearly exterminated the Shawnees who had once lived on the Ohio—a possible reference to seventeenth-century warfare. Langundo-Utenünk, March 16, 1771, 1/2/137/8.

23. Fred Anderson, *Crucible of War: The Seven Years' War and the Fate of Empire in British North America, 1754–1766* (New York: Vintage Books, 2000), 17–18, 23–32; Eric Hinderaker, *Elusive Empires: Constructing Colonialism in the Ohio Valley, 1673–1800* (Cambridge: Cambridge University Press, 1997), 136–39; McConnell, *Country*, 89–90, 101–3; *EAID*, 2:266–67; *MPC*, 5:599–600; Francis Jennings, *Empire of Fortune: Crowns, Colonies, and Tribes in the Seven Years War in America* (New York: W. W. Norton, 1988), 52–53; Louis M. Waddell and Bruce D. Bomberger, *The French and Indian War in Pennsylvania, 1753–1763: Fortification and Struggle during the War for Empire* (Harrisburg: Commonwealth of Pennsylvania, Pennsylvania Historical and Museum Commission, 1996), 3.

24. McConnell, *Country*, 95–96; *EAID*, 2:266 ("that they must"), 267 ("expressed"); "The Treaty of Logg's Town, 1752," *Virginia Historical Magazine* 13 (July 1905): 167–68.

25. *MPC*, 6:110–20; Weiser to Peters, October 12, 1754, p. 1, vol. 1, WP ("the Purchase"); Proprietors of Pennsylvania's observations on Sir William Johnson's Letter to the Lords of Trade, December 11, 1756, p. 108, vol. 2, PM ("would have been better"); Jennings, *Empire*, 104.

26. Beverly W. Bond Jr., "The Captivity of Charles Stuart, 1755–57," *Mississippi Valley Historical Review* 13 (June 1926): 63 (exchange between Shingas and Braddock); Hinderaker, *Elusive*, 140; Jennings, *Empire*, 151–60, discusses the impact of Braddock's policies.

27. *MPC*, 5:510 (translation of the statement on the lead plates); McConnell, *Country*, 83–87, 66–67; Hinderaker, *Elusive*, 140; Anderson, *Crucible of War*, 47–48.

28. *MPC*, 6:51, 589 (Scarouady quotation); Anderson, *Crucible of War*, 5–7, 52–65; Matthew C. Ward, *Breaking the Backcountry: The Seven Years' War in Virginia and Pennsylvania, 1754–1765* (Pittsburgh: University of Pittsburgh Press, 2003), 43–45.

29. John Craig deposition, March 30, 1756, p. 78, vol. 2, PM (Lamullock quotations); Ward, *Breaking*, 45–47; *MPC*, 6:685–86; 8:198 ("The French . . . came"). This Ohio Indians' message was transmitted through the Oneida Thomas King.

30. *GMP*, 15, 16; Erminie Wheeler-Voegelin, "Ethnohistory of Indian Use and Occupancy in Ohio and Indiana Prior to 1795 . . . ," in *Indians of Ohio and Indiana Prior to 1795* (New York: Garland, 1974), 1:150, 118–20, 142, 150, 235, 226, 228–29, 212, 237–41; *AGL*, 41, 50; *MPC*, 6:37 ("let Us live"); Peters to Weiser, October 18, 1755, p. 58, vol. 1, WP ("Chiefs of the Shawonese"). For other examples of associations between Shawnees and Delawares in this period: *MPC*, 6:140, 152–60, 675, 643; 7:510. On the attack at Wills Creek: *MPC*, 6:457–58, 459. "A brief Narrative of the Incursions and Ravages of the French Indians in the Province of Pennsylvania," p. 34, vol. 2, PM; Hunter, *Forts*, 177, 366.

31. Elisabeth Tooker, "Wyandot," in *HNAI*, 15:398–400; Charles Garrad and Conrad E. Heidenreich, "Khionontateronon (Petun)," in *HNAI*, 15:394–96; Conrad E. Heidenreich, "Huron," in *HNAI*, 15:368–69; Hunter, "Ohio Valley," 590; Georges E. Sioui, *Huron-Wendat: The Heritage of the Circle* (Vancouver: UBC Press, 1999), 3–5; White, *Middle Ground*, 193–96; *NYCD*, 10:162; *MPC*, 5:350–51; *GMP*, 486 n. 83, 11; Wheeler-Voegelin, "Ethnohistory," 1:132–33, 137–39, 206.

32. Anderson, *Crucible of War*, 187–88; Hunter, "Ohio Valley," 591; Charles Callender, "Miami," in *HNAI*, 15:686–87; Callender, "Fox," in *HNAI*, 15:636–37; *AGL*, 42; *MPC*, 5:351; E. S. Rogers, "Southeastern Ojibwa," in *HNAI*, 15:769; *GMP*, 11; Wheeler-Voegelin, "Ethnohistory," 1:133–34; White, *Middle Ground*, 220, 191; McConnell, *Country*, 67; Goschgoschunk, September 23, October 22, 1768, 1/2/135/8; Gregory Evans Dowd, *War under Heaven: Pontiac, the Indian Nations, and the British Empire* (Baltimore, Md.: Johns Hopkins University Press, 2002), 9, 48–49, 90–94.

33. *MPC*, 5:463.

34. Account of conference at John Harris's, May 9, 1757, p. 6, vol. 3, PM ("must first go," "much affraid," and "fast up"); *MPC*, 5:349 (quotations about Beaver River town), 531 ("Southward Indians"); Information from John Adam Long, September 30, 1756, p. 102, vol. 2, PM.

35. McConnell, *Country*, 105–12; Hinderaker, *Elusive*, 137–38; Jennings, *Empire*, 401–3; *MPC*, 5:479; 4: 739 (Thomas's comments); 5: 615 ("deputed"); Conrad Weiser to W. Parsons, February 13, 1756, pp. 103–4, vol. 1, HF ("the Six Nations . . . sent"). Tanaghrisson died at John Harris's place in October 1754; thus he was not around for much of the early phase of the conflict. *MPC*, 6:184.

36. My view departs from that of Jennings (*Empire*, 262), who draws a sharper distinction between eastern and western Delawares and says that "they acted quite independently of each other." *IVPN*, 139. Donehoo places Secaughkung on the Cowanesque in the area of Academy Corners, Tioga County, Pennsylvania (*IVPN*, 176–77). *MPC*, 7:726 (Teedyuscung "Being likewise asked who the Unamies were, he said they were a distinct Tribe of Delaware Indians, and that Alomipus was formerly the King of that Tribe."); *DS*, 29.

37. Wallace, *King*, 70–72; Merritt, *Crossroads*, 183; *MPC*, 6:642 ("An Indian from Ohio"); 7:12 ("settled at Wyoming"), 53; Horsfield to W. Parsons, July 3, 1756, pp. 161–64, vol. 1, HF ("to hold a Conference"); *MPC*, 6:645–46, 648–49.

38. *MPC,* 7:676–77 ("the Land," "the Cause"); Charles Thomson, *An Enquiry into the Causes of the Alienation of the Delaware and Shawanese Indians from the British* . . . (London: J. Wilkie, 1759); *MPC,* 5:441 ("twenty-five Miles from the mouth," "a Place"); ibid., 4:648; Merritt, *Crossroads,* 182–83; David L. Preston, "Squatters, Indians, Proprietary Government, and Land in the Susquehanna Valley," in *FEPW,* 180, 198; Jennings, *Empire,* 191–92; Anderson, *Crucible of War,* 160–61; *SWJP,* 3:794–99; "List of Persons killed and Houses Burnt in the Menisinks and Forks of Delaware in Northampton County," p. 52, vol. 2, PM; *MPC,* 6: 756; Hunter, *Forts,* 187, 215, 266–67; Edward Biddle to his father, November 16, 1755, and Weiser to Gov. Morris, November 19, 1755, in Rupp, *Berks and Lebanon,* 50, 54–56.

39. Petrus Boehler to Gov. James Hamilton (English), October 10, 1763, 1/5/127/7, *RMM* ("the Christian Indians"); Address to Gov. Morris from Gnadenhütten Indians, November 1755, pp. 531–34, vol. 2, HF ("It is now," "none of us"); "The Examination of John Shmick and Henry Fry at their Return from a Journey to Wayoming," pp. 51–54, vol. 1, HF; *MPC,* 7:52–53; Merritt, *Crossroads,* 186–87; Governor's Answer to Indians at Bethlehem, March 31, 1757, pp. 365–68, vol. 2, HF; Timothy Horsfield to the Governor, November 26, 1755, pp. 55–58, vol. 1, HF.

40. Richter, *Ordeal,* 30 ("spiritual and temporal"); Dowd, *Spirited,* 3.

41. Anderson, *Crucible of War,* 163–65; Wallace, *King,* 87–89, 96–97; Timothy Horsfield to W. Parsons, July 7, 1756, pp. 177–78, vol. 1, HF; Horsfield to Parsons, July 8, 1756, pp. 183–86, vol. 1, HF; Gov. Morris to Timothy Horsfield, July 9, 1756, pp. 193–94, vol. 1, HF ("in want of provisions"); Indian Intelligence, 1756, pp. 322–29, vol. 2, HF ("some Indians"); *MPC,* 6:443 (quotations about situation at Ostonwakin); *IVPN,* 139–40, places Ostonwakin "at the mouth of Loyalsock Creek" at present Montoursville; Information from "Jo: Puby an Indian now in Bethlehem a Delaware," p. 56, vol. 2, PM (quotations about Niagara).

42. *MPC,* 7:209. I thank Jim Rementer for linguistic advice about this term.

43. Ibid. ("Whish Shiksy"); Dowd, *Spirited,* 3.

44. *MPC,* 7:213, 215, 216–17, 316, 650, 700; 8:32–33, 35 (claims to connections to many nations); 7:509, 538, 651–52 (evil spirit blamed). About the notion of evil spirits, Zeisberger wrote, "when crimes had been committed, the guilty ones laid the blame on an evil spirit who had seduced them. They have also been accustomed to admonish one another in time of war not to give ear to the evil spirit but to the good spirit who counseled peace." Hulbert and Schwarze, *Zeisberger's History,* 130.

45. *MPC,* 7:651.

46. *MPC,* 7:652 ("unite . . . as firmly"), 678 (other quotations).

47. Thwaites, *Early Western Travels,* 1:213 ("we have great reason"); Anderson, *Crucible of War,* 108–216, 275–78, 237; *MPC,* 7:686; 8:199, 203–4, 213, 222, 257–66; Jennings, *Empire,* 405–9; McConnell, *Country,* 126–33; Hinderaker, *Elusive,* 144.

48. *BP,* 3:164–65 ("from over"), 502 ("Eighty Indians"), 508–11.

49. McConnell, *Country,* 157, 161–68, 177; Anderson, *Crucible of War,* 469–71; *KJ,* 28 ("above one Hundred Houses"), 169 ("Ague"), 172; *MPC,* 9:78 ("the English have killed"; the message involved the following Delawares: Newoleka transmitted it to Papounan, who then transmitted it to Pennsylvania officials through Job Chilloway); White, *Middle Ground,* 256–58.

50. *KJ*, 184 ("about Juniata," "to break out"); Dowd, *War*, 121–31, 140–41; *MPC*, 9:35, 63; Indian Commissioners Papers, Accounts, 1764, Examination of Gersham Hicks, case 17, Simon Gratz Collection, Collection 250B, HSP; Jonas Seely to Gov. James Hamilton, September 17, 1763, in Rupp, *Berks and Lebanon*, 77–78; *Scotch-Irish of Northampton County*, 237–38.

51. Wallace, *King*, 182–89, 258–64; Paul Moyer, " 'Real' Indians, 'White' Indians, and the Contest for the Wyoming Valley," in *FEPW*, 225–27; Anderson, *Crucible of War*, 530–34.

52. Milo Milton Quaife, ed., *The Siege of Detroit in 1763: The Journal of Pontiac's Conspiracy and John Rutherford's Narrative of a Captivity* (Chicago: R. R. Donnelley and Sons, 1958), 5–16 ("drive off," "dogs" on 16); Heckewelder, *History*, 291, 292 ("country," "lost"), 293; *KJ*, 171–72.

53. Quaife, *Siege*, 16 ("do not fight," "When ye meet"); Dowd, *War*, 101 (quoted material about Neolin's name).

54. Dowd, *Spirited*, 29–32; *MB*, 238 (Brainerd quotations); Charles E. Hunter, "The Delaware Nativist Revival of the Mid-Eighteenth Century," *Ethnohistory* 18 (Winter 1971): 39–49; Alfred A. Cave, "The Delaware Prophet Neolin: A Reappraisal," *Ethnohistory* 47 (Spring 1999): 265–90; Quaife, *Siege*, 11 (about woman in white and "in his own tongue"); Goschgoschunk, July 8, 1768, 1/1/135/8.

55. Krista Camenzind, "Violence, Race, and the Paxton Boys," in *FEPW*, 215–16; Merritt, *Crossroads*, 266–82, 280–301. Also on the construction of "whiteness" in Pennsylvania, see Gregory T. Knouff, "Whiteness and Warfare on a Revolutionary Frontier," in *FEPW*, 238–57. *MPC*, 9:112 ("Back inhabitants" "got it into"); 9: 68 ("enraged and provoked," "in revenge"); *PG*, August 4, 1763, item no. 31315 ("distressed," "Barns, Stables"); December 8, 1763, item no. 32218; *Scotch-Irish of Northampton County*, 237. On suspicions against the Great Island Indians: *MPC*, 9:65, 139; and Gov. Hamilton to Horsfield, September 20, 1763, pp. 487–90, vol. 2, HF. For quotation about Nutimus, see Gov. Hamilton to Horsfield, September 1, 1763, pp. 483–86, vol. 2, HF. B. A. Grube to Horsfield, October 13, 1763, pp. 503–505, vol. 2, HF; Dowd, *War*, 140–41.

56. Kent, *Susquehanna's Indians*, 62–63; *MPC*, 9:476, 95 ("a number," "armed & mounted"), 96 ("killed Six"), 100–102, 103 ("fifty or Sixty," "armed with Rifles," and "Tomahawks"), 411 ("Noon-Day," "in the Presence of many spectators"). Another account indicated that the killings occurred around two o'clock (*MPC*, 9:103). *MPC*, 9:108 ("Inhabitants of the Townships"), 104–6, 110, 111 ("about 140 other friendly Indians"), 120, 121–23, 126–27, 131, 137 ("a very considerable"), 139; Camenzind, "Violence," 201–2; Philadelphia sojourn diary (Grube), January 24, 1764, and April 3, 1765, 1/2 and 4/127/7, RMM.

57. *MPC*, 9:252–53 ("be able to drive" on 253); Dowd, *Spirited*, 40–42.

58. *MPC*, 9:45 (quotations); *The Journal of John Woolman and a Plea for the Poor* (Secaucus, N.J.: Citadel Press, 1975), 134–57; Camenzind, "Violence," 217–18; Dowd, *War*, 164–65; Ward, *Breaking*, 247–51.

59. *MPC*, 9:254–55 (quotations on 255).

60. For an attempt by the Six Nations to make peace for Ohio Indians, see *MPC*, 9:209–10; *EAID*, 10:471–72 (quotations), 485. Treaty with Delawares, 1765: *EAID*, 10:491–94.

"All the people which inhabit this Continent"

1. MPC, 9:252.
2. Ibid.
3. Ibid., 254.
4. Ibid., 254–55.

Chapter 5

1. SWJP, 4:321, 323, 329 ("several Woodsmen"), 336, 344, 359, 349, 352 ("new Oneida Village"), 365, 392–93, 403, 405–6 ("two large towns" and "sixty good houses" on 405) and 405 n. 3, 361, 369; ibid., 11:36 ("composed cheifly"). Colin G. Calloway, *The American Revolution in Indian Country: Crisis and Diversity in Native American Communities* (Cambridge: Cambridge University Press, 1995), 108–10; Grumet, ed., *Journey*, 12–13; Andrew Montour appears as "Henry" in some records. Wallace, *Indians in Pennsylvania*, 178; Alexander Scott Withers, *Chronicles of Border Warfare . . .*, ed. Reuben Gold Thwaites (Cincinnati: Robert Clarke Company, 1895; repr., Arno Press, 1971), 136n.

2. SWJP, 4:392–93 ("three Lar[ge] Towns," "Little out Villages" on 393); Dolores Elliott, "Otsiningo: An Example of an Eighteenth-Century Settlement Pattern," in *Current Perspectives in Northeastern Archeology: Essays in Honor of William A. Ritchie*, ed. Robert E. Funk and Charles F. Hayes III (*Researches and Transactions of the New York State Archeological Association* 17, no. 1 [1977]), 97–100.

3. MJNY, 27–28; MB, 176.

4. DS, 20, 31; MPC, 7:506. The evidence for Munsees at Wapwallopen is the following: Eleonora (#587) had a father living there, and Erdmuth (#565) had a "Freundin" from there. Both of these women were Minisink, according to Moravian records. It appears that when Moravians used the word "Freund" (male form) or "Freundin" (female form), they may have used it to mean "friend" but that at other times, perhaps quite frequently, it meant more specifically a relative. Fliegel, the indexer of the Moravian mission records, translates "Freund" as "relative" at times; see his entry for Salome (#542) April 25, 1768 (FL 1: 359), and compare it to Friedenshütten, April 25, 1768 (1/5/131/7). Also see Gottlieb (#73), January 11, 1747, FL, 1:134, and Gnadenhütten, Pa., January 11, 1747, 1/1/116/4. Of course, it is possible that only Eleonora's mother, and not her father, was Minisink or Munsee. Friedenshütten, December 20, 1769, 1/6/131/7 (Eleonora or "Lorel"), and May 8, 1769, 1/6/131/7 (Erdmuth). The Moravian records referred to Wapwallopen as "Hallobank" or "Wambhallobank." IVPN, 247–48. Friedenshütten, February 21, March 8, 1768, 1/5/131/7 (Achcohunt). Sheshequin appears as "Tschechschequanik" in these references. IVPN, 202. For indications of Munsees at Chemung ("Shammungk"): Friedenshütten, June 24 (quotation about Chemung and refers to the Minisink Phoebe #568), April 29 (Anna Johanna #552, Minisink, had an uncle there), and August 27, 1768, 1/5/131/7 (Anna Johanna's "friends" from "Shammunk"); ibid., April 30 (Joseph #558, Minisink, had "friends" visiting from there) and May 9 (Phoebe's "Freundin" from "Shommunk"), 1769,

1/6/131/7. *IVPN*, 23–24; *FL*, 3:807. On Newollike (or Augustinus #760): *MPC*, 9:426, 773–75; Friedenshütten, April 21, 1769, 1/6/131/7; ibid., July 20, 1770, 1/7/131/7; Schönbrunn, May 20, 1774, 1/4/1411/9; *FL*, 3:51. *MPC*, 8:152 ("Eghkoohunt" was "the Munsy Chief"), 159 ("Ego-ho-houn" was "the Chief Man of the Munseys"). The total number of inhabitants at Friedenshütten in 1769, for example, was 178. Friedenshütten, end of year total, 1/6/131/7. Philadelphia barracks, end of year total, 1764, 1/2/127/7, *RMM* (indicates fifty-six people died in 1764); John Heckewelder, A *Narrative of the Mission of the United Brethren* . . . (Philadelphia: McCarty and Davis, 1820), 87–88; Schmick travel diary, April 3–May 24, 1765, 1/1/131/7, *RMM*.

5. Z. travel diary, September 20–November 16, 1767, 1/14/227/31, *RMM*; Goschgoschunk, June 9, 10, 11, 14, 17, 1768, 1/1/135/8; ibid., December 18, 1768, 1/2/135/8; M. H. Deardorff, "Zeisberger's Allegheny River Indian Towns, 1767–1770," *Pennsylvania Archaeologist* 16 (January 1946): 2–19 (p. 19 for translation of Damascus). On a trip down the Allegheny in 1769, Zeisberger indicated that the residents along the river were "purely Monsy Indians," with a few exceptions. Goschgoschunk and Lawunakhannek, July 23, 1769, 1/3/135/8. For an indication that Allemewi acted as a sachem of the Munsees, see ibid., July 11, 1769, 1/3/135/8. On his blindness, see ibid., July 19, 1768, 1/1/135/8.

6. *IVPN*, 85–87, 201; Z. to Seidel, November 22, 1771, 22/3/229/32, *RMM* (long quotation); Langundo-Utenünk, May 5, 1770, 1/1/137/8; Schönbrunn, September 20, 1773, 1/3/1411/9 (short quotation). Also, ibid., November 13, 1773, 1/4/1411/9.

7. See the relationships involving individuals at Wapwallopen, Chemung, and Friedenshütten cited in note 4 above. For a kin connection between individuals at Friedenshütten and Otsiningo (or "Zeninga"): Friedenshütten, August 27, 1768, 1/5/131/7. The Friedenshütten resident Amalia (#562) was the daughter of the sachem Achcohunt, who was living at Sheshequin. Friedenshütten, April 20, 1767, 1/4/131/7. On Kawunschannek: Goschgoschunk and Lawunakhannek, July 11, 1769, 1/3/135/8; and Lawunakhannek, January 27, 1770, 1/4/135/8; *IVPN*, 51. Goschgoschunk, July 21, 1768, 1/1/135/8; Lawunakhannek, January 21, 1770, 1/4/135/8; Lagundo-Utenünk, May 16, 1770, 1/1/137/8. Tschechquoapesch's name appears on a petition against the rum trade along with other "Headmen, Chiefs & Sachems of the Monsy Nation." "A Petition of the Indians at Kushkushink on Ohio River to all Justices, Magistrates & Commanders at Fort Ligonier & Pittsburgh," January 13, 1769, 1/3/229/32, *RMM*.

8. *MPC*, 9:344; Clarence Walworth Alvord and Clarence Edwin Carter, eds., *The New Régime, 1765–1767* (Collections of the Illinois State Historical Library, vol. 11, British Series, vol. 2, Springfield: Illinois State Historical Library, 1916), 488 ("a great number," "Murder of some"); *SWJP*, 12:296 ("Scuffle" with Ryan); *MPC*, 9:479 ("three Delaware Chiefs," "Chief of the Six Nations"), 462 ("killed a considerable"). Also on murders of Indians: *MPC*, 9:322, 351–52; Clarence Walworth Alvord and Clarence Edwin Carter, eds., *Trade and Politics, 1767–1769* (Collections of the Illinois State Historical Library, vol. 16, British Series, vol. 3, Springfield: Illinois State Historical Library, 1921), 43. On a Delaware response to Euro-American complaints of Indians killing whites: *MPC*, 9:524.

9. *MPC*, 9:470, 414 ("One Woman," "killed, in order to prevent"), 462–63 ("large body"), 484–85, 487–88, 489–90, 441.

10. McConnell, *Country*, 225–29 (on Delaware consolidation efforts); Wheeler-Voegelin, "Ethnohistory," 1:196–98, 204; Guy Soulliard Klett, ed., *Journals of Charles Beatty, 1762–1769* (University Park: Pennsylvania State University Press, 1962), 67; Langundo-Utenünk, June 21, 1770, 1/1/137/8; *SWJP*, 7:316; Goschgoschunk and Lawunakhannek, June 14, 1769, 1/3/135/8 (last quotation).

11. Goschgoschunk and Lawunakhannek, April 11, June 14, May 12, and July 22, 1769, 1/3/135/8; Z. to Thrane, Seidel, and Hehl, August 14, 1770, 17/3/229/32, *RMM*; McConnell, *Country*, 226–29; Langundo-Utenünk, May 8, 1771, 1/2/137/8 (first quotation); ibid., May 5 and 6, June 6, and July 21, 1770, 1/1/137/8; ibid., May 27, 1771, 1/2/137/8; ibid., July 23 (second quotation); Z. to Hehl, May 20, 1770, 14/1/229/32, *RMM*. By August 1, 1772, Kawunaschannek only had two families of inhabitants remaining: Ettwein and Roth travel diary, Roth's portion, August 1, 1772, 1/4/1371/8, *RMM*. Susquehanna Delawares also relocated to Goschgoschunk in this same period. See movement of residents of Wilwane (on the Chemung) to Goschgoschunk. Travel diary of Z. and Gottlob Sensemann, May 19, 1768, 1/1/135/8. On Wilawane or Willawanna: *IVPN*, 254.

12. Schönbrunn and Gnadenhütten, February 28, 1773, 1/3/141/8; Gnadenhütten, Ohio, July 7, August 6, 12, 1774 and February 10, March 19, August 4, and September 18, 1775, 1/3, 4, and 5/144/9; Travel diary in Schönbrunn, September 17–23, 1773, 1/4/1411/9; Lichtenau, July 7, 1776, 1/2/147/9; Hanna, *Wilderness*, 2:204; Heckewelder, *Narrative*, 59–65; Wheeler-Voegelin, "Ethnohistory," 1:196–98, 204; "Esquisse des Rivieres Muskinghum et Grand Castor," in *RUO*; Klett, *Beatty*, 61 ("200 men"); Z. travel diary, March 13, 1771, in Langundo-Utenünk, March 23, 1771, 1/1/137/8 (other quotations).

13. Langundo-Utenünk, March 23, 1771 (see subentry of March 13), 1/2/137/8 (first and second quotations); *DS*, 36–37; Hunter, "Note on Unalachtigo," 148–51; C. A. Weslager, "More about the Unalachtigo," *Pennsylvania Archaeologist* 45 (1975): 40–44; Wallace, *King*, 12; John G. E. Heckewelder, Communications made to the Historical and Literary Committee and to members of the American Philosophical Society on the subject of the history, manners and languages of the American Indians [1816–1821], APS (response to query 12); Travel diary in Schönbrunn, September 20, 1773, 1/3/1411/9; Goschgoschunk and Lawunakhannek, July 23, 1769, 1/3/135/8; Zeisberger, "History" (German, last quotation). Shoemaker points out that "the word *nation*" had an imprecise meaning "in early modern English . . . , sometimes referring to a formal political entity and at other times to a vaguely defined body of people linked by a common language and culture" (*Strange Likeness*, 6).

14. Amy C. Schutt, "Female Relationships and Intercultural Bonds in Moravian Indian Missions," in *FEPW*, 89–90; Schutt, " 'What will become of our young people'? Goals for Indian Children in Moravian Missions," *History of Education Quarterly* 38 (Fall 1998): 284; Hunter, "Note on Unalachtigo," 149–51. For an example of how Delawares may have come to place an emphasis on language as a marker of Delaware groupings in Ohio, see Gnadenhütten, Ohio, March 26, 1776, 1/6/144/9 (Netawatwees requested that one Moravian town—Lichtenau—be designated a place where he could "hear," as he said, "my language, that is Unamie."). Wallace (*King*, 10) notes the potential for European bias. "To the classical scholars who studied them," he writes, "the Delawares, like all Gaul, had to be divided into three parts."

15. Goschgoschunk and Lawunakhannek, August 30, 1769, 1/3/135/8 (death of Tamaqua reported); Lichtenau, April 22, 1776, 1/1/147/9; ibid., January 10, February 12, 1777, 1/2/147/9; Klett, *Beatty*, 61, 65, 66; *FL*,1:367; Diagram of Meniolagomekah, 4/122/6, *RMM*; Goschgoschunk, June 10 (first quotation) and 12, 1768, 1/1/135/8; Gnadenhütten, Ohio, December 27, 1773 and January 1, April 22, 23, 24, 1774, 1/2 and 3/144/9; Tepisscowahang ("Tepiscochan") probably attended the Fort Pitt meeting in the spring of 1765 (*MPC*, 9:256); Gnadenhütten, Ohio, October 17, 1773, July 17, 1774, April 15, 1776, 1/2, 3 and 6/144/9 (on Nutimus or Nutumer family); Gnadenhütten, Pa., March 19 and 20, and April 4, 1750, 1/7/116/4 (these references suggest that Isaac "Nutumer" was the son of Nutimus); *FL*, 1:316.

16. *EAID*, 10:294–96, 305–7; *MPC*, 9:514; Weslager, *Delaware*, 268–73; *SWJP*, 12:305–6; Friedenshütten, March 26, May 20, 1767, 1/4/131/7; Thomas Brainerd, *The Life of John Brainerd, the Brother of David Brainerd, and His Successor as Missionary to the Indians of New Jersey* (Philadelphia: Presbyterian Publication Committee, 1865), 309–10, 317; Langundo-Utenünk, June 22, 30, 1770, 1/1/137/8; ibid., September 14 (quotation), October 21, 1771, 1/2/137/8; ibid., January 13, 1772, 1/3/137/8; *MPC*, 9:737–39; Friedenshütten, April 29, 1771, 1/8/131/7.

17. Friedenshütten, July 17, 18, 1768, 1/5/131/7 (on Gagohunt); ibid., July 4, 1768, 1/5/131/7 ("The Indian Achcohunt returned from Wyoming and found his wife and her mother, a Shawnee."). On evidence of a Delaware presence at Otsiningo: ibid, August 27, 1768, 1/5/131/7 (indicates that the mother of the Minisink Salome [#609, wife of Levi], died at Otsiningo, where she apparently lived with her twelve-year-old son). MCT; Z. and Sensemann travel diary, May 13, 1768 (Eng.), 1/7/135/8, *RMM* (quotation). The Chemung residents were not identified, but probably included Munsees. They made their statement at the home "on the Tiaogu" of a brother of Salome (#542), a Minisink. MCT.

18. *MPC*, 9:470 (quotation). The Seneca came from "Peemeekannink," which was an Algonquian name for the Genesee (also "Pemidhannek"). Goschgoschunk, October 23, 1768, 1/2/135/8.

19. Friedenshütten, April 24, 1771, 1/8/131/7; ibid., April 30, 1771 (quotation); MCT (Lydia #566).

20. Friedenshütten, memorabilia, 1766, 1/3/131/7 (quotation). For illness in the neighboring towns, see ibid., May 20, 1767, 1/4/131/7. For smallpox outbreak, see ibid., May 12–June 20, 1767.

21. Friedenshütten, January 26, February 24, March 25, 26, and 28, April 6, 7, 9, 10, 21, May 8, 9, 21, and 22, September 24, October 8, 1767, 1/4/131/7; ibid., September 21, 22, 1767 (quotations about Nanticokes); ibid., May 7, 1769, 1/6/131/7 (Gagohunt's comment); ibid., April 26, 1769; ibid., March 1, 1769 (Otsiningo situation).

22. G. H. Loskiel, *The History of the Moravian Mission among the Indians in North America . . .* (London: T. Allman, 1838), 190–91; Friedensstadt Conference Minutes, 1/9/137/8, *RMM*; "Br. Ettweins Bericht von seinem Besuch in Langundo-utenünk an der Beaver-Creek u. Welhik-Tuppek am Mushkingum-River," August 14, 1772, 1/5/137/8, *RMM*; *NYCD*, 8:135–37 with accompanying map; *IVPN*, 232. On hunting areas: Friedenshütten, October 26, 1767, 1/4/131/7 (Wyoming); ibid., October 22, November 3, 1767 (Shamokin); ibid., May 12, 1769, 1/6/131/7 (Tunkhannock or

"Tenkanneck"); ibid., May 25, 1769 (quotation). Schmick to Seidel, January 7, 1771, 5/11/221/29, *RMM* (on fencing on Great Island); Friedenshütten, July 26, 1769, 1/6/131/7 (on reserving five-mile tract around Friedenshütten). The Delaware Job Chelloway (or Chillaway) held an interest in the Wyalusing property after the mission left. "A draught of a Tract of Land called Wyaloosing . . . Surveyed for Job Chilloway," September 16, 1773, Job Chillaway Papers for Wyalusing, 1772–1774, Records of the Land Office, RG-17, PSA.

23. On Delawares at the Fort Stanwix treaty: *SWJP*, 8:113; 12:617–29. Friedenshütten, November 9, 1768, 1/5/131/7, *RMM* (indicates that the Delaware Billy Chelloway attended); ibid., April 4, 1772, 1/9/131/7 (quotation); *NYCD*, 8:135–37.

24. Friedenshütten, April 20, 21, 1769, 1/6/131/7 (first and second quotations); ibid., February 8 (third quotation) and April 4 (fourth quotation), 1772, 1/9/131/7; ibid., November 9, 1768, 1/5/131/7; ibid., June 18, 1770, 1/7/131/7 (references include vague suggestions that the Friedenshütten land might still be secure for the mission Indians).

25. *MPC*, 9:735 (Killbuck's association with Netawatwees); "Proceedings of Sir William Johnson with the Indians at Fort Stanwix," 113. Benevissica (or Beniwesica) attended the treaty at Fort Pitt in May 1765: *MPC*, 9:256; *SWJP*, 6:536 ("Every thing that could").

26. *NYCD*, 8:136, 135 ("intrusions & encroachments") with accompanying map; McConnell, *Country*, 244–45; White, *Middle Ground*, 308; Friedenshütten, December 12, 1768, and January 1, 2, 1769, 1/5 and 6/131/7 (Killbuck's visit and return to Ohio); ibid., March 27, January 1, 1769, 1/6/131/7 (Killbuck quotations).

27. Goschgoschunk and Lawunakhannek, June 14, 1769, 1/3/135/8 (first and second quotations). For Johnson quotation, see note 25 in this chapter. Johnson seems to have found somewhat appealing the notion that Indian affairs would become more orderly if each nation consolidated around particular locations. Alvord and Carter, eds., *New Régime*, 45. Following the Stump murders, he urged Mahicans, whose people had been among those killed, to find one place where they could live together "under his eye and his maintenance." Friedenshütten, April 5, 1768, 1/5/131/7; ibid., November 9, 10, 1768 (last quotation); Billy Chelloway (later Wilhelm #663). MCT. The Munsee sachem Allemewi in the Allegheny Valley suggested that the Fort Stanwix cession promoted the movement of his people to the west. Lawunakhannek, June 16, 1769, 1/3/135/8.

28. *SWJP*, 12:621, 628–29 (on numbers at the treaty); McConnell, *Country*, 250–52; *SWJP*, 7:184 ("complained much"); *NYCD*, 8:135–37 with accompanying map; *AGL*, 58–59; *EAID*, 10:715 n. 33; *SWJP*, 7:315 ("Ohio Senicas, Shawanese & Delawares"); *EAID*, 18:147.

29. McConnell, *Country*, 248, 246, 250–51; Fenton, *Great Law*, 535–40; Peter Marshall, "Sir William Johnson and the Treaty of Fort Stanwix, 1768," *American Studies* 1 (October 1967): 173–76; *SWJP*, 7:184 (Senecas' and Cayugas' view of the treaty); *SWJP*, 8:76.

30. McConnell, *Country*, 259–60; *SWJP*, 7:140 ("a Confederacy"), 315 (meeting on the Detroit River); Lawunakhannek, July 24, 1769, 1/3/135/8 (last quotation).

31. *MPC*, 10:10 ("Council Fire at Fort Pitt," "Council Fire in these middle Provinces"), 62–63 ("I cannot agree"); *PA*, 1st ser., 4:469–70.

32. For 1765 quotation, see note 59 in Chapter 4 above; Goschgoschunk, June 13–14, 1768, 1/1/135/8 (second quotation); Langundo-Utenünk, June 24, 1771, 1/2/137/8 (Killbuck and son's trip); *MPC*, 9:737 (appears to refer to this same trip and indicates that Killbuck was in Philadelphia with "Kellalamind, or John," that is, Gelelemend or John Killbuck). On John Killbuck, see Lichtenau, April 16, 21, 1776, 1/1/147/9; Schönbrunn and Gnadenhütten, December 26, 1772, 1/3/141/8 ("Jo Peepi" visit to Philadelphia with the information that a schoolteacher as well as a preacher had been requested); *MPC*, 10:61–64 (also reports on "Joseph Peepy" in Philadelphia). Another request for a Quaker preacher was sent in fall 1769. Lawunakhannek, February 5, 1770, 1/4/135/8.

33. For examples from the Seven Years' War of Delawares as "grandfathers," see *MPC*, 6:37 (Shawnees called Delawares "Grandfathers"); 7:49 (Shawnees referred to Delawares as "our Grandfathers"); 8:197 (Delawares as "Grandfathers" of the Shawnees), 311, 497–98 ("Kickabouses" or Kickapoos called Delawares "their Grandfathers"); Hulbert and Schwarze, *Zeisberger's History*, 27 ("some old people," "how peaceably"). The Mahican Hendrick Aupaumut wrote that his people had a long history of calling Delawares "grandfathers." Hendrick Aupaumut, "A Narrative of an Embassy to the Western Indians," *Memoirs of the Historical Society of Pennsylvania* 2 (1827): 76–77.

34. Kraft, *Lenape*, 165.

35. Hulbert and Schwarze, *Zeisberger's History*, 76 (first quotation); Schönbrunn, June 4, 1774, 1/5/141/8 (second quotation); Gnadenhütten, Ohio, May 19, 1774, 1/3/144/9 (last quotation).

36. On Delawares as grandfathers, mentioned at the time of Dunmore's War, see *PA*, 1st ser., 4:532; Schönbrunn, May 8, 30, June 4, July 29, August 6, 1774, 1/5/141/8; ibid., October 6, 1774, 1/6/141/8; Gnadenhütten, Ohio, May 19, June 6, August 6, 1774, 1/3/144/9. McConnell, *Country*, 268–69; White, *Middle Ground*, 351–57; Jack M. Sosin, *The Revolutionary Frontier, 1763–1783* (New York: Holt, Rinehart and Winston, 1967), 57–60, 85–87; K. G. Davies, ed., *Documents of the American Revolution, 1770–1783* (Dublin: Irish University Press, 1975), 8:75–78; *MPC*, 10:140–42, 168.

37. *DW*, 10–11, including nn. 17, 19 (on John Gibson), and 20, 36 n. 64 (Location for Pipe Creek comes from correlating the information in this note with the information in the reminiscences on 11; "lived long enough" on 10), 16 (mentions that the Indians who were killed came from "the Town Fork of Yellow Creek, where the Indian town was, a small one."); Hanna, *Wilderness*, 2: map between pp. 144 and 145. Moravian records indicate that the dead included "1 Shawnee chief and 6 Iroquois (*Maquaische*)": Gnadenhütten, Ohio, May 8, 1774, 1/3/144/9; *DW*, 15 ("was in the habit"), 17 (Baker's Bottom); *PA*, 1st ser., 4:512 ("nine Indians," "Murthered and Scalped"); Gnadenhütten, Ohio, May 12, 1774, 1/3/144/9 (mentions killing of Gibson's wife); *PA*, 1st ser., 4:499.

38. *MPC*, 10:196 ("took their Revenge"); *DW*, 36 and nn. 62, 63, and 64, 43 ("being killed"), 151–54 ("took three scalps," and "one prisoner" on 152), 155–56; *PA*, 1st ser., 4:513 ("into the river Monongahela near Cheat river"); Gnadenhütten, Ohio, June 15, 1774, 1/3/144/9; ibid., May 8, 1774 (Shawnee captain quotations); *PA*, 1st ser., 4:533 ("sattisfied for the loss of his Relations," "Thirteen Scalps"), 545; McConnell, *Country*, 274–77; *MPC*, 10:196–97 ("attacked, and one of them wounded" on 197); *DW*, 66–67,

xix; Gnadenhütten, Ohio, June 30, 1774, 1/3/144/9 (in area of Beaver or "Sackung"); Schönbrunn, June 30, 1774, 1/4/1411/9; Schönbrunn, August 4, 1774 ("abgebrannt," "die Welschkorn . . . niedergehauen . . . hatten."), 1/5/141/8; PA, 1st ser., 4:559 (indicates "four Hundred of the Virginians are marched to destroy Wagetomica, the Town the Shawanese lately abandoned"), 553 ("the Shawanese are all Gone from Waketummike to Assemble themselves at the lower Towns"). On Tachnedorus and the attack near Yellow Creek, see introduction to Anthony F. C. Wallace, *Jefferson and the Indians: The Tragic Fate of the First Americans* (Cambridge, Mass.: Belknap Press of Harvard University Press, 1999).

39. Gnadenhütten, Ohio, May 14, 16, 17, and 19, 1774, 1/3/144/9; Schönbrunn, May 22, 1774, 1/4/1411/9 (indicates the meeting with the Shawnees was at "Woaketammeki" or Wakatomica); ibid., June 9, 14, 1774 (continuing efforts with Shawnees); Gnadenhütten, Ohio, July 16, 27, August 12, 16, 1774, 1/3/144/9 (meetings with Virginians); PA, 1st ser., 4:531–32.

40. Beverly Prior Smaby, *The Transformation of Moravian Bethlehem: From Communal Mission to Family Economy* (Philadelphia: University of Pennsylvania Press, 1988), 38–39; Linda Sabathy-Judd, trans. and ed., *Moravians in Upper Canada: The Diary of the Indian Mission of Fairfield on the Thames, 1792–1813* (Toronto: Champlain Society, 1999), xxii–xxiii; Heckewelder, *Narrative*, 151–52 (quotation), 189; Langundo-Utenünk, July 11 (sachem's quotation), June 6, 1770, 1/1/137/8; Z. to Hehl, May 20, 1770, 14/3/229/32; Travel diary in Schönbrunn and Gnadenhütten, September 20, 1773, 1/3/1411/9 (last two quotations).

41. Langundo-Utenünk, July 26, 1771, 1/2/137/8 (first quotation); Schönbrunn and Gnadenhütten, January 19, 1773, 1/3/141/8 (Shawnees' statement); Langundo-Utenünk, February 3, 1772, 1/3/137/8 (remaining quotations). On *Beson* as "medicine," see Schönbrunn and Gnadenhütten, December 25, 1772, 1/3/141/8.

42. Gnadenhütten, Ohio, May 14 (first quotation), June 11, 1774 ("3 Mahicander" and "3 Mennissinger"); on Echpalawehund's significance, see Schönbrunn and Gnadenhütten, January 14, 1773, 1/3/141/8; Schönbrunn, August 24, 1774, 1/5/141/8 (Z.'s remark); PA, 1st ser., 4:552 (the context of this speech suggests that the speaker was White Eyes, though the document is not explicit about the speaker; note that the speech accompanies "Intelligence" provided by White Eyes); Gnadenhütten, Ohio, July 27, 1774, 1/3/144/9 (indicates that White Eyes had just returned from a meeting with Virginians, which further suggests that he had delivered the speech of July 23); Z. to Seidel, September 13, 1774, 20/4/229/32, RMM (on concern about involvement in "Chief Affairen"); also on this matter: Schönbrunn, August 17, 1774, 1/5/141/8.

43. Fenton, *Great Law*, 533–35; Lawunakhannek, August 24, 25, and December 2, 1769, 1/3 and 4/135/8 (on Iroquois-Cherokee peace); DW, 5 n. 8, 20, 26, 48 and n. 85, 72; Friedenshütten, April 16, 1771, 1/8/131/7; Gnadenhütten, Ohio, March 8, 1774, 1/3/144/9; ibid., April 14, 1774 ("100 Cherokeesen"); ibid., June 21, 1774; EAID, 18:199. For developments in Delaware-Cherokee relations during the Revolutionary War: Tanner, "Cherokees in Ohio," 96–98.

44. PA, 1st ser., 4:531–32 (quotations).

45. Wheeler-Voegelin, "Ethnohistory," 211–12; Schönbrunn, June 11, 1774, 1/4/1411/9 (first and last two quotations); ibid., May 20, 1774 (on war dance); ibid., July 7, 1774

(Munsees forwarded a message from the Shawnees to encourage Schönbrunn Indians to leave), 1/5/141/8; Z. to "Geschwister" in Bethlehem, Nazareth, and Lititz, July 22, 1774, 17/4/229/32, *RMM* (indicates the message to move originated with Munsees); Schönbrunn, May 20, August 24, 1774, 1/5/141/8 (Schönbrunn was the residence of prominent Munsees, including Glikhikan [Isaac #659], Gendaskund [Jacob #658], Newollike [Augustinus #760], and Allemewi [Salomo #642]). See MCT and *FL*, 1, under these names; "Esquisse des Rivieres" (shows "Moughweassing" just east of "Waccatomeca" area).

46. Schönbrunn, July 7, 1774, 1/5/141/8 (first and second quotations); *RUO*, 81; *AGL*, 72; *DW*, 269–74 and n. 83, 256 ("We had 7 or 800 Warriors"), 268 ("there are many conjectures"). Wyandots also fought against the Virginians during Dunmore's War, as noted in the condolence ceremony at the Pittsburgh treaty of 1775 (*RUO*, 81). Caughnawagas were mainly Mohawks from the St. Lawrence. (ibid., 81n). On the numbers of Indian warriors at Pt. Pleasant being exaggerated: *NYCD*, 8:517; and White, *Middle Ground*, 364 n. 96.

47. *PA*, 1st ser., 4:557 ("join the Virginia"); *RUO*, 40 ("some Satisfaction," "serving with him"); *PA*, 1st ser., 4:553 ("Mischief," "Grand father's, the Delawares"); *DW*, 254 ("hard fought"), 256 ("lasted from "); Z. to Seidel, January 6, 1775, 21/4/229/32, *RMM* ("Schwoneks"); Schönbrunn, November 5, 1774, 1/6/141/8 ("Schwonnack oder Virginier" applied to Netawatwees); *NYCD*, 8:517, 535.

48. *PA*, 1st ser., 4:532–33.

Chapter 6

1. Z. to Seidel, March 10, 1772, 23/3/229/32, *RMM* (about Mahicans in the area of Gekelemukpechunk); Langundo-Utenünk, Conference Minutes (Eng.), August 12, 1772, 1/9/137/8; "Br. Ettweins Bericht von seinem Besuch in Langundo-Utenünk . . . ," September 7, 1772, 1/5/1371/8, *RMM*; Schönbrunn, October 2, 5, 9, 1772, 1/1/1411/9. The Gnadenhütten missionary Johann Schmick stated in March 1776, "16 Mahicans are here and the rest Delawares." Gnadenhütten, Ohio, March 26, 1776, 1/6/144/9. The population of the town at this time seems to have been between 136 and 151 inhabitants. Gnadenhütten, Ohio, end of year totals, 1775 and 1776, 1/6 and 8/144/9. Schmick may not have distinguished Mahicans from Wompanosch, some of whom lived at Gnadenhütten, including Esther (#10) and Christina (#134), both identified as Wompanosch in earlier records. *FL*, 1:87, 115; Gnadenhütten, Ohio, December 1, 1773, 1/2/144/9 (Christina); ibid., October 28, 1775, item 1, folder 5, box 144 (Esther). The Onondaga man was Thomas (#910), and his son was Nicolaus (#911). Schönbrunn, January 1, 1775, 1/6/141/8. The Cherokee man was Noah (#732), and his wife was Wilhelmina (#733). Ibid., July 4, 1773, 1/3/1411/9. The Nanticoke individual was Samuel (#551). Lichtenau, July 20, 1778, 1/7/147/9. The Conoy ("Canai") individual was Augustus (#554). Gnadenhütten, Ohio, November 25, 1774, 1/4/144/9. Heckewelder, *History*, xlii (on "Canai" as "Conoys"); *FL*, 1:315, 424, 369–70, 54. On Agnes (#667), see Langundo-Utenünk, February 27, 1771, 1/1/137/8, *RMM*. MCT.

2. On Thompson, see Chapter 5 above. Z. to Geschwister, August 6, 1777,

10/5/229/32, *RMM* (on missionaries' locations); *FL*, 2:534, 686, 684, 558, 562, 493–94 (for an overview of individual missionaries); Loskiel, *History*, 215–18; Schönbrunn, February 24, May 4, 8, 1775, 1/4/1411/9 (on Conners); Lichtenau, August 1, 1777, 2/3/147/9 (on Peggy Conner); Charles N. Thompson, "Sons of the Wilderness: John and William Conner," in *Indiana Historical Society Publications* (Indianapolis: Indiana Historical Society 1937), 12:9–18; John Lauritz Larson and David G. Vanderstel, "Agent of Empire: William Conner on the Indiana Frontier, 1800–1855," *Indiana Magazine of History* 80 (December 1984): 301–28; Lichtenau, July 21, 1777, 2/3/147/9; ibid., November 30, 1777, 1/5/147/9.

3. *RUO*, 123–25 ("two Negro Women" on 124–25), 105 ("runaway from the Mouth of Hockhockan"); Schönbrunn, January 11, 1776, 1/4/1411/9 (Jonathan [#173] and his wife); *MCT*; *PA*, 1st ser., 1:330 ("Severall"); *KJ*, 13 and 16 ("run away with the Indians"); Hulbert and Schwarze, *Zeisberger's History*, 124. See also William B. Hart, "Black 'Go-Betweens' and the Mutability of 'Race,' Status, and Identity on New York's Pre-Revolutionary Frontier," in *Contact Points*, ed. Cayton and Teute, 96–100; Claudio Saunt, "'The English Has Now a Mind to Make Slaves of Them All': Creeks, Seminoles, and the Problem of Slavery," in *Confounding the Color Line: The Indian-Black Experience in North America*, ed. James F. Brooks (Lincoln: University of Nebraska, 2002), 47–75.

4. *EAID*, 10:484 ("we are very glad"); *RUO*, 116 (Cornstalk quotations); Hulbert and Schwarze, *Zeisberger's History*, 124. For negotiations over African American captive returns, see *SWJP*, 4:746; *EAID*, 10:470; *RUO*, 105–6; *MPC*, 9:219. For a Delaware individual's observations of the cruelties of slavery: Heckewelder, *Narrative*, 206–7.

5. For charges of witchcraft: note 7 below; Goschgoschunk, August 16, 1768, 1/2/135/8 (first quotation); Lawunakhannek, February 5, 1770, 1/3/135/8 (second quotation); Schmick to Seidel, November 19, 1776, 18/12/221/29, *RMM* (third quotation); Heckewelder to Ettwein, February 23, 1777, no. 250, *JEP* (fourth and fifth quotations).

6. *KJ*, 34–35 ("a Root," "grew of a short," "if they would obey"); Lawunakhannek, May 16, 1769, 1/3/135/8 (last quotation); Annemarie Shimony, "Eastern Woodlands: Iroquois of Six Nations," in *Witchcraft and Sorcery of the American Native Peoples*, ed. Deward E. Walker Jr. (Moscow: University of Idaho Press, 1989), 149, 151–52.

7. Goschgoschunk, August 16, 1768, 1/2/135/8; Schönbrunn, June 7, 1773, 1/3/141/8 (quotations about the powder); Friedenshütten, September 23, 1771, 1/8/131/7; Roth to Seidel, September 30, October 15, 1771, 15 and 16/7/221/29, *RMM* (on accusations at Friedenshütten); Schmick to Seidel, September 25, 1771, 10/11/221/29, *RMM* (accusations at Friedenshütten); Schönbrunn, November 5, 1774, 1/4/1411/9 (quotations in last sentence); Gnadenhütten, Ohio, April 5, 1775, 1/5/144/9; Shimony, "Eastern Woodlands," 141–65 (on the opposition between "in-group loyalty" and witchcraft, 147–48); White, *Middle Ground*, 331–32.

8. Goschgoschunk, July 20 (first quotation), July 15 (second quotation), July 4 (third quotation), July 8 (fourth quotation), July 15 (fifth quotation), 1768, 1/1/135/8; Z. to Hehl, July 22, 1768, 27/2/229/32, *RMM*; Goschgoschunk, June 13, 1768, 1/1/135/8; ibid., January 26, 1769, 1/2/135/8.

9. In particular, the discussion in Shimony, "Eastern Woodlands," 147–48, has helped me develop my thoughts about how witchcraft may have been perceived.

Goschgoschunk, October 10, 1768, 1/2/135/8 (first quotation); Lawunakhannek, August 31 (second quotation), June 8 (Glikhikan as brother of Wangomen), June 7 (third and fourth quotations), 1769, 1/3/135/8; Langundo-Utenünk, July 14, 1770, 1/1/137/8 (fifth quotation); Lawunakhannek, March 12, 1770, 1/4/135/8 (middleman); Langundo-Utenünk diary, June 9, 1770, 1/1/137/8; Hulbert and Schwarze, *Zeisberger's History*, 19.

10. Langundo-Utenünk, June 21, 1770, 1/1/137/8 (first quotation); Schönbrunn, May 31 (second quotation), June 3 (third quotation), June 7 (fourth quotation), 1773, 1/2/1411/9; Hulbert and Schwarze, *Zeisberger's History*, 111–12.

11. Schönbrunn, June 20, 25 (quotations), 1773, 1/3/1411/9.

12. Schönbrunn and Gnadenhütten, January 14, 1773, 1/2/1411/9 (first quotation); Gnadenhütten, Ohio, October 21, 1773, 1/2/144/9 (second quotation); Schönbrunn, April 22, 1774, 1/4/1411/9 (remaining quotations).

13. Hulbert and Schwarze, *Zeisberger's History*, 93 ("to lay all affairs"), 97 ("often very thoroughly," "chiefs and counsellors"), 32 ("An alliance"); Langundo-Utenünk, July 11, 1770, 1/1/137/8; Schönbrunn, June 25, 1773, 1/3/1411/9.

14. Newcomb, *Culture*, 48–51 (names from Morgan on 49); Harrington, "Preliminary Sketch," 209–11; *MPC*, 9:212–29; Hulbert and Schwarze, *Zeisberger's History*, 112–13; "Some Remarks and Annotations concerning the Traditions, Customs, Languages &c of the Indians in North America . . . ," no. 100, JEP. For additional references to the divisions, see Lawrence Henry Gipson, ed., *The Moravian Indian Mission on White River: Diaries and Letters, May 5, 1799, to November 12, 1806* (Indianapolis: Indiana Historical Bureau, 1938), 166–67, 151. On leadership structure, see below.

15. A Delaware reported in 1823 that Munsees included representatives from all three Delaware divisions. Weslager, *Delaware*, app. 3, 480–81; Harrington, "Preliminary Sketch," 209. Hunter has pointed out that Heckewelder introduced errors in discussion of Delaware organization. He mistakenly likened the Munsees to the Wolf phratry, the Unamis to the Turtle, and the Unalachtigos to the Turkey. Heckewelder, *History*, 51–52. A translation of a portion of Zeisberger's writing perpetuated this confusion. *DS*, 36–38; Weslager, "More about Unalachtigo," 42; Weslager, *Delaware*, 43–44; Elisabeth Tooker, "Clans and Moieties in North America," *Current Anthropology* 12 (June 1971): 360–61; *EAID*, 18:125 (on Pipe seemingly as successor to Custaloga); *RUO*, 88 (Ohokon as alternative name for Pipe); *FAUO*, 281 (mention of the three divisions, here called "tribes").

16. Hulbert and Schwarze, *Zeisberger's History*, 112–13; "Some Remarks and Annotations concerning the Traditions, Customs, Languages &c of the Indians in North America . . . ," no. 100, JEP. All quotations in this paragraph are from Zeisberger, "History," except for "to be Chief in the Place of the Deceased" and "to be obedient . . . , "which come from "Some Remarks and Annotations." Apparently the three phratry heads in 1775 were Gelelemend ("Kalalamint"), Welapachtschiechen ("Walapachakin"), and Captain Pipe ("Ohokon"). Gelelemend was of the Turtle phratry (*FRUO*, 317); Captain Pipe was associated with the Wolf phratry (*FRUO*, 132 [Pipe speaks of "my men belonging to the Woolf Tribe"]; *BDZ*, 1:220); *RUO*, 88 (White Eyes stated, "there are three tribes of us" and then named these three individuals as "the Cheifs Appointed for the Delaware Nation.").

17. Shoemaker, *Strange Likeness*, 90–95; *EAID*, 2:201 (quotation).

18. *MPC,* 10:61–62 ("I am ready," "I desire" on 62); Schönbrunn, July 30, 1773, 1/3/1411/9 (last quotation); ibid., August 3, 12, 1773.

19. Gnadenhütten, February 27, 1775, 1/4/144/9 (quotations); see Chapter 4 above, including note 6, on Captain John and Tatamy.

20. *RUO,* 40 ("a very poor Man," "Lord Dunmore"); Schönbrunn, February 2, 1775, 1/4/1411/9 (quotation about deed); Z. to Seidel, January 6, 1775, 21/4/229/32, *RMM* ("wie bisher immer geschehen ist"); *RUO,* 19.

21. Gnadenhütten, Ohio, February 27, 1775, 1/4/144/9 (first quotation); "Br. Ettweins Bericht von seinem Besuch in Langundo-utenünk . . . ," August 30, 1772, 1/5/1371/8, *RMM* (second quotation); *IVPN,* 203–6.

22. *RUO,* 85–87 ("that Tract of Country" quotation on 86–87); *EAID,* 18:115 (includes the following in a speech from Congress: "You [Delawares] tell us that your uncles, our brothers, the *Wyandots,* have given your nation a large tract of country, comprehended between the River *Ohio* on the south, the west branch of the River *Muskingham* and *Sandusky* on the west, Lake *Erie* on the north, and *Presque-Isle* on the east"); *FAUO,* 320–21. Glikhikan (Isaac) spoke with Ohio Iroquois (*Minque*), who stated, "the Wyandots [Delamattenoos] gave land to the Delawares." Lichtenau, November 12, 1776, 1/1/147/9. See also the claim that the Delawares' land at Kaskaskunk was a gift from the Wyandots: Goschgoschunk, August 9, 1768, 1/1/135/8. Netawatwees sent a message to Langundo-Utenünk, however, that raised a question about the validity of the Delawares' claim to Kaskaskunk. Langundo-Utenünk, January 13, 1772, 1/7/137/8.

23. Z. to Seidel, January 6, 1775, 21/4/229/32, *RMM* (first quotation); Schönbrunn, April 7, 1775, 1/4/1411/9 (second quotation); ibid., November 5, 1774, 1/4/1411/9; Gnadenhütten, Ohio, April 4, 1775, 1/4/144/9; *RUO,* 43–44 ("Great Council," "Wiandots Towns").

24. *RUO,* 87 ("Acquaint," "Uncles"); see Chapter 5 above, including note 31.

25. *EAID,* 18: 141 (quotations from White Eyes) and 573 n. 96; Heckewelder, *History,* 47–51 (other quotations on 48 and 50).

26. *RUO,* 40–41, 51–53 ("disputes subsisting" on 41, comments of War Post on 51 and 52), xiii; Calloway, *American Revolution,* 26–29; James H. Merrell, "Indians and the New Republic," in *The Blackwell Encyclopedia of the American Revolution,* ed. Jack P. Greene and J. R. Pole (1991; Oxford, Eng.: Blackwell, 1994), 392–93.

27. *RUO,* 95–96 ("we only ask"), 166; Acting Superintendent Guy Johnson quoted in introduction to Davies, *Documents,* 11:15; *EAID,* 18:1; John K. Mahon, "Indian-United States Military Situation, 1775–1848," in *HNAI,* 4:144.

28. *RUO,* 80, 82; Schönbrunn, October 29, 1775, 1/4/1411/9; MCT and FL, 1:305 (Nathanael #621); Lichtenau, November 16, 1776, 1/2/147/9 (indicates Welapachtschiechen was at the treaty); *EAID,* 18:125 (Custaloga's death), 131 (death of Netawatwees); *RUO,* 28 and n. 57, 202–3; Gnadenhütten, Ohio, September 15, 19, 1776, 1/6/144/9; Worthington Chauncey Ford, ed., *Journals of the Continental Congress, 1774–1789* (Washington, D.C.: Government Printing Office, 1905), 3:433; 4: 208, 266–68; Z. to Provincial Helpers Conference, May 12, 1776, 1/5/229/32, *RMM;* Lichtenau, May 3, 7, 11, 17, 1776, 1/1/147/9; Ettwein to missionaries, [1776?], no. 1046, JEP ("eine Mühle, miller, ein paar Bauern"; and on seeking help from Quakers). For ex-

amples of Moravian contact with the continental army: *FDUO*, 18–19, 27–29, 93–95, 101–3,164–67.

29. *EAID*, 18:169 (quotations); *FAUO*, 138–45.

30. *RUO*, 98–99.

31. Ibid., 53 (War Post), 61 (Kishanosity).

32. Ibid., 27 ("shot at by two Men"); *FDUO*, 35 ("If White Eyes passes"), 48 ("the situation"); *FAUO*, 157 n. 3; *AGL*, 83; Heckewelder, *Narrative*, 158–59 ("Americans . . . fired on a body of Senecas" attempting to enter into negotiations at Pittsburgh in July 1777).

33. *PA*, 1st ser., 5:445 ("the waters of Turtle Creek"), 287 (attack "near the Kittanning"); *IVPN*, 235–37, 167; *FDUO*, 15 (mentions attack on Allegheny "about twenty miles above Pittsburgh"); *RUO*, 245 (attack at Kittanning), 250 (attacks on the Ohio), 254 ("the widow").

34. *RUO*, 253 n. 1, 254, 210 n. 54; *PA*, 1st ser., 5:446–47 ("24 Warriors"); Lichtenau, August 15, 1777, 1/2/147/9; ibid., September 5, 7, October 2, 1777, 1/4 and 5/147/9; Z. to Geschwister, September 3, 1777, 11/5/229/32, *RMM*; *AGL*, 80; *RUO*, 236 ("Repeated hostilities"); Calloway, *American Revolution*, 32; Hanna, *Wilderness*, 2:210; *PA*, 1st ser., 5:445 ("Wapanaws"). The "Wapanaw" and "Woaponos" Indians may have been former New England Indians, as were the Wompanosch who had joined the Moravians.

35. *FDUO*, 96 ("Wiondoughwalind with his Men"), 100–101, 54–55, 67 and n. 28, 134, 95; the Delaware "Windohale" appeared at a conference at Pittsburgh in 1759. *MPC*, 8:383; *GMP*, 15–16 ("small Delaware Town," "last Town"); Wheeler-Voegelin, "Ethnohistory," 1:150. On Walhonding and Cuyahoga: *FDUO*, 164; Lichtenau, October 13, 1777, 1/5/147/9; ibid., March 7, 11, 1777, 1/2/147/9 ("wurde . . . an der Walhonding . . . ein Minque entdeckt"); Gnadenhütten, Ohio, July 28, 1777, 1/9/144/9 ("6 Minques u. 1 Mennissinger"); Schönbrunn, March 15, 1777, 1/9/1411/9.

36. *RUO*, 31n–32n; *EAID*, 18:152 ("intend to"); Lichtenau, July 23, 1777, 2/3/147/9 (last quotation).

37. Lichtenau, April 5, 1778, 1/6/147/9; ibid., December 25, 1777 (Welapachtschiechen was baptized and renamed Israel), April 5, 1777, 1/6/147/9; ibid., June 18, 1777, 1/2/147/9 (first quotation); *FDUO*, 102 ("all agreed"); *PA*, 1st ser., 8:250 ("influence"), 140 (mentioned how the Delawares had "numerous alliances").

38. Lichtenau, April 7, 1777, 1/2/137/9; *PA*, 1st ser., 5:446 ("were sent to Pluggys Town & Sandusky"); *FDUO*, 164–66 n. 28 ("the greater part" on 165); *PA*, 1st ser., 6:588 ("Head Chief," "take hold," and "join").

39. *FDUO*, 215 ("only one Man," Impetuous"), 216–20 ("small Indian boy" on 219).

40. *FDUO*, 244; *FAUO*, 82.

41. *FAUO*, 320 ("some of their Chiefs," "Tomhawk and Belt," "have created"), 318 ("The Delaware Nation have ever been"), 201 ("rumor"), 217 ("There never was a Conference"), 216, 203–4 ("I have now looked" on 203); *EAID*, 18:167–68 ("to join the troops").

42. Heckewelder, *Narrative*, 181 (paraphrases White Eyes's address to the Delawares—"they had never"); *EAID*, 18:167–68; Lichtenau, September 16, 26, 1778, 1/8/147/9. Remaining quotations in order: ibid., October 30, 23, 28, 1778, 1/8/147/9; *FRUO*, 132–33; *FAUO*, 321.

43. *FAUO*, 254–55, 178–79, 188–89, 197; *PA*, 1st ser., 7:569 ("to furnish," "not to be

procured," "People in the Back Counties," "so violent"), 465 ("Herbs Salt & Cowhides"); Heckewelder, *Narrative*, 207 ("Was it not for the English").

44. *FAUO*, 313, 317–19 and 319 n. 1 ("sent down" and "one People" on 319), 387–88; *PA*, 1st ser., 8:640; *FRUO*, 41, 43–44; *PA*, 1st ser., 7:505 ("a young Delaware chief named Nanowland"), 172 ("Young Men"); Lichtenau, August 2, 1779, 1/9/147/9 (quotations about Gelelemend's speech).

45. *FRUO*, 333–34, 301–2, 321 ("I conceive that much confidence"), 339–40 ("every body here," "near relations," "a Friend," "towards Wheeling"), 296 (on William Penn), 342–43 ("very few excepted"), 373, 378–79; Brodhead to Washington, October 17, 1780, from *Olden Time*, 2:374–75, in Delaware volume for 1780, THDC; *PA*, 1st ser., 8:596 ("forty men," "attempt to destroy"); Salem (Heckewelder), April 19, 20, 1781, 1/1/148/10, *RMM*; *PA*, 1st ser., 9:161 ("about three hundred men").

46. Heckewelder, *Narrative*, 212, 219 ("your fields shall yield"; place mentioned was the Miami), 155 ("ascribed," "to the influence"); *BDZ*, 1:29–30, 83; *FL*, 3:887. ⸙

47. Heckewelder, *Narrative*, 208–9, 231, 170, 240 (comments of Pomoacan); *AGL*, 80; *BDZ*, 1:3, 4, 26 n. 1, 8 ("not of one mind"), 15–21.

48. *BDZ*, 1:33 n. 1, 37, 38 (quotations related to Major de Peyster); Jacob Haymaker, letter (Eng.), September 7, 1781, 7/7/151/10, *RMM*.

49. John Joseph Schebosch to Seidel (Eng.), November 4, 1781, 3/6/151/10, *RMM*; Leinbach document, April 5, 1782, 8/6/151/10, *RMM* (last two quotations); *PA*, 1st ser., 9:524–25.

50. *BDZ*, 1:78–83; *PA*, 1st ser., 9:524 (first and second quotations); "An Account of the Massacre at Gnadenhütten, written by John Ettwein to refute charges against the mission made by 'Gentlemen from Washington County' in a newspaper," no. 103, JEP; Letter of L. Weiss, attachment D from Ettwein, 9/6/151/10, *RMM* (quotations about Williamson); Smaby, *Transformation*, 23–24.

51. "Account of the Massacre," no. 103, JEP (first quotation); Leinbach document (about the soldier with hatchet); *PA*, 1st ser., 9:525 ("The Militia chose"); Muskingum-Sandusky-Huron River diary (Z.), March 23, 1782, 1/1/151/10, *RMM* (last quotation). List of Indians killed at Gnadenhütten, March 8, 1782, 1/1/151/10; Register of Baptisms, Marriages, Deaths, etc., 1769–1870, pp. 278–80, 1/8/313/33, *RMM*; A. Everly to A. Hübner (Eng.), May 7, 1, 1782, 10/6/151/10, *RMM*; Weiss letter. For the number of children killed, see Register of Baptism, Marriages, Deaths, etc., 1769–1870. Heckewelder, *Narrative*, 312–26.

52. Phillipus (#128), Christina (#134), Johannes (#842), Joseph (#1375), Anna Benigna (#862), Lucia (#759), Rebecca (#874), Christian (#256), MCT; List of Indians killed at Gnadenhütten, March 8, 1782; *FL*, 1:217. To trace the probable tie between the three women and Teedyuscung, see Phoebe (#762) who is named as sister to Rebecca and Lucia (ibid., 338) and in MCT also appears as the daughter of Teedyuscung. "A Brief Account of the Christian Indians formerly Settled on the Muskingum River," no. 102, JEP.

53. *BDZ*, 1:34, 103–14, 200, 165, 180, 86, 61 (indicated Shawnees lived "a good day's journey" from Upper Sandusky in 1782), 126–27, 139, 141, 109 ("had given him," "scattered"), 113, 114; *AGL*, 85; MCT (Mark or Marcus #217); Heckewelder, *Narrative*, 336–42; *Narrative of a Late Expedition against the Indians; with an Account of the Barbarous Execution of Col. Crawford* . . . (Andover, [Mass.]: Ames & Parker, [1798?]) in

Early American Imprints, ser. 1, Evans no. 35689, Readex Digital Collections, Archives of Americana, American Antiquarian Society and NewsBank, 2002; *AGL*, 85.

54. *BDZ*, 1:126, 134, 172, 181–83, 164, 165, 184, 187, 188, 192, 194, 200, 195, 189–90 ("block up the creek").

55. *BDZ*, 1:194, 197, 198, 167, 188, 193, 194, 205.

Epilogue

1. William N. Fenton, "Structure, Continuity, and Change in the Process of Iroquois Treaty Making," 16–17, and Francis Jennings, "Iroquois Alliances in American History," 38, in *HCID*; Robert A. Williams, *Linking Arms Together: American Indian Treaty Visions of Law and Peace, 1600–1800* (New York: Oxford University Press, 1997), 53; Merritt, *Crossroads*, 1; Shoemaker, *Strange Likeness*, 86–90.

2. *BDZ*, 1:232 ("Delawares and other Indians"), 379–80, 429–30, 361 ("Delawares and Shawnese"), 429 ("Delawares in Gigeyunk," "given the Delawares"), 230, 240, 296, 300, 326, 452; ibid., 2:40; *AGL*, 88–89, 81; *SCP*, 2:16–17 n. 1 (Pakongekalas); Helen Hornbeck Tanner, "The Glaize in 1792: A Composite Indian Community," in *American Encounters: Natives and Newcomers from European Contact to Indian Removal, 1500–1850*, ed. Peter C. Mancall and James H. Merrell (New York: Routledge, 2000), 405–6.

3. *AGL*, 88–89; *BDZ*, 1:301 (Titawachkam called "head-man in his town" at Sandusky), 336, 364, 365, 372, 369, 265, 278–289, 239, 279–82, 313–14, 327, 329, 340–41; Sabathy-Judd, *Fairfield Diary*, xxi; *SCP*, 2:92.

4. *BDZ*, 1:295–66 ("severe fever" on 296), 300 ("prevalent," "swollen necks"), 407 ("fifteen men"), 440 ("burnt," and "built"), 442, 369 ("yellow fever"), 362, 359, 344 ("very great famine," "no corn"), 396, 454, 57 ("hard night-frosts"), 63 ("most people").

5. *EAID*, 18:280, 326–27; Charles J. Kappler, comp. and ed., *Indian Affairs, Laws and Treaties* (Washington, D.C.: Government Printing Office, 1904; repr., New York: AMS Press, 1971), 2:7; *SCP*, 2:9–10, 10n, 11n ("The Indian representation" on 9 and "had the effect" on 10), 11–12, 11n–12n; Hurt, *Ohio*, 95–99; Randolph C. Downes, *Council Fires on the Upper Ohio: A Narrative of Indian Affairs in the Upper Ohio Valley until 1795* (Pittsburgh: University of Pittsburgh Press, 1940), 288–98 (hunting rights stated at Fort McIntosh, see p. 295); Weslager, *Delaware*, 320; White, *Middle Ground*, 417, 436–40.

6. *SCP*, 2:15 ("The murders"), 4n, 9 ("five or six people"), 18–19, 21; Hurt, *Ohio*, 98–99, 104–5.

7. Hurt, *Ohio*, 100–119; White, *Middle Ground*, 441–43, 445 ("fragile unity"); Tanner, "Glaize," 405–6; Dowd, *Spirited*, 103–4.

8. *AGL*, 90, 88; Tanner, "Glaize," 405–10; Aupaumut, "Narrative," 69, 96, 87, 97–98, 109, 122, 123.

9. Hurt, *Ohio*, 129–35, 139; *AGL*, 91; White, *Middle Ground*, 466–68; Weslager, *Delaware*, 330–33; Kappler, *Treaties*, 2:39–45.

10. Thompson, "Sons of the Wilderness," map opp. p. 42, 196n–205n; Weslager, *Delaware*, 327, 332–33; Kappler, *Treaties*, 2:44; Gipson, *Moravian Indian Mission*, 23 ("the successor"), 102, 454, 151 (Hockingpomska was of the Wolf division), 223n, 109 ("given us this entire river"), 109n.

11. Goshen (Eng.), October 4, 1798, 1/2/171/19; ibid., Oct. 9, 1803, 1/13/171/19; *FL*, 1:124; Henry Howe, *Historical Collections of Ohio* . . . (Cincinnati: R. Clarke and Co., 1875; Ann Arbor: University of Michigan Library, 2005, http://name.umdl.umich.edu/ AJ2911.0001.001), 343, 428 ("it was a village"). Pipe was said to have lived "near the road to Mansfield" in the area of the Jerome settlement (ibid., 36); *AGL*, 101, 80 (map 16), 99 (map 20); Weslager, *Delaware*, 351; James B. Finley, *Sketches of Western Methodism: Biographical, Historical, and Miscellaneous. Illustrative of Pioneer Life* (Cincinnati: Methodist Book Concern, 1854; Ann Arbor: University of Michigan Library, 2005, http://name.umdl.umich.edu/AJ2655.0001.001), 388, 390–91; J. L. Lutz, "The Methodist Missions among the Indian Tribes in Kansas," in *Transactions of the Kansas State Historical Society, 1905–1906* (Topeka, Kans.: State Printing Office, 1906), 213; Goshen, November 21, 1799, 1/5/171/19 ("had agreed").

12. Weslager, *Delaware*, 338–39, 351; Kappler, *Treaties*, 2:64–65, 70–72, 77–78, 80–82, 101–2; Dowd, *Spirited*, 139–41; R. David Edmunds, *The Shawnee Prophet* (Lincoln: University of Nebraska Press, 1983), 80–82, 138–42; Benjamin Douglass, *History of Wayne County, Ohio, from the Days of the Pioneers and First Settlers to the Present Time* (Indianapolis: Robert Douglass, 1878; Ann Arbor: University of Michigan Library, 2005, http://name.umdl.umich.edu/AFK4254.0001.001), 225; Howe, *Historical Collections*, 428–30; Goshen, August 8, July 26, 1812, 1/9/173/20 ("above 20 men," "Many declared"); Gayle Thornbrough, ed., *Letter Book of the Indian Agency at Fort Wayne, 1809–1815* (Indianapolis: Indiana Historical Society, 1961), 181–83, including nn. 69, 70, and 73, 186–87 and nn. 76 and 77; *BDZ*, 2:158, 166–88; Sabathy-Judd, *Fairfield Diary*, xxv, 512–15.

13. Kappler, *Treaties*, 2:170 (quotations from St. Marys Treaty); Weslager, *Delaware*, 360–62, 353, 363, 373; Francis Paul Prucha, *The Great Father: The United States Government and the American Indians* (Lincoln: University of Nebraska Press, 1984), 243–48; Richard C. Adams, *The Delaware Indians: A Brief History* (Saugerties, N.Y.: Hope Farm Press, 1995), 37. Leaving the St. Marys/St. Joseph area, the Delaware leader Welandawecken headed to Spanish territory about 1789. The son of the Munsee captain Titawachkam was apparently in the vicinity of New Madrid in 1788–89 but returned to the Lake Erie region by 1790. *BDZ*, 2:62, 88; *SCP*, 2:140; David J. Weber, *The Spanish Frontier in North America* (New Haven, Conn.: Yale University Press, 1992), 198–203, 281.

14. Samuel A. Allinson, "A Fragmentary History of the New Jersey Indians," *Proceedings of the New Jersey Historical Society* 4 (1873): 46–48; *EAID*, 10:657, 659, 662–68; J. N. Davidson, *Muh-he-ka-ne-ok: A History of the Stockbridge Nation* (Milwaukee, Wis.: Silas Chapman, 1893), 16–17; Electa F. Jones, *Stockbridge, Past and Present; or, Records of an Old Mission Station* (Springfield: Samuel Bowles and Co., 1854), 85–87; Weslager, *Delaware*, 274–76; Frazier, *Mohicans*, 237–39, 241–45.

15. Davidson, *Muh-he-ka-ne-ok*, 19, 20 ("When we rise," is quoted in Davidson; he does not give a source or explain how he obtained this quotation), 21 ("when they arrived"—this is a quotation from the missionary John Sergeant; Piqua on 21); Jones, *Stockbridge*, 100 (also on Piqua).

On Munsees among the Stockbridges: Davidson, *Muh-he-ka-ne-ok*, 18–19. Based on Moravian reports of the tribal affiliations of Moravian converts, the Munsee background of some Stockbridge, Massachusetts, Indians can be guessed. The sister of Eva

(#57), a Highland Indian, was living at Stockbridge, as was the son of Jephta (#48), an Esopus Indian. Both the Highland and the Esopus, as we have seen, were Munsee groups. Pachgatoch diary (Sensemann), May 26, 1751, 1/3/114/3, *RMM*; MCT.

16. Marion Johnson Mochon, "Stockbridge-Munsee Cultural Adaptations: 'Assimilated Indians,'" in *Proceedings of the APS* 112 (June 1968): 195, 199–201; John C. Savagian, "The Tribal Reorganization of the Stockbridge-Munsee: Essential Conditions in the Re-creation of a Native American Community, 1930–1942," in *American Nations: Encounters in Indian Country, 1850 to the Present*, ed. Frederick E. Hoxie, Peter C. Mancall, and James H. Merrell (New York: Routledge, 2001), 291; Davidson, *Muh-he-ka-ne-ok*, 22; Reginald Horsman, "The Origins of Oneida Removal to Wisconsin, 1815–1822," in *The Oneida Indian Journey: From New York to Wisconsin, 1784–1860*, ed. Laurence M. Hauptman and L. Gordon McLester III (Madison: University of Wisconsin Press, 1999), 58–66; Jones, *Stockbridge*, 103–5; Reuben Gold Thwaites, ed., *Collections of the State Historical Historical Society of Wisconsin* (Madison: Democrat Printing Co., 1900), 15:6–8 (quotations), 49.

17. In August 1832, the missionary Cutting Marsh reported, "It is now quite probable that the Stockbridge Indians will remove in the course of two years to a place about 15 miles distant on the E. side of Winnebago Lake" (Thwaites, *Collections of Wisconsin*, 71). In February 1834, Marsh stated that the Stockbridge group "are making preparations as fast as possible to remove, but a majority doubtless will not go before the winter 1834–5" (ibid., 94); Jones, *Stockbridge*, 105–6; Savagian, "Tribal Reorganization," 291–92; Mochon, "Stockbridge-Munsee Cultural Adaptations," 202; Loretta Metoxen, "The Oneidas in Wisconsin: The Early Years, 1822–1848," in *Oneida Indian Journey*, ed. Hauptman and McLester, 134; Thwaites, *Collections of Wisconsin*, 164. With the closing of the small Goshen, Ohio, mission in 1821, much of its population had moved to the Thames site. Darryl K. Stonefish, *Moraviantown Delaware History* (Thamesville, Ont.: Moravian Research Office, 1995), 15, 23–27, 30–31. See this volume also on the modern-day Moraviantown Delaware Nation in Canada. Sabathy-Judd, *Fairfield Diary*, xxvi; Weslager, *Delaware*, 352; Earl P. Olmstead, *Blackcoats among the Delaware: David Zeisberger on the Ohio Frontier* (Kent, Ohio: Kent State University Press, 1991), 171; Kappler, *Treaties*, 2:574–82, 742–55. *NASP*, 2:177–78; 1:580–81.

18. Thwaites, *Collections of Wisconsin*, 68 (mentions a Munsee family emigrating from New York and states that one member of the family had died while visiting friends at Cattaraugus); Weslager, *Delaware*, 352–53; Speck, *Celestial Bear*, 1–13 and nn. 15–16.

19. Kappler, *Treaties*, 2:304 ("extending up," "for the permanent"); Weslager, *Delaware*, 369, 363–64, 400; *NASP*, 1:61, 303, 647 ("sixty-nine souls").

20. Tooker, "Wyandot," 402–3; Lutz, "Methodist Missions," 213–14; *NASP*, 1: 170 (quotations about Delawares with Wyandots in Ohio), 356, 581; ibid., 2: 14, 51.

21. *NASP*, 1:306, 453; H. Allen Anderson, "The Delaware and Shawnee Indians and the Republic of Texas, 1820–1845," *Southwestern Historical Quarterly* 94 (1990): 233–37, 242–43, 246–60 ("virtually omnipresent" on 247); Callender, "Shawnee," 632; F. Todd Smith, *The Caddos, the Wichitas, and the United States, 1846–1901* (College Station: Texas A & M University Press, 1996), 12; David La Vere, *The Texas Indians* (College Station: Texas A & M University Press, 2004), 171–76; Dorman H. Winfrey, ed., *Texas Indian Papers, 1844–1845* (Austin: Texas State Library, 1960), 32 (quotation from St.

Louis), 43, 54 (St. Louis referred to the following groups as grandchildren: Waco, Caddo, Anadarko, Ioni, and Shawnee).

22. Smith, *Caddos and Wichitas*, 15, 17, 19–20, 25–42, 43 (location of Delawares on Brazos Reserve), 40–69, 70–72, 73, 70–105; La Vere, *Texas Indians*, 200–201; Winfrey, *Texas Indian Papers*, 44 (words of Bintah).

23. Weslager, *Delaware*, 399, 401, 421–28, 12–14, 17–18; H. Craig Miner and William E. Unrau, *The End of Indian Kansas: A Study of Cultural Revolution, 1854–1871* (1978; Lawrence: University Press of Kansas, 1990), 5–18, 28–43, 109–15; Adams, *Delaware*, 54–56 (quotation on 56); C. A. Weslager, *The Delaware Indian Westward Migration . . .* (Wallingford, Pa.: Middle Atlantic Press, 1978), 223–29. Goddard, "Delaware," 224 ("continuum of contacts"); Robert S. Grumet, *Voices from the Delaware Big House Ceremony* (Norman: University of Oklahoma Press, 2002); Herbert C. Kraft, *The Lenape-Delaware Indian Heritage: 10,000 B.C.–A.D. 2000* (n.p.: Lenape Books, 2001), 515; Claudia Haake, "Delaware Identity in the Cherokee Nation," *Indigenous Nations Studies Journal* 3 (Spring 2002): 19–45. Haake points out that there continued to be "legal ambiguities" about the Delawares' position after the 1867 agreement (28–29).

24. Richard W. Cummins, Indian Agent, Fort Leavenworth Agency, September 15, 1845, from Cong. Doc. Series no. 470, doc. 1, pp. 539–40, copy in Delaware volume for 1837–49, THDC; Smith, *Caddos and Wichitas*, 51; *NASP*, 1:61; "Appeals Court Nullifies Delawares' Sovereignty," *Tulsa World*, November 17, 2004, LexisNexis; "Delawares Lose Federal Recognition," March 25, 2005, in ibid; Kraft, *Lenape-Delaware Indian Heritage*, 514, 532; Weslager, *Delaware*, 10; Haake, "Delaware Identity," 19–45.

Index

Page numbers in italics refer to illustrations and maps.

Acknowledgments

I am immensely grateful to the many individuals who have helped me over the years as I developed my ideas about the history of the Delawares. Bernard Sheehan alerted me to the importance of the Moravian mission records, and I became immersed in those documents because of his influence. I am thankful for his guidance and for that of others, including David Edmunds, Bill Reese, Stephen Stein, Ed McClellan, Jim Madison, and the late Paul R. Lucas. Grants from the Phillips Fund of the American Philosophical Society and the Indiana University History Department as well as a fellowship from the Center on Philanthropy were helpful in launching my research, and I gratefully acknowledge this support. I appreciate the invaluable lessons in German script reading that I received at the Moravian Archives in Bethlehem, Pennsylvania, through the teaching of Rev. Vernon H. Nelson.

More recently I had the wonderful opportunity to work as a postdoctoral researcher with the McNeil Center for Early American Studies under Cooperative Agreement CA4560-B-0028 between the University of Pennsylvania and the National Park Service, to complete a study of the relationships among local groups of Lenape/Delaware people, other Indians, and Euro-American newcomers during the early colonial period. This book emerged from that effort. For their assistance in many ways, I thank Dan Richter, Amy Baxter-Bellamy, and Zelini Hubbard of the McNeil Center. Dan Richter has been a thorough and insightful reader of various drafts of my manuscript, and I have appreciated his excellent advice and the great deal of time he has devoted to helping me improve my work. I am also very grateful to Chuck Smythe of the National Park Service for his support and his helpful comments about my study. Richard Dunn and Jane Merritt read and commented on an early draft, and I am thankful for their suggestions as well as for those of an anonymous reviewer. Bob Grumet gave generously of his time in helping me consider the best approach to my subject and alerting me to useful documents and other readings. Many other people have aided me with advice about sources or about the content of specific chapters. These include Kate Carté Engel, Tom Hamm, Emily Hutton, Jordan Kerber, Ricki Mueller,

Jim Rementer, Darryl Stonefish, Susan Taffe, Cami Townsend, and Chris Vecsey. Also for help along the way, I am grateful to George Boudreau, David W. Adams, Laurie Moses Hines, Sarah Curtis, Kay Johnston, Jo Anne Pagano, Heidi Ross, George DeBoer, and my colleagues in the history department of the State University of New York College at Cortland. I thank all the scholars who offered suggestions regarding my various conference papers and other presentations. I also appreciate the editorial expertise of Bob Lockhart, Erica Ginsburg, Laura Miller, Mary Tederstrom, and other staff at the University of Pennsylvania Press, who have helped guide this book to publication.

I have benefited from the kind assistance of many librarians and archivists. I thank the following institutions and their staffs: the Moravian Archives, Bethlehem, Pennsylvania; the Pennsylvania State Archives, Harrisburg; the American Philosophical Society; The Historical Society of Pennsylvania; the Library Company of Philadelphia; the Pennsylvania State Library, Harrisburg; Special Collections, Haverford College Library; Friends Historical Library, Swarthmore College; the Ohio Valley-Great Lakes Ethnohistory Archive, Glenn Black Laboratory of Archaeology, Bloomington, Indiana; Herman B. Wells Library, Indiana University, Bloomington; Everett Needham Case Library, Colgate University; Archives and Special Collections, Dickinson College; Hamilton Public Library, Hamilton, New York; Stevens-German Library, Hartwick College; Burke Library, Hamilton College; and Van Pelt Library, University of Pennsylvania.

In addition to the support of many good friends, my family has offered me tremendous amounts of care and encouragement. My parents, Ralph and Martha Slotten, and my brother, Hugh Slotten, shared their enthusiasm for history and were always ready to converse with me about my latest research findings. I also lovingly thank my sons, Tom and David, who have sustained an interest in my work and buoyed my spirits through the years. With the deepest appreciation for his great patience and constant love, I dedicate this book to my dear husband, Rob. Through it all, he has been a calm and abiding presence in my life.

CPSIA information can be obtained at www.ICGtesting.com
Printed in the USA
BVOW08s0704201213

339479BV00003B/765/P